MECHANICS-
MERCANTILE
LIBRARY.

Arthur F Mathews '06

POWER MENTORING

POWER
MENTORING

How Successful Mentors and Protégés Get the Most Out of Their Relationships

Ellen A. Ensher

Susan Elaine Murphy

JOSSEY-BASS
A Wiley Imprint
www.josseybass.com

Published by Jossey-Bass
A Wiley Imprint
989 Market Street, San Francisco, CA 94103-1741   www.josseybass.com

Chapter 7 epigraph: From OH, THE PLACES YOU'LL GO! by Dr. Seuss, copyright TM & copyright © by Dr. Seuss Enterprises L.P. 1990. Used by permission of Random House Children's Books, a division of Random House, Inc.

Chapter 8 epigraph: From *The Prophet* by Kahlil Gibran. Copyright 1923 by Kahlil Gibran and renewed 1951 by Administrators C.T.A. of Kahlil Gibran Estate and Mary G. Gibran. Used by permission of the Gibran National Committee, address: P.O. Box 116-5375, Beirut, Lebanon; phone and fax: (+961-1) 396916; email: kgibran@cyberia.net.lb.

Jossey-Bass books and products are available through most bookstores. To contact Jossey-Bass directly call our Customer Care Department within the U.S. at 800-956-7739, outside the U.S. at 317-572-3986, or fax 317-572-4002.

Jossey-Bass also publishes its books in a variety of electronic formats. Some content that appears in print may not be available in electronic books.

Library of Congress Cataloging-in-Publication Data

Ensher, Ellen A.
  Power mentoring : how successful mentors and protégés get the most out of their relationships / by Ellen A. Ensher, Susan Elaine Murphy.
    p. cm.
  Includes bibliographical references and index.
  ISBN-13: 978-0-7879-7952-2 (alk. paper)
  ISBN-10: 0-7879-7952-X (alk. paper)
  1. Mentoring in business. 2. Career development. I. Murphy, Susan E. II. Title.
  HF5385.E57 2005
  658.3'124—dc22   2005015654

Printed in the United States of America
FIRST EDITION
HB Printing   10 9 8 7 6 5 4 3 2

Contents

POWER MENTORING

For Mom and Dad, who gave me a love of books. For Sean, who is my best promoter, and especially for our Mark—may you have many wise mentors to help you along your journey.
Ellen

For my mother and father, and my husband, Copil.
Susan

CHAPTER ONE

INTRODUCTION TO POWER MENTORING

And when the event, the big thing in your life, is simply an insight—isn't that a strange thing? That absolutely nothing changes except you see things differently and you're less fearful and less anxious and generally stronger as a result: Isn't that amazing that a completely invisible thing in your head can feel realer than anything you've experienced before?
—JONATHAN FRANZEN, *THE CORRECTIONS*

As a child, what did you want to be when you grew up? Maybe it did not work out that you would be a movie star or an Olympic athlete, but have you found the level of joy in your work that you had hoped for? When you chose your major in college and then later changed it, or perhaps recently made a job or career switch, why did you do it? Maybe it was because you suddenly had the Great Career Insight—I will spend the majority of my waking hours for the rest of my life at work, so if I am not as happy at work as I want to be now, then I am wasting my life! We spend more time working than doing anything else we do in our lives. Those of us in the United States have the dubious distinction of working more hours and taking less vacation time per year than our counterparts in nearly any other industrialized nation.[1] Nearly 40 percent of U.S. workers spend at least 50 hours on the job per week, and that number is even higher for the professional class.[2]

Why do we work so much? Maybe because in the United States we see work as central to who we are as individuals. An Associated

Press survey showed that 91 percent of respondents said their jobs were important to their overall satisfaction in life.[3] Given that we spend many hours at work, how we view it is important. Work can be a joy or drudgery, and an overwhelming amount of research conclusively shows that this often depends on our relationships with other people at work. *Power Mentoring* is about helping you gain more fulfillment at work by showing you how to actively develop and improve your relationships with others there, and in doing so gain all of the career outcomes that you have always imagined.

Consider the following situation: What would you do if you found out that your colleagues were corrupt and stealing money from one of Southern California's poorest cities? Imagine you were a young public servant and felt as though you had no one to trust or turn to about this crisis. This is the situation that Araceli Gonzalez, former council member for the city of Cudahey, found herself in a few short years ago. She had no one to turn to, except, that is, for her mentor, Rosario Marin (41st U.S. Treasurer). What would you do if you were the mentor in this situation? Rosario Marin told Araceli to "do the right thing" and turn in her colleagues. Araceli did so and found that "everyone turned against her, except Rosario." Marin stood by her young protégé and helped her get back on her feet politically and career-wise. Gonzalez has gone on to become a successful small business owner and received national recognition as an up-and-coming leader.

In this book, we share many stories like this and insights from interviews with 50 of America's most successful mentors and protégés in leading industries. We reveal secrets from academia and present our own research that demonstrates how having a network of good mentoring relationships can make your work environment, your job, and your career better.

Power Mentoring is for professionals and managers who want to make the most of their careers. We have written this book for those of you who want to obtain a protégé or mentor, or who simply want to improve a current mentoring relationship. The book can also help you regardless of whether you are well established in your career or are just starting out. You might be a manager, a technical specialist, or even an entrepreneur. Our intention is that *Power Mentoring* will be helpful to people at all stages of their careers and in many types of positions. It is also for administrators of mentoring programs and anyone who teaches or conducts training about mentoring.

Regardless of whether you are thinking about finding a mentor, becoming a mentor, or extending your vast experience with mentoring, there is always much to learn. Some of our interviews provide examples of traditional mentoring relationships, in which an older, more experienced mentor takes a younger protégé under his or her wing and guides the protégé through career twists and turns. We found, however, that most of our interviewees did not rely on a single traditional mentor for support, but instead had a broad network consisting of a variety of mentors to support them. We call this network approach to mentoring *power mentoring*. We found that all those involved in power mentoring, both as mentors and as protégés, received mutually beneficial outcomes related to their personal career growth and development. In this book you'll learn more about the various forms of power mentoring, how it differs from traditional mentoring, and the benefits associated with these relationships.

In this chapter, first we briefly introduce you to the power mentors and protégés in our research. Next we take you through a brief, compelling overview of what has changed in the career landscape, and of how power mentoring reflects the most contemporary approach to career development. Finally, we provide you with an overview of the book.

WHO ARE OUR POWER MENTORS AND PROTÉGÉS?

To learn about power mentoring, we had the great fortune to interview 50 top leaders in a variety of industries. To find these individuals, we culled through well-respected lists identifying leading executives, with an eye toward being especially inclusive of women and people of color. While our interviewees represent a variety of industries, there is a marked emphasis on entertainment, technology, and politics. These industries exert tremendous worldwide influence. They also have a high percentage of knowledge workers who represent the cutting edge in career management by moving from project to project, working in teams, and identifying with their profession or party more than with a particular organization.

Next, we did extensive background research on each of these individuals and their experiences as mentors and protégés. We then created a target list of those we felt were not only exemplary leaders but were also highly skilled at developing others via mentoring. As a final step, we employed a network of industry experts to provide feedback on participant worthiness for inclusion in *Power Mentoring*.

Once we identified a top mentor, or in some cases a protégé, we then set out to learn as much as possible about that person's network of mentoring relationships, including their past mentors and current protégés. Often we found that the power mentors had very strong one-on-one relationships with one or several protégés, so in those cases we interviewed mentor-protégé *pairs* such as Lisa Ling, television host and reporter, and her mentor, Mitch Koss, Channel One television news producer. Sometimes we found that power mentors had a one-on-one relationship that blossomed to include not only their relationship with a single protégé but also with the protégé's other mentors and contacts. In those cases we interviewed mentoring *groups* such as Cisco's CFO Larry Carter, his protégé Patty Archibeck, and Patty's other mentor, Debra Martucci, vice president of Information Technology at Synopsys, in California's Silicon Valley.

And finally, we were fascinated to find that mentors sometimes belong to an entire *lineage* of mentoring relationships. In a lineage, all of the mentors and protégés connect to each other through a relationship with a "founding" mentor, as in the Jack Welch lineage at General Electric (GE) or the Lou Gerstner lineage at IBM. Although the majority of our interviews represent pairs, groups, or lineages, in some cases, because of other time commitments or outside events (such as illness or war), we were able to interview the mentor only. In these cases, we relied solely on their reflections about their relationships.

Often when we pick up a book filled with fascinating career details, many of us assume that those experiences have little to do with our own lives, because the people portrayed are at the height of their success. Please do not make that assumption with this book! The individuals we profile in *Power Mentoring* often come from humble beginnings and have compelling mentoring stories with which many people can identify. These people got to where they are not by luck, but because of their superior technical and relationship talents and their ability to persevere. The difference between them and other people with talent is that they were not hesitant to ask for help. They were very eager to learn from others. While some had all the advantages one could wish for, others had very modest starts and overcame many obstacles to reach their current levels of success.

Our interviewees have other unique characteristics. First, rather than interviewing a majority of men or of women, our sample included roughly equal numbers. We also looked at mentoring through diverse eyes. Our interviews represented men and women of various ethnicities, ages, sexual orientations, and childhood economic backgrounds, each difference providing us with some unique ideas about mentoring. Let's start by giving you a preview of some of our very interesting power mentors. Of course, later in the book, you will also get a chance to meet at least one of their protégés as well. To give you an introduction to some of our individuals, we describe three with compelling stories.

First, we have the inspiring story of Dixie Garr, vice president of Cisco's Customer Success Engineering. As the youngest of eight children, Dixie grew up in a small town in Louisiana and graduated from her high school class with a National Merit Scholarship. In her role at Cisco, relationship building is her forte, because she leads teams responsible for world-class customer service. When you meet Dixie, you notice her radiant self-confidence, which comes from knowing that she has worked hard to get where she is and that she has much to share with others. She does so often—for example, in addition to her responsibilities at Cisco, she is a sought-after motivational speaker. Her mentoring relationships have been characterized by candor and honesty. As far as her success goes, Dixie says that "there was never a time that I didn't expect to . . . be all that I could be. My parents helped me to understand that I could not be passive, but proactive." Dixie is a glass-ceiling breaker as a black woman in a white male–dominated field. She is also living proof of her belief that technology is a great leveler for women and minorities—she sometimes paraphrases James Brown's lyrics, "Don't give me anything, just open the door and I'll get it myself."

We also had the good fortune to interview a master mentor, Bob Wright, vice-chair of GE and chair and chief executive officer

(CEO) of NBC Universal. Bob joined GE in 1969 and has been an influential mentor for many talented business leaders—you'll meet two of his superstar protégés, Pamela Thomas-Graham, chair of CNBC, and Paula Madison, president and general manager of KNBC, in subsequent chapters. As a protégé of the legendary Jack Welch and thus part of his lineage, Bob's career reads like a primer on how to be successful in American business. Bob enjoys a sterling professional and personal reputation, and under his leadership GE/NBC has made significant inroads in recruiting, retaining, and promoting diverse men and women. In a Columbia Business School lecture in 2003, he shared this observation with his audience: "I've learned that one of the main differentiators between good leaders and great leaders is not necessarily intelligence or experience or personal charisma. It is passion—intense passion for your work and for the success—not of the self—but of the larger enterprise."[4] In future chapters you'll learn a lot more about how Bob brings these words to life through his mentoring relationships.

Now we introduce you to another fascinating and very different power mentor, Rosario Marin, who at the time of our interview was serving as the U.S. Treasurer and was the highest-ranking Latina in the administration of President George W. Bush. Rosario emigrated to the United States from Mexico when she was 14 years old. She spoke no English. A few years later she graduated from Harvard, and judging from her career success since, you might assume that she has led a charmed life. Not so. As a result of having a son with Down syndrome she became frustrated with the available state and federal services for the disabled, and her passion to help her son galvanized her to get involved in politics. Initially she was drawn to work for former California Governor Pete Wilson, because when she heard him speak on behalf of people with disabilities she knew "he was a man of compassion." Wilson became a mentor for her, and she served as deputy director of the Governor's Office of Community Relations. Years later, even in her very busy and highly visible role as U.S. Treasurer, Rosario stayed active in her Latino community and the world of Southern California politics by mentoring several young, aspiring politicians in state government.

These are just three of our extraordinary interviewees. We provide a complete list of our participants in Exhibit 1.1 and more detailed biographical information about each person in the

EXHIBIT 1.1 INTERVIEW PARTICIPANTS

Name	Title	Organization	Role	Name
Fran Allen	Senior technical consultant and vice president, IBM Services	T. J. Watson Research Center, IBM	Mentor to:	Anita Borg
Patty Archibeck	Senior manager, Executive Communications	Cisco Systems, Inc.	Protégé of:	Larry Carter Debra Martucci
Lilach Asofsky	Senior vice president, Marketing/Research/ Creative Services	CNBC	Protégé of:	Pamela Thomas-Graham
Anita Borg (deceased 4/6/2003)	President	Institute for Women and Technology	Protégé of:	Fran Allen
Marc Buckland	TV director	NBC, ABC, CBS	Mentor to:	Laura Medina
Lee Butler	Former commander of U.S. Nuclear Forces	Strategic Air Command	Mentor to:	Donald Pettit
Joan Buzzallino	Vice president of Human Resources, enterprise on demand transformation, the next phase of e-business	IBM Storage Systems	Protégé of:	Linda Sanford
Larry Carter	Senior vice president and chief financial officer	Cisco Systems, Inc.	Mentor to:	Patty Archibeck

(Continued)

EXHIBIT 1.1   INTERVIEW PARTICIPANTS   (continued)

Name	Title	Organization	Role	Name
Judy Chu	Assembly Member, 49th District	California Legislature	Protégé of: Mentor to:	Hilda Solis Sharon Martinez
Martha Coolidge	President, 2002–2003 Film director	Director's Guild of America	Protégé of:	Francis Ford Coppola Peter Bogdanovich
Barbara Corday	Dean, School of Cinema and Television	University of Southern California Film School	Protégé of:	Frank Biondi
Ron Dellums, Esq.	Peace and AIDS activist	Dellums, Brauer & Halterman	Mentor to:	Ron Kirk Barbara Lee
Nick Donofrio	Senior vice president, Technology and Manufacturing	IBM	Mentor to:	Linda Sanford
David Dreier	Congressional Representative, California (R)	U.S. Congress	Mentor to:	Mary Bono
Kim Fisher	Director	Prologue International	Protégé to:	Jim Robbins
Dixie Garr	Vice president, Customer Success	Cisco Systems, Inc.	Mentor to:	Anthony Hayter
Leeza Gibbons	Executive producer and TV personality	Leeza Gibbons Enterprises	Mentored by:	Dick Clark Arnold Shapiro
Lesli Linka Glatter	TV director	Universal Studios	Protégé of:	Steven Spielberg Clint Eastwood

Name	Title	Organization	Role	Name
Araceli Gonzalez	Former delegate, 33rd Congressional District	California Legislature	Protégé of:	Rosario Marin
Judith Gwathmey, M.D. (biotechnology)	President, chief executive officer, founder	Gwathmey, Inc.	Mentor to:	Numerous graduate students
Anthony Hayter	Director, Technical Sales	Crystal Voice Communications	Protégé of:	Dixie Garr
Gale Anne Hurd	Producer (*Terminator 1, 2, and 3*), president	Valhalla Productions	Protégé of:	Roger Corman
Ron Kirk, Esq.	Former senatorial candidate, Texas (D)	Gardere, Wynne, & Sewell, LLP	Protégé of:	Ann Richards Ron Dellums
Kay Koplovitz	President	USA Network	Mentor to:	Doug Holloway
Mitch Koss	Producer	Channel One: A Primedia Company	Mentor to:	Lisa Ling
Charles Lickel	Vice president, Development	IBM Storage Systems	Protégé of:	Linda Sanford
Lisa Ling	Host and TV reporter (formerly of *The View*, ABC)	National Geographic Explorer	Protégé of:	Mitch Koss
Paula Madison	President and general manager	KNBC NBC/ Telemundo Los Angeles	Protégé of:	Bob Wright

(Continued)

EXHIBIT 1.1 INTERVIEW PARTICIPANTS *(continued)*

Name	Title	Organization	Role	Name
Rosario Marin	Former U.S. Treasurer	California State Integrated Waste Management Board	Mentor to:	Araceli Gonzalez Juan Noguez
Sharon Martinez	Former mayor, previous council member	City of Monterey Park, California	Protégé of:	Hilda Solis
Debra Martucci	Vice president, Information Technology	Synopsis, Inc.	Mentor to:	Patty Archibeck
Laura Medina	Film director	DGA Mentoring Program	Protégé of:	Marc Buckland
Ron Meyer	President and chief operating officer	Vivendi Universal Entertainment	Mentor to:	Nikki Rocco Richard Lovett
Martha Morris	Vice president, Global Services Procurement	IBM	Protégé of:	Linda Sanford
Juan Noguez	Vice mayor, Huntington Park, California	Huntington Park City Hall	Protégé of:	Rosario Marin
Donald Pettit	Former deputy director, Manned Space Flights	NASA	Protégé of:	Lee Butler
Jim Robbins	President and founder	Software Business Cluster	Mentor to:	Kim Fisher
Diane Robina	Executive vice president and general manager	TNN: The National Network	Protégé of:	Anne Sweeney

Name	Title	Organization	Role	Name
Nikki Rocco	President, Universal Pictures Distribution	Universal Studios	Protégé of:	Ron Meyer
Bethany Rooney	Film director	Universal Studios	Mentored by:	The late Bruce Paltrow
Linda Sanford	Senior vice president	IBM Storage Systems	Protégé of: Mentor to:	Nick Donofrio Charles Lickel Martha Morris Joan Buzzallino
Hilda Solis	Congressional Representative, 31st District	U.S. House of Representatives	Mentor to:	Sharon Martinez Judy Chu
Anne Sweeney	President and cochair of Media Networks	ABC Cable Networks Group & Disney Channel Worldwide	Mentor to:	Diane Robina Kathleen Von der Ahe
Pamela Thomas-Graham	President and chief executive officer	CNBC	Protégé of: Mentor to:	Bob Wright Lilach Asofsky
Kathleen Von der Ahe	Senior vice president	ABC Network	Protégé of:	Anne Sweeney
Louise Wannier	CEO and founder	Enfish (Knowledge Management Corporation)	Peer mentor to:	Henry Yuen

(Continued)

EXHIBIT 1.1 INTERVIEW PARTICIPANTS   *(continued)*

Name	Title	Organization	Role	Name
Jackie Woods	President	American Association of University Women	Mentor to:	Eboni Zamani
Bob Wright	Vice chair and executive officer Chair and chief executive officer	GE NBC	Mentor to:	Paula Madison Pamela Thomas-Graham
William Wulf	President, National Academy of Engineering, AT&T Professor of Computer Science	University of Virginia	Mentor to:	Numerous graduate students
Henry Yuen	Former chair and chief executive officer	Gemstar-TV Guide International, Inc.	Peer mentor to:	Louise Wannier

appendixes. Appendix A contains the full list of interviewees as well as biographical information on each. Appendix B provides more detail on our interview and analysis process.

THE CHANGING CAREER LANDSCAPE

Most people agree that we are living in a time of great change—much of which has occurred in the past 20 years. The face of working America has been transformed, not only in terms of who is in the workforce, but in the kind of work we do and how it is done. In today's workforce, we see more women, working mothers, and people of color. In fact, dual-career couples made up 78 percent of the workforce in 2002, compared to 66 percent in 1977.[5] The type of work we do has changed significantly as well. Instead of building things or working at manufacturing jobs, we are providing services. According to the U.S. Bureau of Labor Statistics, service-providing industries are expected to account for approximately 20.8 million of the 21.6 million new wage and salary jobs generated in the 10 years between 2002 and 2012.[6] Many more jobs are outsourced than ever before.[7] What's changed is who we do business with, in the sense that our employees and customers are more diverse, more international, and more pressured for time. We are sure you have heard it before—to succeed in today's work environment, managers must be able to successfully manage diversity, enable employees to balance their work and personal lives, and respond adeptly to the changing needs of their customers.

What we do at work and how we do our work are changing as well. Advances in technology result in a decreased availability of the more rudimentary jobs and an increased need for higher-level jobs requiring technical skills. Technology products drive our consumer lifestyle, because last year, customers spent more than $867 billion on information technology.[8] Due to technology, we experience a blurring of boundaries between work and our personal lives. We are hooked into work 24/7 by our Blackberries, Palm Pilots, e-mail, instant messaging (IM), and chat rooms. Current estimates indicate that 839 million people worldwide access the Internet.[9] E-mail and the Internet have dramatically changed how we related to each other—40 percent of employees surveyed in 2003 said they "couldn't live without e-mail."[10] All of these workplace changes have a dramatic impact on individuals' careers and on how best to manage them.

Twenty years ago, a good job for nonprofessionals was usually with a union that ensured that its members enjoyed decent pay and benefits. Now, union membership is dwindling and represents 13.2 percent of private sector jobs, as compared to 20.1 percent in the early 1980s.[11] For professionals, the idea was to climb the corporate ladder in a hierarchical fashion, with ascending to the ranks of management the ultimate goal. All this has changed. Today, employees have more choices and more demands. We have an army of contingency workers (for example, temporary, part time, contractors), and in fact one of the biggest employers in the United States outside of Wal-Mart and the federal government is ManPower Plus, a temporary agency.[12] It is predicted that by 2010, 50 percent of workers will be contingency workers. Today, careers are likely to be protean and boundaryless, with an emphasis on projects and temporary assignments—a situation requiring that employees learn to manage their own careers adeptly and respond readily to change.[13] It is no wonder, then, that the average person changes careers approximately five to seven times over his or her working life. A survey by the Bureau of Labor Statistics found that Baby Boomers typically have approximately ten jobs in their work lives between the ages of 18 and 38.[14] This pattern raises two questions: First, how does the changing landscape affect you, and second, has career advice kept up with these changes?

We have talked about the broad career landscape, and now let's talk about how this relates to you as an individual. In light of these recent changes, are you happy at work? Do the words of the poet Kahlil Gibran, "Work is love made visible,"[15] resonate for you, or do you feel more like Dilbert on a daily basis: underappreciated and overworked? Or does it vary for you from day to day or depending on what else is happening in your life? Next, consider the members of your organization or profession. Think specifically about your coworkers, or your employees if you are a manager, and how they might respond to these questions. Chances are good that their responses have a lot to do with whether they will remain in your organization or profession. If employees are mentally disengaging by showing less interest or enthusiasm for their work, or physically disengaging by increasing their absenteeism and turnover, your organization will suffer.

Beverly Kaye, a best-selling author and career consultant, reported some interesting findings and analysis from an ongoing Gallup study.[16] Gallup reports that 26 percent of the U.S. population are engaged (loyal and productive), 55 percent are not engaged (just putting in their time), and 19 percent are actively disengaged (unhappy and spreading their discontent). Gallup estimates that the cost of this widespread disengagement is $350 billion per year in lost productivity to American business. Along the same lines, consider this example: A national clothing chain must sell 3,000 pairs of $35 khakis to cover the price of replacing a salesperson who quits, which includes the cost of recruitment, training, and lost productivity. Moreover, the tab to replace a white-collar middle manager runs about $100,000, and the costs increase the higher up the organizational structure you go.[17] Even more troubling than the direct costs of turnover, however, are the indirect and even higher costs of lost productivity.

If you are concerned about costs like these, you are not alone. Many CEOs and managers today are very concerned about what it takes to attract and retain talented employees. Beverly Kaye and Sharon Jordan-Evans recently completed their own survey of 15,000 employees in a wide variety of industries, and from this identified the main drivers of employee retention.[18] We list the top five drivers here:

1. Exciting work and challenge
2. Career growth, learning, and development
3. Working with great people and relationships
4. Fair pay
5. Supportive management/great boss

It probably comes as no surprise that pay was not ranked first, second, or even third. (Of course, that does not mean you can underpay people and they will be happy.) You might be wondering how managers' attitudes differ from employees' with respect to what they think makes a motivating workplace. In fact, Marcus Buckingham and Curt Coffman wrote a book based on interviews and surveys conducted by the Gallup organization with 80,000 managers in Fortune 500 companies.[19] They found that according to managers, 12 core elements make up a great place to work. Take a look at this list and ask yourself to what degree these items apply to your own work environment:

1. Do I know what is expected of me at work?
2. Do I have the materials and equipment I need to do my work right?
3. At work, do I have the opportunity to do what is best every day?
4. In the last seven days, have I received recognition or praise for doing good work?
5. Does my supervisor, or someone at work, seem to care about my development?
6. Is there someone at work who cares about my development?
7. At work, do my opinions seem to count?
8. Does the mission/purpose of my company make me feel my job is important?
9. Are my coworkers committed to doing quality work?
10. Do I have a best friend at work?
11. In the last six months, has someone at work talked to me about my progress?
12. This last year, have I had opportunities at work to learn and grow?

Did you notice how important relationships with others were in both of these workplace surveys? This brings us back to the subject of this book, which is mentoring relationships. Simply put, factors that determine whether employees and managers stay engaged at work can be influenced by solid mentoring relationships. After all, research shows conclusively that good mentors provide two major forms of assistance to their protégés: emotional support and career help, which includes presenting an example of a positive career role model.[20] Mentors furnish many types of career support by offering challenges and growth opportunities, career advice, and access to learning opportunities and resources. Mentors also provide emotional support in terms of encouragement, recognition, feedback, and coaching. And yes, studies have shown that those who have mentors make more money than those who do not![21]

What else can mentors do? Mentors can help you clarify work expectations, give you an opportunity to do your best, enable you to receive recognition and praise, make you feel cared about, encourage your development, make you feel like your opinions matter, provide you with friendship at work, talk to you about your progress, and provide opportunities for you to learn and grow. As we have mentioned, past research has also found that people with mentors get more promotions and experience greater job and career satisfaction than those without mentors.[22] Of course, this list might make it seem like only the protégé benefits—not so in power mentoring! We think you will be pleasantly surprised to find out about all the ways that mentors benefit from mentoring as well. These benefits include an improvement in mentors' feedback and coaching skills, an enhanced reputation, and a greater sense of personal fulfillment.[23] We elaborate on these points by relating stories and ideas from our interviewees in Chapter Three. In sum, past research shows that good mentoring relationships can improve your work life, job satisfaction, and happiness quotient at work.

In the spirit of learning from the best, we conclude with a quote from Jeffrey Immelt, GE's current CEO, when asked about the most important lesson he learned from mentor Jack Welch: "The importance of people," he says, "attracting them, inspiring them. I spend at least 50% of my time on people. I teach, I develop, I encourage, I reward, I challenge. I do those things to motivate people."[24]

We turn now to the second question posed earlier: Has career advice kept up with what we know about the changing career landscape? The answer is yes in some respects and no in others. Professionals today are exhorted to build a network, develop a portable portfolio of skills, and be prepared for frequent and unexpected changes. Most career books and professionals tout the importance of having a mentor, and some even offer advice about how to get a mentor. However, much of the advice about mentoring seems predicated on outdated assumptions about work. One of these assumptions is that most professionals want to pursue a hierarchical career path, when today we are just as likely to see horizontal career paths in which professionals gain skills in different arenas by moving sideways rather than up. Also, most professionals today are likely to exhibit greater loyalty to their professions than to their organizations, so having a mentor in the same organization—or even just one mentor anywhere—is no longer sufficient. Today, because knowledge becomes outdated so quickly, having access to a diverse group of confidants in the form of power mentors can help a person stay ahead of change.

Although careers have changed dramatically in the past 20 years, most of the advice readily available on mentoring has not taken these dramatic changes into account, until now. We do not work, manage our careers, or even have relationships (for example, think about e-mail and online relationships) the same way we used to 20 years ago, so why should we assume that our mentoring relationships operate the same way? We can't. Earlier we defined traditional mentoring as a relationship in which an older, more experienced, and higher-level mentor takes a younger protégé under his or her wing and guides the protégé through career twists and turns. Usually, in a traditional mentoring relationship there is an implied expectation of exclusivity between the mentor and the protégé. Traditionally, the flow of benefits was seen as one-way, with the mentor giving and the protégé partaking. Recent research, particularly in the past 10 years, has exploded many of the old myths about mentoring. Mentoring relationships today are different, and *Power Mentoring* reflects the new work environment and career challenges.

We are certainly *not* saying that traditional mentors are no longer useful. In fact, if you have a great traditional mentor, then treat him or her like gold. Also, if you have more than one traditional mentor, or what we call a *network,* then you are already enjoying some of the benefits of a power mentoring approach. Power mentoring is about having more than one mentor and/or different forms of mentors. Times have changed, and many people, like us, may not have access to traditional mentors; therefore this book is about encouraging you to expand your thinking about mentoring. Given the importance of mentoring, it is not surprising that 60 out of the 100 best organizations identified by *Fortune* magazine support formal mentoring programs.[25] On the federal level, the U.S. House of Representatives has approved a bill increasing federal funding of mentoring grants to $100 million for formal youth-mentoring programs.[26] Mentoring is often touted as the answer to many of our societal, organizational, and employee career dilemmas.

Unfortunately, recent research has revealed that those in formal mentoring programs often fail to deliver on their rosy promises, and the participants may be left helpless and disillusioned.[27] Possible reasons for this include a shoddy formal mentoring program structure, a matchmaking system that mimics blind dates from hell, or simply inadequate resources or rewards to support these programs. We notice a strange disconnect between academics and practitioners with respect to formal mentoring programs. Researchers continue to find that formal mentoring programs are less effective than spontaneously developed relationships, yet organizational decision makers continue to invest more resources in the formal programs. Organizations and nonprofits often expend a large amount of resources on formal mentoring programs, when instead perhaps they should be expending these resources on creating an infrastructure that enables mentoring relationships to grow and thrive organically.

Should academics and practitioners throw up our hands out of frustration with each other? No! This disconnect is one of the reasons for this book. We need to communicate across the academic-practitioner divide, share what we know, and partner together. We believe that formal mentoring programs can be made much better and even rival informal relationships if they are made to look and feel like informal relationships. This book will give you lots of ideas about how to do this, because we draw from both formal and informal relationships. We revisit the idea of applying power mentoring approaches to formal mentoring in Chapter Eight.

Research clearly shows that spontaneously developed or informal mentoring relationships are, on the whole, more effective than those developed under the auspices of formal programs. But even informal mentoring relationships may not be the answer for everybody. In fact, many of the successful corporate executives we know are busy being masters of their own universe and may not have time to mentor all of us who might really thrive under their tutelage. Therefore, while traditional mentoring, which can take place in a formal program or as part of an informal relationship, is great, it has four main drawbacks. Traditional mentoring is limited because it is

1. Based on outdated career assumptions.
2. Often part of formal mentoring programs, which while common, have been found to be less effective than spontaneously developed relationships.
3. Difficult to obtain because the demand for mentors outweighs the supply.
4. May be particularly difficult for women and people of color to obtain. Research has found that often mentors tend to mentor in their own image, based on the idea that "like attracts like,"

FIGURE 1.1 CHARACTERISTICS OF POWER MENTORING

High
Level of
Reciprocity

Self-Directed

Transcends
Organizational
Boundaries

Difficult
Tests and
Challenges

**Power
Mentoring**

Multiple
Mentors and
Networks

Facilitates
Leadership
Succession
Planning

High Quality
Relationships

Nontraditional
Mentoring
Forms

so if you don't look like those in the power structure, you might be at a disadvantage for getting a traditional mentor.[28]

To remedy these drawbacks, we suggest you consider the myriad ways power mentoring differs from traditional mentoring and think about how you can get involved in these relationships. Of course, these ideas are discussed in detail in the rest of the book, but we provide you with a brief preview of these concepts in the following paragraphs.

Power mentoring includes traditional mentoring but also expands and in some cases radically departs from what we consider to be traditional mentoring (see Figure 1.1).

- Power mentoring is about networks and may involve having access to groups or even an entire lineage of mentors, rather than simply being in a dyadic relationship.
- It is not only about protégés receiving benefits but is also about the rewards mentors receive.
- Traditional mentoring tends to be about mentors and protégés partnering together because "like attracts like." Power mentoring is often about relationships between people who are dissimilar but who have complementary skills and needs.

- In traditional mentoring, the mentor frequently chooses the protégé, whereas in power mentoring the protégé often makes the first advance.
- Instead of being a monogamous, one-on-one relationship, power mentoring involves an open, even polygamous relationship.
- While the purpose of traditional mentoring is often related to the planning of organizational succession and staff development, power mentoring does this and more, because it is about developing a talent pool for an entire profession.
- While traditional mentoring often takes place in or is bounded by an organization's corporate membership or structure, the boundaries of power mentoring relationships are permeable and often defy intuitive logic. In some cases, even competitors can be mentors, because in today's environment, people's loyalty may be tied to their profession rather than to their temporary corporate home.

In short, our academic colleagues have recommended that having a diverse network of mentors is the best solution for today's career dilemmas.[29] We also recommend that if you are a protégé, you take an active approach to getting a mentor rather than waiting to be chosen. Look outside typical boundaries when considering whom to target. If you are already a mentor or a would-be mentor, you can learn a great deal about the many benefits you can gain, not just what you can give, from this book. These ideas and others represent an important part of the *Power Mentoring* prescription for success.

OVERVIEW OF THE BOOK

Power Mentoring is structured around three questions: (1) What is power mentoring? (2) What's in a power mentoring relationship for you? (3) How can you develop power mentoring relationships to enhance your own career and professional happiness?

CHAPTER TWO: THE MANY FACES OF POWER MENTORING

Chapter Two begins with a provocative question: Can you make it in your career without a mentor? We provide proof through examples that perhaps you can without a traditional mentor, but not without a power mentor! In this chapter we expand our definition of power mentoring by providing compelling examples from our participants and describe how power mentoring differs from traditional mentoring in what it does, how it looks, and where it lives. Specifically, Chapter Two

- Answers the question, Do you need a mentor to get ahead?
- Explains how traditional and power mentoring are similar and different
- Profiles 10 new forms of mentoring relationships and their challenges and benefits through case examples
- Will help you become inspired to develop power mentoring relationships by highlighting the vast array of choices open to you

CHAPTER THREE: MENTORING AS A TWO-WAY STREET: BENEFITS OF GIVING AND RECEIVING

In this chapter we want you to become enthusiastic about all of the terrific benefits you and your organization can gain from being part of a power mentoring relationship. We do this by introducing our power mentors and protégés through their stories about what they give and get from their relationships with each other. We highlight the benefits that both mentors and protégés gain by featuring mentor-protégé pairs such as retired Five-Star General Lee Butler (former commander of the U.S. Nuclear Forces) and his protégé, Brigadier General Donald Pettit. We show how reciprocity or a mutual exchange of benefits is the key ingredient enabling power mentoring relationships to thrive. We conclude the chapter with a summary of benefits gained by protégés, mentors, and organizations. Therefore, the chapter

- Answers the question, What can I gain from power mentoring?
- Introduces our cast of characters and their mentoring successes
- Compares traditional and power mentoring rewards and benefits
- Shows that power mentoring is a two-way street and that both parties engage in valuable exchanges
- Highlights both mentor and protégé ideas about what they give and get

CHAPTER FOUR: THE MIND OF THE MENTOR

The purpose of this chapter is to shed light on the mind of the mentor in power mentoring relationships. An important key to understanding mentoring relationships lies in determining why people choose to mentor others. We delve into the mind of the mentor to uncover some of the typical philosophies the mentors in our study held with respect to the mentoring relationship. We also look at (1) the characteristics of a perfect protégé in the eyes of the mentor; (2) the purpose and nature of the possible tests and challenges that mentors might pose to protégés; and (3) the ways the mentoring relationship can develop successfully. These topics help would-be protégés and mentors enrich their potential relationships. More specifically, this chapter will help you

- Answer the question, What's in it for me to be a power mentor and what can I learn from power mentors?
- Get into the inner workings of the mentor's mind by learning about mental models and mentoring philosophies
- Uncover the secrets of why mentors are first attracted to their protégés and what makes the "perfect protégé"
- Understand the tests and challenges of powerful mentoring pairs as well as the skills needed to pass these tests

CHAPTER FIVE: THE PROTÉGÉ'S PERSPECTIVE: HOW TO GET AND KEEP A POWER MENTOR

In this chapter, we examine initiation and attraction from the perspective of the protégé. We fully develop the idea of trust as a foundation for power mentoring and suggest specific categories and outcomes related to trust. Along with this, we discuss goal setting, because many of our stories revealed that successful protégés engage in specific career goal-setting activities to determine what types of mentors will work well for them. We provide specific strategies that protégés involved in the various types of power mentoring relationships (for example, peer, barrier-busting, and so on) can use to obtain power mentors. In summary, this chapter

- Answers the question, How do I get and keep a power mentor?
- Gives specific strategies for finding 10 different types of power mentors

- Uncovers targeting and wooing techniques for getting and keeping a power mentor
- Encourages you to set goals for getting what you want out of power mentoring
- Shows how trust and loyalty can enhance power mentoring

CHAPTER SIX: UNLOCKING THE SECRETS OF GREAT POWER MENTORING RELATIONSHIPS

In this chapter we uncover the specific strategies both the mentor and the protégé use to deepen their relationship by sharing examples of relationships that worked to achieve great things for both parties. We specifically focus on examples of good people skills, communication, and continued trust building. To understand the secrets of the successful mentoring relationship itself, we frame our findings in the context of important research on interpersonal relationships. Specifically, the chapter

- Answers the question, How does one bring a power mentoring relationship to its full potential from the perspective of both the mentor and the protégé?
- Introduces the building blocks of other effective relationships (for example, friendships, marriage) and shows how these apply to power mentoring
- Illustrates the importance of defining moments in power mentoring relationships
- Highlights the role of emotional intelligence in mentoring relationships and the important communication strategies employed by our power mentoring pairs and clusters
- Shares strategies to gracefully extricate oneself from the mentoring web of connections, especially if a relationship has become dysfunctional
- Makes the reader aware of when it is time to bring others into the mentoring network

CHAPTER SEVEN: POWER MENTORING AND YOU

The purpose of this chapter is to help you integrate learning from previous chapters and provide you with concrete and immediately applicable ways to improve your own career through power mentoring. We introduce the road map for entering into power mentoring relationships by providing a structure for readers to create a personal Relationship Development Plan (RDP). This chapter

- Answers the question, What's my plan of action for making power mentoring work for me (and possibly my organization) right now?
- Integrates key concepts from previous chapters to create a personal Relationship Development Plan for power mentoring

Chapter Eight: Conclusion: What We Have Learned About Mentoring in Today's Work Environment

In Chapter Two, we discussed the drawbacks of formal mentoring programs. In this final chapter we revisit these problems, offering suggestions for addressing them by incorporating power mentoring strategies. We provide a brief review of the best practices of formal mentoring programs and assess how power mentoring can be integrated into the existing workplace framework and organizational reward structures. In short, this chapter

- Answers the question, How does power mentoring apply to formal mentoring programs?
- Gives strategies to improve formal mentoring programs in organizations by incorporating power mentoring concepts

In Chapter Two, we introduce power mentoring by extending what you may know about mentoring. We give you an idea of the many forms of power mentoring. We specifically address how contemporary power mentoring differs from classic mentoring in *what it does, how it looks,* and *where it lives,* by providing illustrations from our interviews.

CHAPTER TWO

THE MANY FACES OF POWER MENTORING

*Young people will have an older person in the
organization to look after them in their early years to
ensure that their careers are off to a good start. Out of
these relationships it is hoped that young people learn to
take risks, accept a philosophical commitment to sharing,
and learn to relate to people in an intuitive empathic way.*
—HARVARD BUSINESS REVIEW, 1978

*Success is a lousy teacher. It seduces smart people into
thinking they can't lose.*
—BILL GATES

"Everyone Who Makes It Has a Mentor" was the title of the classic 1978 *Harvard Business Review* article that the first of the two chapter epigraphs was taken from. This article details the mentoring relationship among three successive chief executives at the Jewel Companies. The debate about making it in your career with or without a mentor still rages today. So, do you think that you can make it in your career without a mentor? Are the larger-than-life stories of the self-made man or woman really true? What about someone like Bill Gates? He is often depicted as a rumpled Ivy League dropout turned master of the universe who made it to the top all by himself. But did Gates really make it entirely on his own? Absolutely not.

While Bill Gates may not have had a traditional mentor, he derived many benefits from power mentoring. In fact, Gates obtained his first computer industry job through the guidance and on the recommendation of one of his high school teachers, Fred Wright. Mr. Wright was a mentor to Gates and his group of computer-savvy friends, including fellow Microsoft founder Paul Allen. (It's interesting that three others in the computer club at Lakeside High School—Marc McDonald, Richard Weiland, and Chris Larson—became some of the first programmers for Microsoft.) Wright was the group's center and driving force, encouraging all the members to explore computers and enabling them to connect with Computer Center Corporation (a Seattle-based technology organization). Moreover, to this day, even Gates, one of the most successful men in the world, has a team of advisors that he draws from, including Microsoft chief executive officer (CEO) Steve Ballmer and fellow billionaire Warren Buffet.

If you carefully examine the careers and lives of successful people, you may find that many were indeed fortunate enough to have "traditional" mentors who helped them along the path to success. In fact, there is even a Mentor Hall of Fame Web site that identifies celebrities, political and business leaders, and their respective mentors. Mentor-protégé pairs include Madonna and Gwyneth Paltrow and William Fulbright and Bill Clinton. But what about other successful people who insist that they made it on their own? We suggest that while these people may not have been lucky enough to enjoy the help of traditional mentors, an examination of their career journeys would reveal some reliance on a network of power mentors. Can you make it in your career without a mentor? Perhaps you can without a traditional mentor, but not without a power mentor!

In Chapter One, we provided a brief introduction to the classic approach to mentoring, known as *traditional mentoring,* as well as to the more contemporary approach known as *power mentoring,* noting similarities and differences. Specifically, we covered in brief:

- The changing career environment, which leads to new demands on mentoring relationships
- Limitations of classic mentoring approaches
- The advantages of new forms of mentoring embodied in power mentoring

Now, we expand on these ideas by weaving in compelling examples from our participants that tell the story of power mentoring relationships. We describe how contemporary power mentoring differs from classic mentoring in *what it does, how it looks,* and *where it lives,* by providing illustrations from our interviews. Before we get into the details of the differences, we provide an overview of what we mean by classic mentoring and discuss the need for the more contemporary approach that we call *power mentoring.*

CLASSIC VERSUS CONTEMPORARY APPROACHES TO MENTORING

Most discussions of the classic approach to mentoring start by recalling the tale of Odysseus, the protagonist of Homer's *Odyssey* and other works. In setting out for the Trojan War, Odysseus entrusted the education of his son, Telemachus, to Mentor, a wise elder (in some versions Mentor was later revealed to be the goddess Athena in disguise). This view of mentoring as a relationship in which an older, more knowledgeable individual takes a younger protégé under his wing hasn't changed much since the inception of Greek mythology. Because we've spent the past decade immersed in mentoring by writing articles, speaking about mentoring, and designing mentoring programs, we've started to see some new ideas emerge about contemporary approaches to mentoring. In addition, we owe a debt of gratitude to our academic colleagues doing mentoring research; unfortunately many of their great ideas have been hidden away in the proverbial ivory tower— until now.[1] All of these ideas formed the basis of our conversations with our 50 executives, which led to our identifying the approach to mentoring that we call power mentoring.

In the past, mentoring has taken one form only: traditional mentoring. This type of mentoring in corporate America has for many years followed a basic pattern that goes something like this: The older, wiser, top executive would choose a young person who may have reminded him of himself when he was younger, or perhaps had attended the same college or university. He would groom that person in his own image, passing along the wisdom of his profession, and, more important, the secrets of the organization. In traditional mentoring, the emphasis is on grooming the protégé for a key position within the same organization, and the relationship is expected to be monogamous. As you will see, this dynamic is often very different in power mentoring relationships.

Scholarly interest in traditional mentoring relationships (in their prevalence, function, and benefits) began in the early 1980s and was reflected in influential works like Kathy Kram's *Mentoring at Work* and Michael Zey's *The Mentor Connection*.[2] Numerous research studies over the past 20 years have confirmed the benefits of these traditional one-on-one relationships for improving protégés' rates of promotion, career satisfaction, and salary. In fact, as mentioned in Chapter One, many companies have been so enamored of the positive effects of mentoring on employee career success that they have attempted to replicate spontaneously developed mentoring relationships by establishing formalized programs. These formal mentoring programs, in which the organization pairs mentors with protégés (often people they have never met) in one-on-one relationships where they get together periodically, have in general proved only marginally effective. These relationships are something like short-term arranged marriages. Some have been successful, but many started out as mismatches. If the people involved have nothing in common or no common goals to work toward, the relationship would not develop as fully as a spontaneous relationship based on mutual attraction and similar expectations would develop. Power mentoring suggests innovative ways that formal mentoring programs can be improved for a better return on investment for organizations and their stakeholders.

In traditional mentoring relationships, whether formal or spontaneous, mentors support protégés in three ways.[3] First, they offer career guidance—for example, by making suggestions on assignments a protégé might take, or suggestions on what career path might be most advantageous. Second, mentors can provide emotional support around issues such as the inherent conflict between work and family, or can recommend methods for coping with a difficult boss or with work stress. Third, a mentor may provide support to protégés by serving as an effective role model who demonstrates appropriate behaviors for different situations. For example, a protégé might observe a mentor using persuasion techniques during a meeting to effectively convince upper management of the merits of an idea. Alternatively, a mentor may demonstrate how to handle a difficult employee. In sum, there are many advantages to the traditional mentoring relationship, and for that reason we want to make it very clear that traditional mentoring should *not* be discarded. In fact, we suggest that traditional mentoring be considered part of the power mentoring system. It is because today's organizations and careers are different from those of the past that the traditional "one-size-fits-all" approach to mentoring does not fit everybody, all the time. Therefore, by providing an array of options, power mentoring is better suited for the changing workplace.

How do you know if your current or anticipated mentoring relationship is a traditional mentoring relationship or a power mentoring relationship, and what are the major differences? First, rest assured that *power mentoring* is not just a cute term. The word *power* has several specific implications here. First, power mentoring is unique because it gives those involved the power of choice in terms of relying not just on one mentor, but many. Second, this approach to mentoring can empower you to make more money, get more promotions, and make your career goals and dreams come true. Third, power mentoring is empowering in that it can help you to have better professional relationships and ultimately derive more satisfaction and meaning from your work.

Think of power mentoring as serving as an umbrella under which are gathered a number of different types of mentors, including traditional mentors but also other types of mentors, like electronic mentors (e-mentors), reverse mentors, peer mentors, and many others that we discuss later in this chapter. In short, power mentoring is defined as a network approach to mentoring that gives those involved mutually beneficial outcomes related to career growth and development. Exhibit 2.1 presents a summary comparison of the major differences between the classic form of traditional mentoring and the contemporary approach of power mentoring.

Many of you are probably already engaged in power mentoring. A typical scenario might look like this: Perhaps there's an influential member of your profession whom you don't know well but whom you look to for inspiration by watching and learning from their example (for example, if you are in media maybe this is Barbara Walters). When you find yourself in a tight spot, you might even ask, "What would Barbara do here?" At the same time perhaps you are fortunate enough to have a boss who provides you with career advice and job-related feedback. While this is all well and good, you find that it isn't quite enough. Barbara Walters might be a terrific role model, but you don't exactly have her home phone number handy so you can run your daily concerns by her. Likewise, your boss is wonderful when your question is work related, but what about when your need really blurs the boundaries of work and home, or you just need to kvetch? You still need something more, so you find yourself turning to a *peer mentor* for emotional or more personal support. This network approach to relying on a set of different mentors for your various needs is just one example of how power mentoring can be helpful to you.

We encourage you to take an additive approach to mentoring. If you are fortunate enough to have a wise and successful godfather or godmother mentor, by all means enjoy the benefits of this relationship and hang on tight! If however, like us, you aren't fortunate enough to have this one perfect traditional mentor, or you just want to make a good thing better, then consider the many options power mentoring offers you. Start by thinking about your needs and wants and what you can give a potential mentor in exchange for their assistance and support. Next, take a look at the various types of mentors we discuss in the next section of the chapter, and then think about whom you know or would like to get to know who might fill these roles for you. We will be giving you lots of specific ideas and strategies about exactly how to do this in the following chapters. Developing your own personal posse of power mentors is likely to be exactly what you need to help you reach your full potential in your career.

WHAT POWER MENTORING DOES

In this section we outline the five unique components of what power mentoring does in comparison to traditional mentoring.

ORGANIZATIONAL PURPOSE

One of the most important reasons organizations support traditional mentoring relationships is to facilitate short-term succession planning for key positions. Power mentoring goes a step beyond this limited approach because it also focuses on long-term succession planning at various levels of the organization. In addition, power mentoring places a greater emphasis on diversity than traditional mentoring has done in the past. We examine two well-known organizations to exemplify these points.

Disney's Disneyland promotes itself as the "happiest place on earth." While its visitors may still be happy, the evidence indicates

EXHIBIT 2.1 COMPARISON OF CLASSIC AND CONTEMPORARY APPROACHES TO MENTORING

	The Classic Approach: Traditional Mentoring	The Contemporary Approach: Power Mentoring
What Power Mentoring Does		
Organizational purpose	Short-term succession planning for key positions	Long-term succession planning and organizational diversity
Relationship initiation and maintenance	Initiated and driven more by mentor's wishes and needs	Initiated and driven more by active protégé
Tests and challenges	Less apparent and well documented	Nearly always profound and integral to the relationship development
Reciprocity	Benefits tend to be perceived as unidirectional, with mentor giving and protégé receiving	A greater focus on complementary skills in that protégé and mentor exchange different but important benefits
Generative nature (giving back to the next generation)	Late in career	Throughout career
What Power Mentoring Looks Like		
Style	Monogamous (exclusive, one-on-one relationship)	Polygamous (open relationship)
Source of mentor	Intraorganizational (usually relationships occur within same organization)	Extraorganizational (relationships often outside the organization)
Diversity	Like attracts like in terms of demographic similarity	Less demographic similarity—instead mentors and protégés thoughtfully seek out diverse relationships

	The Classic Approach: Traditional Mentoring	*The Contemporary Approach: Power Mentoring*
Where Power Mentoring Lives		
Loyalty base	Organization	Profession
Where it works	Organizations or professions with clearly defined and linear career paths	Any type of organization but especially thrives in boundaryless organizations or careers
Mentor centrality	Can vary (mentor can be very skilled but not tapped into power mainstream)	Mentor is part of and provides access to powerful lineage of mentors

that its stockholders and employees are less than happy. Traditional mentoring does exist at Disney, because the organization does have a formal mentoring program. In fact, Michael Eisner (former Disney CEO) enjoyed a close traditional mentoring relationship with former Disney President Frank Wells. However, Eisner was severely criticized in the press, not only for a number of management missteps, but also because he failed to develop an heir apparent to succeed him as CEO. Many see this as a conscious strategy employed by Eisner to maintain his indispensability and powerful position.[4] Eisner was not a power mentor or even a traditional mentor to others. Though Eisner brought Michael Ovitz to Disney and tried to mentor him, this relationship ended acrimoniously for both parties and perhaps contributed to Eisner's reluctance to mentor others. However, many pundits believe that Eisner's lack of long-term succession planning and executive development greatly contributed to his loss of position and power and was ultimately a major contributing factor in his demise.

In contrast, Jack Welch, former CEO of General Electric (GE), spent a great deal of time developing a circle of potential successors, ensuring a smooth leadership transition as well as the long-term viability of GE. Jack Welch is a master traditional mentor and consummate power mentor. This is evident from the former Welch protégés who have gone on to succeed in leadership positions. These include a long list of executive luminaries such as Mark Bulriss (CEO of Great Lakes Chemical), Robert Collins (chair of Scott Technologies), and David Cote (chair of Tupperware), as well as the current CEO of GE, Jeffrey Immelt.[5] We interviewed and share the stories of three phenomenally successful former Welch protégés, including Bob Wright, CEO of NBC, and his protégés Pamela Thomas-Graham, CEO of CNBC, and Paula Madison, president of KNBC. A close examination of Jack Welch's mentoring legacy reveals that not only was he concerned about his immediate successor, but he also cared about the development of the pipeline of future talent. It is well known, too, that he could be ruthless in ousting nonperformers and did not suffer fools gladly. Jack knew the future of GE was in developing a diverse talent pool: people of varied ethnicity and gender as well as those who brought new and different skill sets. Therefore, he focused not only on mentoring others for the purpose of succession planning but also to ensure diversity and thus the long-term success of GE.

Power mentoring contrasts with traditional mentoring in four other important ways besides organizational purpose. Power mentoring differs (1) in who initiates the relationship (in power mentoring it is often initiated by the protégé), (2) in the extensive role of tests and challenges (while these may also occur in traditional relationships, to date they have not been well documented or studied extensively in those relationships), (3) in the prevalence of true reciprocity (the mentor as well as the protégé benefits in power mentoring), and (4) in the generative focus (giving back to the next generation occurs throughout the power mentor's career, rather than just later in life, as in traditional mentoring). We provide a compelling example that illustrates these four aspects of what the power mentoring relationship does in the story of protégé Araceli Gonzalez, manager and owner of AG Business Services, and her mentor, Rosario Marin, 41st U.S. Treasurer.

Araceli Gonzalez is a Mexican American woman who has begun to make a mark in Republican politics in Southern California. She enjoyed the backing of the George W. Bush White House during her run for the California State Senate in a typically Democratic district. How did a young woman in local politics find herself linked to the Washington, D.C., power elite? Through the wise mentoring of Rosario Marin, former U.S. Treasurer and another Mexican American Republican. On first meeting Rosario, Araceli described herself as awestruck. To Araceli, Rosario was an incredibly poised woman who served as a leader in politics in a neighboring town in Southern California, and who believed in the same things Araceli believed in. She never dreamed that they might become friends, let alone that Rosario might be her mentor.

When initially thinking about the possibility of Rosario helping her, Araceli described her feelings this way: "I never thought of her as someone I would have a relationship with because she's way up there, and I am way down here." She continued to watch Rosario's career and found that in addition to the many similarities in their backgrounds, there was a lot she could learn from Rosario. They began to run into one another at meetings, and eventually Araceli began to ask Rosario for career advice in working through some difficult issues in her position as city council member for the Cudahy, a small city in Los Angeles County.

RELATIONSHIP INITIATION AND MAINTENANCE

As we discuss in Chapter Five, we found that in power mentoring relationships protégés tended to initiate relationships with their mentors more often than the reverse. We heard examples of protégés who staked out a claim on a mentor they believed could help them. Protégés approached their targeted mentors with specific goals and plans. This type of approach is much different from traditional mentoring relationships, where the protégé waits to be tapped by the mentor. In power mentoring, the protégé often chooses the mentor and makes a conscious effort to recruit him or her. In contrast to the protocol in traditional mentoring relationships, Rosario did not pick Araceli; instead Araceli knew what she wanted, saw a woman she admired, and sought Rosario out for career advice.

TESTS AND CHALLENGES

Another important factor that differentiates power mentoring from traditional mentoring is the extensive prevalence of tests and challenges. Studies have suggested that in classic mentoring, protégés may sometimes encounter tests and challenges as part of the development of their relationship with their mentors. In an early study of mentoring, Kathy Kram showed that as the mentor and protégé are getting to know one another, a mentor may present the protégé with a test in the form of a difficult work assignment.[6] Other than Kram's early work, there is a dearth of research investigating the phenomenon of tests and challenges. We suspect that tests and challenges are important in traditional mentoring relationships as well as in more contemporary types of mentoring but simply have not been studied extensively. In contrast, we found that in the power mentoring relationships we examined, tests and challenges were integral to relationship development. Moreover, the testing often was a two-way street where the protégés tested the mentors and vice versa. Also, the tests and challenges posed took more complex and diverse forms than those discussed in previous mentoring studies.

Returning to our example, the test and challenge came from Araceli to Rosario. She had put a test to Rosario when she asked her for help in a difficult situation. Araceli began to witness situations such as conflicts of interest and secret dealings in her city and surrounding cities. She realized that it was not something she could talk about openly; she was concerned that her criticisms would get back to those who were involved and who were running in the same political circles as she was. As Araceli put it, "So here I was—in a very difficult situation. It was, do I run for reelection and let these guys beat up on me so that I don't bring out these conflict of interest charges and corruption? Or do I finish out my term and turn them in?" The only person she thought of presenting her dilemma to was Rosario. In Araceli's words: "Rosario said, 'Do the right thing,'. . . so I turned them in." Araceli reflected on what happened next: "Every colleague I had, every person I thought was my friend, was gone. The only ones who didn't turn their backs on me were law enforcement and Rosario Marin. Of course, I was very scared and worried. But I felt that my actions were what serving in public office was all about—speaking your mind and not being afraid. Rosario was there for me and said, 'Look, Araceli, you're doing the right thing. If that's what you feel in your heart, do what's in your heart. I will see what I can do.'" Araceli couldn't get anyone at a higher level in the city to take this on. She admits that if she hadn't had Rosario, she probably would have been intimidated to the point of moving out of the city.

The city council members were all brought before a grand jury to testify. As Araceli recounted the story, she still struggles with what she did. She said, "It's very hard to turn in your colleagues for conflict of interest and corruption charges. It doesn't happen. And I can see why. Because people will pressure you to the point where you think you've done something wrong, when in actuality you really have followed the law." What helped her through the experience was Rosario's advice: "Just do what is right. And you're never going to have to worry." Araceli was testing the depth of the relationship between them. In turn, Rosario provided a challenge to Araceli by telling her, "Araceli, do what is right." The tests and challenges in Rosario and Araceli's relationship came from both sides of the mentoring dynamic—another factor setting power mentoring apart from traditional mentoring relationships.

RECIPROCITY

Often traditional mentoring is perceived as a fairly altruistic practice, with the mentor doing most of the giving and the protégé doing most of the receiving. But researchers have begun to challenge this perception, and an interesting line of research is evolving around what mentors gain from the relationship.[7] Therefore, in line with this newer thinking, we believe that one of power mentoring's most interesting characteristics is its reciprocal nature. What is exchanged might be different on each side of the relationship, but it is perceived as valuable by and to each party. In fact, we were struck by the mentors' conscious development of mentoring relationships with those who had complementary or different skills, rather than seeking protégés with similar skills and trying to mold them in their own image. Power mentors consciously look at what they can give *and* gain—we talk more about these ideas in the next chapter. Many individuals and pairs we interviewed talked about the fact that having a protégé helped them know more about their organization or kept them up to date on technical skills required in their profession. In the case of Araceli and Rosario, while Rosario resides in Washington, D.C., Araceli has helped her maintain her Southern California political connections. In fact, when Rosario declared her interest in running for the U.S. Senate, she found that Araceli was a loyal and hardworking supporter.

Generative Nature

One of the final ways power mentoring differs from traditional mentoring relates to the stage of life in which one undertakes the role of mentor. Power mentors recognize that the generativity (giving back to the next generation of workers) that comes from mentoring someone should be undertaken early in one's life rather than waiting until later, which is more typical of traditional mentoring relationships. The term *generativity* comes from psychologist Erik Erikson's study of the phases of a person's life.[8] Generativity represents Erikson's seventh developmental stage, in which individuals assist the younger generation in developing and leading useful lives. If individuals do not engage in generativity during middle age, Erikson argues, there is stagnation in their lives. What does generativity mean for mentoring relationships? Acting on one's motivation to mentor early on enables the mentor to relish the accomplishments of others throughout their careers. In addition to altruistic benefits, choosing to give back early in one's career helps hone the mentor's employee development skills that are now part of managers' performance appraisals in many organizations. In the case of Araceli, Rosario Marin recognized what she enjoyed about mentoring and believed she would benefit from the success of her protégé; as she said, "I think that what you get back when you actually see them accomplish their goals or be successful at whatever endeavor it was that they were after is tremendous joy. You are able to share in their successes. And their successes become your own."

In addition, the mentor passes along the lessons he or she has learned from others throughout their own careers. Rosario Marin noted the generative importance of the mentoring help she provides for people such as Araceli. As Rosario put it:

> Just deciding to run for a Senate seat is not easy [Araceli ran for the California State Senate]. I mean, you know you're going against an incumbent. It's hard. And she's [Araceli's] calling to find out whether she should do it or not. And I am not going to tell her run for it or don't run for it. I'm going to utilize the same tactics that my mentors used on me. They didn't make the decisions for me. But they helped clarify what the questions were that I needed to answer. Hopefully I was able to do that for her, I think that you can guide the questioning versus providing the answer.

Rosario was helping Araceli in the prime of her own career before waiting until the end. Mentors who engage in generativity at a younger age and early in their careers sacrifice a sizable chunk of their own time when they can perhaps least afford it. For many power mentors, however, this sacrifice is well worth it. They mentioned significant benefits such as enjoying a communication conduit with the younger generation, gaining a trusted ally, and enhancing their own reputation as a developer of the next generation. Rosario did not wait until she was U.S. Treasurer to take an interest in advancing the careers of others but did so from the beginning, and she has reaped many rewards that have made the investment in others worthwhile. In turn, as Rosario continues to ascend in politics, the protégés she has developed become a loyal band of helpful supporters.

WHAT POWER MENTORING LOOKS LIKE

Power mentoring differs from traditional mentoring along dimensions like the following:

- Does the relationship involve one mentor and one protégé

(monogamous), or a protégé with multiple mentors (poly-gamous)?

- What is the source of the mentor—that is, is the person internal to the protégé's organization, as is often is the case in traditional mentoring, or external to the organization, as in power mentoring?
- What is the degree of diversity (with respect to ethnic and gender similarity) in the mentor-protégé dyad?

The following case presents an illustration of these points.

At first glance it might appear that Patty Archibeck (senior manager, Executive Communications, Cisco) was in a traditional mentoring relationship with Larry Carter (former chief financial officer (CFO) of Cisco), because he was much older, much higher up in the hierarchy of Cisco, and an established icon in the industry (in Patty's words, "a big dog"). But their relationship had all the hallmarks of a power mentoring relationship. Larry's style was non-threatening, nonexclusive, and characterized by a lack of jealousy. In fact, Larry encouraged Patty to get other mentors. He openly acknowledged his own limitations, because, for example, he could certainly not offer her a female perspective on work-family balance. So he encouraged Patty to reach out and develop relationships with other female mentors and even suggested top women she might contact. Moreover, he encouraged her to reach beyond Cisco and look for mentors in unusual places. Patty did just that, since her favorite 6:00 a.m. step-aerobics instructor, Debra Martucci, also happened to be the highly regarded vice president of Information Systems at Synopsys (a world leader in electronic design automation (EDA) software for semiconductor design). Larry and Patty's relationship captured a number of the distinguishing features of power mentoring.

STYLE

In a traditional mentoring relationship, it is expected that there is one mentor for each protégé. The typical model involves an older and wiser mentor taking a younger, less experienced, albeit promising protégé under his or her wing. In the past, there was an expectation, often implicit, of monogamy and a sense of betrayal should the protégé develop mentoring relationships with other mentors.

In other words, there was an expectation of exclusivity. In comparison, power mentoring is not jealous or exclusive, as evidenced by the situations of Larry, Patty, and Debra.

SOURCE OF MENTOR

A second important feature of this relationship is the fact that one of Patty's mentors was within her organizational home at Cisco and the other was outside it at Synopsys. There are many advantages to having mentors both internal and external to a person's home organization. Mentors internal to the organization help individuals navigate the power structure of the organization by telling them who can help facilitate work or who may have specific resources. An internal mentor would also help make sense of organizational decisions and policies. Mentors external to an organization provide a different perspective on the protégé's career and profession, as well as on the situations they witness in their organization. Being too entrenched in one organization can lead to less innovative decision making, possibly embracing only a particular style of management, and finally an inability to imagine a career outside of that organization. Individuals involved in power mentoring realize the benefits of external mentors and use them to their advantage throughout their careers.

DIVERSITY

A third feature of the mentor-protégé relationship more typical of power mentoring situations is diversity. In the past, traditional mentoring relationships were about "like attracting like." *Like* refers to variables such as gender, race, social class, organizational affiliation, education, and profession. Even today, the majority of mentoring pairs are homogeneous. This is not necessarily bad; it may just be part of human nature, reflecting our greater comfort with people who are more like ourselves. But mentoring research has increasingly found that having diverse mentoring relationships, particularly those across gender and racial lines, yields tremendous benefits on both sides. Diverse mentoring relationships give protégés access to people in power positions who can support them and increase their organizational visibility.[9] Research also shows that people different from the dominant group (in terms of numbers) often bring different opinions, encouraging creative decision making.[10] We saw many examples of this among our interviewees, because 30 percent were in either cross-race or cross-gender dyads, like Patty and Larry.

WHERE POWER MENTORING LIVES

Power mentoring tends to live in situations that characterize the workplace of the 21st century. Today's organizations, especially those that have gone through extensive downsizing, find much less company loyalty among employees than in earlier periods. What used to be loyalty to one's organization has been replaced by increased loyalty to one's profession. Another change related to downsizing and restructuring is that many organizations tend to be less hierarchical than in the past. These flatter organizational structures, in addition to having more fluid work arrangements, often leave employees with unclear career paths.

Power mentoring lives in unique types of organizations for somewhat unique groups of employees. This doesn't mean that power mentoring is necessarily reserved for just a select few; instead it fulfills the needs of individuals who work under the new employment contracts in organizations. These organizations employ individuals who understand that their career development is really in their own hands. These employees know that to get ahead, they need to be aligned with the movers and shakers of their organizations.

Take the example of Bethany Rooney, an up-and-coming television director who has worked with some of the best television directors in Hollywood, including the late Bruce Paltrow, with whom she both worked as a director and served as associate producer. Her early career was spent working with.him on such hits as *St. Elsewhere*. She talked about what she learned from Bruce:

> He had a really strong work ethic. He believed that the job of a television director was to do the best job that you could, given the constraints of time and money, which are a part of the television world. Therefore, it was incumbent upon the director to plan the day and work within that day to get the work the best that you can, but it didn't mean going over, and it didn't mean being self-indulgent, and it didn't mean putting the crew into overtime. It meant be prepared. Spend the time where it's important for the story and spend less time where you can. And it meant being

responsible for the budget. And that's really an old-fashioned attitude that hasn't been prevalent much in Hollywood the last few years.

That relationship with Bruce began as a traditional employer-employee relationship, although it ended as she was, in her words, "kicked out of the nest." Here is how she described the incident: "The second year I directed an episode. I went to him and said I felt I should be promoted to be a full producer instead of associate producer. This was after five years on the series. And he was very old-fashioned. He said, 'Why? I already have a producer, and two writing producers.' So I said, 'Well then, I think it's time for me to go.' He said, 'I'll give you a directing spot for next year so everybody knows we like you. Good-bye and good luck.'"

In retrospect, Bethany realized that by forcing her to move on from her role as associate producer, Bruce was giving her great career advice. At the same time he gave her credibility and a safety net by providing her with a directing gig. By continuing on that show in her current position, she never would have moved ahead. People change jobs or organizations to get promotions in Hollywood. Loyalty to one employer will only stall one's career. After moving on, Bethany has worked with other directors and producers from whom she has learned many different things about the business. She has received mentoring, but not in the traditional form as we think of it. As she talked about Alice West, a coproducer on shows written or produced by the award-winning David E. Kelley (*The Practice, Ally McBeal, Boston Public,* and *Chicago Hope*), Bethany noted, "She has over the years brought me as a director to the shows which she is now producing. Though we've never sat down and had a formal mentoring conversation, the fact that she likes my work and makes an effort to bring me in to whatever show she is working on, is her way of mentoring me."

LOYALTY BASE

In entertainment, especially the creative arena of television and films, individuals have a craft that resides outside the parameters of a particular workplace. Put differently, they have marketable skills that transcend the boundaries of their organization. Individuals in many professions have these types of relationships with their organizations. In our study, this career type was very prevalent for people in technology as well as in entertainment and media. But the pattern is not limited to these industries. Many professionals work independently of their firms. Bethany, for example, felt loyalty to certain people and to her profession, but for her, as for others in her industry, following her craft was of paramount importance.

WHERE IT WORKS

Besides reflecting changing loyalties, organizations today are less likely to resemble bureaucracies with many layers of management and stringent job responsibilities. New organizations are also less likely to be operating strictly within their own boundaries; instead they often operate together with other organizations, perhaps in different industries and cultures.[11] Along with these changes in organizational forms have come commensurate changes in the types of careers held by individuals. Rather than moving up in an organization by following a linear career path, which often occurs in more hierarchical, bureaucratic organizations, careers today are more fluid and cross over into other organizations and even industries. As mentioned earlier, entertainment, technology, and politics are prime examples of industries where boundaryless careers abound. Bethany Rooney, as a boundaryless careerist, found it necessary to have multiple mentors along the way as she moved from project to project. It is simply the nature of the entertainment business to quickly form intense alliances and then move on to new relationships.

MENTOR CENTRALITY

While traditional mentoring can reside anywhere in an organization, and anyone can start a mentoring relationship, a power mentoring relationship is different and more powerful because its participants are plugged into the lineage of an organization or profession's top leadership—a concept we call *mentor centrality*. Bethany Rooney began her career attached to a successful lineage of powerful mentoring relationships, because she started with the "A list" crowd and was allowed to stay there. She did not have to prove herself in low-budget directing jobs or directing for cable. Because of the people she was attached to, she was able to move in the "A" world. Within more hierarchical and traditional organizations, the lessons power mentors deliver often come from a long, distinguished line of leaders within the organization. Knowledge of the organization's culture—the way decisions are made by the most powerful individuals—accrues to those tapped into these relationships. Therefore, mentor centrality can be very helpful to those involved in power mentoring.

SUMMARY: CLASSIC VERSUS CONTEMPORARY MENTORING

Power mentoring is a contemporary approach that differs from classic mentoring in important ways. We have outlined how power mentoring—as a new form of mentoring—has a different purpose, looks different, and lives in different types of organizations than traditional mentoring. We reiterate that traditional mentoring still contains many benefits for individuals, but power mentoring is an enhanced form of mentoring for today's employees in fast-paced, competitive organizations and fields. Power mentoring is contemporary, flexible, and dynamic and takes many forms. In the next section we describe how the unique characteristics of power mentoring lead to 10 new and exciting types of mentoring.

THE MANY TYPES OF POWER MENTORING

The unique aspects of power mentoring we described in the previous section combine to produce 10 innovative forms of power mentoring relationships that can be useful in addition to traditional mentoring. These forms of power mentoring are important to identify because they provide solutions for today's career situations or dilemmas. For example, if you have little access to an appropriate mentor due to geographic constraints, e-mentoring, in which protégés are matched with potential mentors over the Internet, might be helpful to you. To gain an in-depth understanding of the many forms of power mentoring, we introduce them to you in the context of the various business sectors (for example, technology, media, nonprofit, education), companies, and executives that participated in our study. Of course, you will be introduced to others throughout the rest of the book, because this chapter covers only a small sample of our interviewees. Even though you may not work in any of these industries, the lessons they provide about mentoring are still applicable, since we have found that career dilemmas and aspirations are universal.

POWER MENTORING AT IBM

While it is well known that IBM is an acronym for International Business Machines, IBMers joke that it stands for "I've Been Moved," because IBM is well known for its frequent redeployment of personnel. However, we suggest that perhaps it ought to stand for "Innovative Business Mentoring," since this organization encapsulates several unique mentoring practices and has woven the practice of mentoring into the daily fabric of its organizational culture. Nick Donofrio, senior vice president (VP) of Technology and Manufacturing, commented that "I probably mentor 100 people and another 300 think I am their mentor." We interviewed a cluster of IBM mentors and protégés and use their stories to illustrate three forms of power mentoring: *boss, reverse,* and *electronic* mentoring.

Meet Linda Sanford, a master multitasker and power mentor. She had proven herself to be chameleon-like, because she has excelled at managing not only in highly technical environments but also in a sales environment. She is one of IBM's highest-ranking female senior executives, one of *Fortune*'s "Power 50" (the magazine's ranking of top women in business) in 2001, and a member of the Women in Technology International Hall of Fame. Linda is as comfortable discussing strategy with IBM's CEO as she is toting her son's baseball equipment across Manhattan en route to meet him for dinner. She is much sought after as a leader, a speaker, and especially as a mentor. In fact, she estimates that she probably has more than 40 active mentoring relationships—an extraordinary feat given her level of management responsibility.

Linda Sanford's experience with mentoring epitomizes power mentoring, because she participates in a wide variety of mentoring relationships in her role as both a mentor and a protégé. First, let's examine her in the role of a power protégé. It is no accident that she tapped herself into a powerful line of mentors by developing relationships with boss mentors such as IBM luminaries Jack Kuehler (former IBM president), Nick Donofrio (senior VP), and Lou Gerstner (former IBM CEO). Linda worked for Jack Kuehler early on in her career as a young executive assistant, and he saw her potential and encouraged her to develop her skills. She also has a long history of working with Nick Donofrio, because Kuehler had introduced them and Donofrio wanted to hire her in the 1980s. However, it wasn't until the early 1990s that Linda worked for Nick, running the IBM mainframe in Poughkeepsie, New York. It's interesting that they teamed again in 2004. As for Gerstner, he came aboard in 1993 at a time when IBM was suffering, and skillfully engineered a turnaround. Linda impressed Lou as an adept leader, and she proved her mettle during the trying times in IBM's massive culture change.

BOSS MENTORS

A *boss mentor* is one who provides emotional and career support to the subordinate-protégé, within the formal boundaries of the relationship as well as informally.[12] We found that many who utilized their bosses as mentors did so in a sequential fashion, akin to serial monogamy. During the period in which the protégé works for the boss, the protégé's professional success depends to a large degree on the performance of the boss mentor. Likewise, the boss mentor must feel a keen sense of loyalty to and trust in the subordinate-protégé, because the boss often shares proprietary and personal information with the subordinate. However, often when the protégé moves on to another position, the mentoring aspect of their relationship either evolves into a lasting friendship or terminates amicably, since the time and energy of both parties is rightly transferred to their new working relationships. Linda Sanford recounted the following lesson gleaned from Lou Gerstner: "He was the one who said, 'Go do sales.' And I remember thinking, 'Sales? Please, I grew up in Catholic school and I couldn't even sell the candy bars. I had to get my father to buy them all.' But Lou said, 'Stretch yourself.' Go learn something new. Go learn a different set of skills and what motivates people."

Linda took his advice and in 1998 was named the chief of IBM's sales force. She was dubbed an "unlikely choice" by the *Wall Street Journal* because she had spent the bulk of her 22-year IBM career developing products like typewriters and printers. She took over a 17,000-person unit that generated about 70 percent of IBM's $80 billion in annual revenue. She was scrutinized not only for her lack of experience in sales but also for her groundbreaking role as a high-flying female executive in the male-dominated IBM environment. Linda helped move IBM from fifth to second in total storage market share in the two years that she was the senior vice president and group executive of the IBM Storage Systems Group. She is a successful power protégé because she is an active protégé whose success reflects well on her mentors, on IBM's executive team, and on the entire organization.

Linda's experiences with past boss mentors exemplify some of the unique challenges and opportunities found in this type of mentoring. First, the reputations of the two parties become inextricably linked—Gerstner took a risk in encouraging Sanford to branch out, and the risk paid off for both. However, we can all think of examples where a risk such as this did not work out and the end result was less than happy. For example, in 1999, Mark Willis, former CEO of Times-Mirror Corporation, encouraged his then-protégé Kathryn Downing, CEO and publisher of the *Los Angeles Times,* to become involved in a risky profit-sharing deal with the newly constructed Staples Center. This deal resulted in a firestorm of criticism regarding journalistic ethics and caused a loss of position for both of them.[13] A further disadvantage is that transitioning away from a boss mentor can be challenging and must be managed with great skill and tact.

However, the advantages far outweigh the disadvantages, because the boss mentor gains a loyal and capable successor and the protégé gains an opportunity for advancement and fast-track learning. In general, when a protégé is mentored by a boss, there is a high degree of job satisfaction, great performance, and enhanced retention.[14] In fact, because of the numerous advantages, many organizations are now encouraging bosses to function as mentors and are rewarding them for doing so in the performance management process.

Reverse Mentoring

Although Linda Sanford and Nick Donofrio are both IBM superstars, they are also smart enough to know they are not omniscient, and both participate in IBM's formal *reverse mentoring* program. This is a program in which senior executives are paired with the next generations of IBM leaders. This might at first seem counterintuitive. However, it is modeled after GE's reverse mentoring program, where a younger, less experienced employee mentors an older, more experienced person. Ideally, both parties involved in reverse mentoring benefit. The senior executive gains a fresh perspective and a communication conduit to junior staffers, whereas the junior reverse mentor gains valuable career advice and a positive role model. Nick recounted unique challenges and lessons in working with a reverse mentor. He smiled as he recalled his initial meetings with his reverse mentor: "When he first came to me his arms were loaded with books, as he thought he was coming to explain to me everything he had been doing in his first six months at IBM. And I said to him, 'Uh-uh. Look, that's not what this is all about. I just want to hear you talk to me about what it's like. What are your problems so that I can get a better perspective [of what goes on at your level].'" This was the first of several meetings, and Nick found that he gained a great deal from meeting with his reverse mentor, since these encounters led to the development of a five-year plan to orient and integrate the next generation of leaders. Nick mentioned that he found reverse mentoring challenging at first, yet ultimately he found it beneficial, because it both validated his own thinking and enabled him to think in different directions.

E-MENTORS

How do power mentors like Linda Sanford and Nick Donofrio mentor so many people and so well? Certainly, their ability to multitask is a huge plus, but they are also assisted by technology and are actively engaged in mentoring those in their network by electronic means. *E-mentoring* involves using computer-mediated communication such as e-mail, instant messaging, and in some cases live chats to initiate and maintain a mentoring relationship.

Past research has found that e-mentoring, while very prevalent, can fall prey to miscommunication unique to online relationships, such as flaming and inappropriate self-disclosure.[15] However, e-mentoring will continue to grow in importance since it offers many of the same benefits as face-to-face mentoring relationships and has unique advantages. For example, while Linda lives and works in New York, her protégés live and work around the globe. Her web of mentoring relationships includes more than 40 protégés and is ultimately effective, because many of her protégés have remained with IBM and have frequently been promoted. E-mentoring makes a range of mentoring relationships possible by removing the constraints of time and geography that limit face-to-face mentoring interactions. Moreover, e-mentoring can remove the markers of status and demographics, making mentors and protégés more likely to respond to the content of their messages, rather than being influenced by superficial characteristics. For this reason, e-mentoring may be particularly helpful for individuals who find themselves initially judged on their appearance or group membership rather than their own skills.[16]

POWER MENTORING IN SILICON VALLEY

California's Silicon Valley has become legendary for its technology gold rush, with the rapid rise and fall of its twenty-something millionaires and their reputation for working and playing hard. Although many dot-com dreams turned to fool's gold in a short time, in reality, there are a number of entrepreneurial ventures that not only survived but thrived during and after the dot-com crash. Cisco is an example of an organization that rose to the top during the dot-com fallout, due in no small part to the skilled leadership of then-CFO Larry Carter. Cisco had a total of $18.9 billion in revenues in 2003 and is currently number 2 on *Fortune*'s list of "America's Most Admired Companies." In addition, it is number 95 on the Fortune 500 list.

We also interviewed the directors of two Silicon Valley technology incubators who have had a number of notable successes. We interviewed Kim Fisher, then executive director of the Women's Technology Cluster, and her peer mentor, Jim Robbins, executive director of the Panasonic Internet Incubator and numerous other incubators. Prior to becoming the executive director of the Women's Technology Cluster, Kim Fisher was CEO and cofounder of AudioBasket, Inc., a firm that creates audio programming that is both personalized and broadcast quality for Web sites and wireless devices. Kim raised over $25 million for AudioBasket from venture capital firms and through strategic partnerships with firms such as AOL/Time Warner and Panasonic.

Jim Robbins was brought onto her board of directors and provided a good sounding board about company issues. Along with being the executive director of the Panasonic Internet Incubator, Jim is also a principal in the Panasonic Ventures Fund and the executive director and founder of the Software Business Cluster (SBC). In addition, he is a popular speaker on new business formation and has been featured in the *Wall Street Journal, CNNfn,* and *Business Week,* among other publications. Within these organizations we found mentoring practices as innovative as their products: *group* and *for-hire mentoring.*

GROUP MENTORING

Group mentoring is where a senior-level mentor provides ongoing coaching to small groups of junior-level employees. Securing a meeting with Cisco's chief financial officer is no small feat, because Larry Carter's time is often booked up months in advance. It is no wonder, since he is an industry icon famous for the innovation of the "virtual close," winning the 2000 Excellence Award from *CFO* magazine; Larry also helped Cisco garner an Alexander Hamilton award for Investor Relations from *Treasury* magazine. Because Larry's time is valuable and so many people want him to be their mentor, he uses an innovative approach: group mentoring. This approach has been very successful and epitomizes his efficient yet warm personal style. Group mentoring involves one executive mentoring small groups of employees. Carter refers to his group mentoring sessions as "Lunch with Larry" meetings; these usually consist of 10–12 junior executives. Larry explains that "there's no agenda, and it's just me and the people. They are usually from different parts of the organization. They are also all about the same level, so they are either managers or directors or individual contributors." As Larry characterizes it, these are great meetings for two-way feedback. He ends up asking just as many questions as he answers. He feels that these sessions are a great way to help individuals learn the ropes in the organization and learn the reasons behind organizational decisions. He also feels that this type of open dialogue is very important for helping to develop trust. As he put it, "There is no better way to do it than sit down, look them right in the eye, and tell them the good, the bad, and the ugly. You develop a rapport, and you also make them feel comfortable [so] that they are not threatened; their job is not in jeopardy."

In sum, group mentoring can be particularly helpful when access to senior executives is limited and when the number of potential protégés far exceeds available mentors. Also, group mentoring can be a terrific way to foster a sense of camaraderie among protégés and even be an important source of peer mentoring. However, if not managed carefully, the downside can be protégés competing for attention. Moreover, it may be difficult for a protégé to secure advice from the mentor on confidential or sensitive issues in a group mentoring situation. Group mentoring has many potential advantages, yet it would be advisable not to rely on this form of mentoring exclusively.

Mentors for Hire

Hiring a mentor sounds like an appealing form of mentoring for those who cannot or do not want to invest resources required in a long-standing relationship. In this form of mentoring, a mentor primarily provides job- or career-specific advice or help in exchange for tangible (usually financial) remuneration. We found this form of mentoring especially prevalent in the technology industry, evolving as a new twist on the incubators of the 1990s. The relationship is short term and oriented toward achieving a handful of finite goals. According to Jim Robbins, an individual who has worked with many incubator organizations in Silicon Valley, "We work like you might think of a consultant doing, the difference being that we're living on a day-to-day basis with people. . . . Sometimes the companies might need coaching, sometimes they might need mentoring, sometimes they might need referrals, sometimes they might need training, sometimes they might need network facilitation. So we do all those kinds of things." In other words, people sign up when accepted in the incubator to work on certain aspects of their business plan with experts. More specifically, Jim noted:

> In the incubator that's the kind of mentoring we're talking about. . . . What I do is describe the process as a wish list that they have the responsibility for preparing, a list of things that they would like help with. And I'll take responsibility for helping them on the list. And if they give me a list with four things on it, I might help them personally with two things. I might refer them to someone else for a third. And I might tell them that they're on their own for the fourth, that I can't help.
>
> I try to get people to take responsibility for saying what they need help on and then figure out how to help them. And mentoring is part of that help. Now, that doesn't mean that I just ignore the companies that don't follow through with that. But that would be the ideal way that I see the incubators working, is that we have a whole range of services, but if you're in the incubator, tell me what you need, "Today I need X."

Mentor-for-hire relationships have evolved online as well and take the form of e-mentoring. Kim's firm, Prologue International, provides incubators with e-mentoring systems that connect entrepreneurs with a network of online mentors. In addition to having a list of mentors from which an entrepreneur can choose online, Prologue incubators have events to bring entrepreneurs and mentors together. As Kim Fisher noted:

> We try to get the mentors to have a network here so twice a year we have mentor events where the mentors and the companies get together, and they interact and network with each other, so people like being part of that community. The last event we had was modeled after speed dating, so we had all the companies with groups around the room in the hotel, and then the mentors had five minutes to talk to each company. We wanted to make sure that, you know, every mentor and every company got a chance to interact, and connections were formed because I don't want to be in the middle of the connections. I want a connection to happen, and then I want them to all go off on their own.

Individuals who facilitate the introduction of would-be protégés to would-be mentors talk about the importance of the matching process to ensure that the mentor hired has the needed expertise. It is emphasized in these specialized mentoring relationships that the connection is made to fulfill a specific need. Once that expectation is clear, protégés involved in these relationships indicate that mentors for hire are indeed very useful in enabling them to overcome myriad challenges related to starting and maintaining successful entrepreneurial ventures, as in our examples. Alternatively, they could continue the relationship on an as-needed basis in other professions.

POWER MENTORING IN POLITICS

The world of politics has brought us some of history's most inspirational leaders and some of our gravest disappointments. Politicians, with their capacity to wield power from the local level to the world stage, are a fascinating group of people. However, while politicians may be impressive, they are essentially high-level temporary workers. Like those who work in the entertainment industry, politicians must continually concern themselves with obtaining their next job. Like those who work in technology, whose job security is dependent on the mercurial whims of the market and consumers, politicians' jobs also depend on the elusive interests of their constituents. We found some very interesting examples of three unique forms of power mentoring among our political participants: *inspirational, family-member,* and *barrier-busting* mentors.

INSPIRATIONAL MENTORS

The importance of mentors as role models and sources of inspiration came up repeatedly in our conversations with our participants. An *inspirational mentor* is one who provides a model of excellence without having a direct relationship with the protégé. This might fly in the face of what we conventionally understand about mentoring; after all, with inspirational mentoring there is no real relationship. However, since role modeling is a key function of mentoring, sometimes an individual can be a role model without the relationship part. This is a special type of power mentoring. An individual can be an inspirational mentor by virtue of a philosophy that he or she espouses, by the way he performs his calling, or simply by the way she lives her life. Martin Luther King Jr. was identified as an inspirational mentor by several of our participants.

Former California Congressional Representative and social activist Ron Dellums spoke eloquently about Martin Luther King Jr. as his inspirational mentor. Dellums credited King with giving him clarity for his life work and a sense of purpose for his career in public service. Ron was elected to Congress in 1970 and served in the House of Representatives until his retirement in 1998. Consistently striving to promote peace and disarmament, Ron Dellums was the leader of the congressional effort to end U.S. support for apartheid in South Africa. Currently, Dellums is the president of Healthcare International Management Company. Here are his reflections about Martin Luther King Jr.:

> Martin Luther King Jr. was a mentor even though I never got a chance to meet him in person. He touched me intimately. For example, he said that peace is more than simply the absence of war; it's the presence of justice. In my very diverse district in the Bay Area, it made it all make sense to me, because the peace movement ultimately was a movement for justice—not just a movement to stop the guns and the bombs. True peace was to find justice. So the civil rights movement, the women's liberation movement, and the gay liberation movement were all matters of justice. The idea of peace being about justice made my politics clear.

MLK also said that there were two kinds of leaders, one who waits until the consensus is formed and then runs in front of the group to say, "I'm the leader," or the person who has the audacity to shape the consensus. And when MLK said, "I am from the latter," that made me willing to take the risk to do that as well.

Another reason MLK was a mentor for me is he said that the most radical thing that our people could do was to assert the full measure of our citizenship. Martin Luther King said, if you really want to be radical, say, "I am a citizen." I have rights and prerogatives. Assume your duties as well. My politics were always shaped by that idea. This is unlike some members of Congress who are good on certain issues and lousy on other issues. They can be great environmentalists, and then they're bad on foreign policy, or whatever. Because of MLK I have a coherent belief system, and a way of codifying things that was holistic. So I have a set of politics, and he was responsible for that.

An inspirational mentor is important in providing a protégé with a sense of identity, purpose, and vision. Often our participants spoke of their inspirational mentors as being crucial at key decision points, as they asked themselves, "What would my inspirational mentor do in this situation?" Of course, having only an inspirational mentor is usually not sufficient. There is an oft-repeated story about a young boy who told his parents that he was afraid of monsters in his bedroom. His parents comforted him and reminded the child that he would be safe because "God was present and would protect him." The child replied, "Yes, but sometimes I need somebody with skin on him to protect me." Thus, in addition to inspirational mentors, most of us also need somebody with "skin on them" to provide us with tangible support when needed.

FAMILY-MEMBER MENTORS

Nearly 20 percent of our participants mentioned specific family members as being important mentors to them as well. A *family-member mentor* is an immediate or extended family member who provides emotional, career, and role-modeling support to the protégé from a young age. Often the family-member mentor is a person of considerable influence and accomplishment within their own family circle and/or community. Most participants who mentioned family members as being important were women or people of color. This is likely due to the fact that few mentors were available for female and minority Baby Boomers because the top ranks of organizations were populated by white males, who tended to mentor younger white males like themselves. In fact, as mentioned previously, there is an entire body of mentoring literature that suggests that women and people of color face greater barriers to obtaining mentors than do white men.

Ron Dellums provides compelling examples of family-member mentors. Dellums was part of a legacy of social activism, learning many important lessons that he directly applied to his life work from his parents as well as extended family members, including his uncle and grandmother:

> My mother is a very important mentor in my life because this was a woman who dropped out of high school to have me and then went back and finished high school. She and my father got married while she was in high school. But she was very thirsty for knowledge. She wanted to learn.
>
> One day in junior high I came home and told my mother that this kid had called me a dirty black African, and so I popped the guy when he called me that. At that point she could have reinforced my anger and violence. Instead my mother sat down with me and got the story. She told me that "because he called you dirty, then that's your decision to fight or not, but don't fight because he called you black or because he called you African because you are both of those. You are a thousand adjectives. Two of them are that you are black, and you are of African descent. And anywhere you go for the rest of your life, you should feel pride when somebody says you're a black African." She was the person who intervened in my life to say it's okay to be black and it's okay to be African. Because she said to me that the reason why you threw your fist at this boy is because you were throwing a brick at a mirror. You weren't striking out at him, you were engaging in your own self-hate. She reinforced my humanity, which became an integral part of my politics. So it made sense that I could be a leader of a coalition movement because she helped me to see that I was [part of] something larger.
>
> This lesson helped me later in life when Ed Koch, then mayor of New York, called me a "Zulu warrior and Watusi prince." So everybody says, "Uh-oh, Ed Koch blew it." So I met with my Black Caucus colleagues from New York. They said, "Hey Ron, we know

you're going to kick butt." And I said, "I have no fear of Mayor Koch, why should I go fight?" I said, "Tell me the basis for my challenge to him. The Zulus were the first indigenous people who stood off an industrial army and beat them in Southern Africa. The Watusi are elegant, smart people. So what's to fight about?"

So when Koch called me up, he said, "I just meant that you were a fighter and an eloquent person." And I said, "Ed, if you're saying that I'm an elegant street fighter, cool, man, no problem. You know, I can't quarrel with that." So, if Ed Koch said to me that he did not mean it in the pejorative, then I accept Ed Koch's comment.

As Dellums and other participants mentioned, having important family-member mentors early in life instilled in them the important perspective that they had a responsibility to mentor others. However, family-member mentors can have their disadvantages as well, because dysfunctional family dynamics can erode the quality of mentoring relationships. Moreover, others' perception of nepotism may cause a loss of self-esteem in the protégé. However, for those we spoke to, it seemed that having family-member mentors gave them an early advantage, particularly when growing up in a social environment that was sexist or racist, or just not supportive of them developing to their full potential. In fact, many youth-mentoring programs today (for example, Big Brothers and Big Sisters) are based on the idea that a mentor serves as a surrogate family member. These programs have been integral in enabling high-potential, low-opportunity youths to thrive. Family-member mentors provide the ultimate in a trusting mentoring relationship because of the deep affection and risk of family social censure or displeasure. This can set the stage for other meaningful relationships down the line.

BARRIER-BUSTING MENTORS

Traditional mentoring is often built on the similarity between people of like backgrounds, organizations, and in the case of politics, ethnic and party affiliations. However, we saw many instances of unique mentoring alliances in which close and successful mentoring relationships were formed across traditional barriers such as competitive organizations or political parties. U.S. Congressional Representative Hilda Solis (D-CA) and California Assembly

Member Judy Chu (Dem.) provide us with a fascinating example of mentoring across the barrier of ethnicity, which in this case was extremely important to their voting constituents.

Representative Hilda Solis is Hispanic, and her protégé, Judy Chu, is Chinese American. The relationship between these women has been tested across ethnic lines a couple of times, but the trust and intimacy they have built in working together over the years have made it possible to weather these challenges. The first involved redistricting for Chu's city and for the cities represented by Solis. Election results in these districts in the past have shown clear patterns of voting for candidates of one's own ethnicity. By working together to develop a redistricting plan, rather than against one another, Chu and Solis both got what their respective communities wanted. Another similar challenge to their relationship occurred when Solis endorsed Chu over her Latino male opponent. To keep the peace in her district, Solis's natural inclination would be to go with the Latino male, and in fact she received a lot of pressure to back him from the Latino community. However, by that time, Solis and Chu had forged a great relationship over a number of years, and Solis went with her loyalty to Chu rather than to the community. As Chu said, "That's when I knew I could really trust her." This act became a pivotal moment of trust building that brought their relationship and the work they did together in the district to a new level. Their example of Latinos and Asians working across ethnic lines enabled them to make significant progress on community issues and drew much attention from the political world.

Barrier-busting mentoring is not without risk, because those who engage in it are vulnerable to considerable social censure from their own group members. Often if they take the risk and it doesn't work out for whatever reason, their reputation can be damaged and their long-term career prospects dimmed. However, those who successfully mentor across barriers find that the rewards often outweigh the risks. Mentoring across barriers offers a fresh perspective and is the ultimate in building empathy for a person whose perspective or interests may diverge radically from your own. Further, in today's dynamic and fast-paced career environment, where alliances and interests often shift unexpectedly, having relationships across actual or virtual party lines can be a keen competitive advantage.

POWER MENTORING IN MEDIA

The entertainment industry provides a compelling example of nomadic or boundaryless careers, because most jobs in this industry are essentially highly creative, well-paid temporary jobs. Entertainment professionals must carefully balance the competing need to succeed in their present gig while simultaneously working on getting their next job. Those who work in entertainment are often passionate about their work and loyal to their professions and guilds. In fact, in a nation where union membership as a whole is decreasing and unions are often decried as weak and powerless, it is interesting to note that entertainment industry unions (for example, the Screen Actors Guild, Directors Guild of America, and so on) wield more influence than ever before. Our last two innovative types of mentoring capture these competing demands: *peer and step-ahead mentoring* and *mentors of the moment*. Peer and step-ahead mentors are mentors who are at the same status level or just one step ahead of the protégé but who have a complementary set of skills and experiences. A mentor of the moment entails a situational, intense relationship that has a lasting, sometimes life-changing impact by virtue of the advice given, the role modeling offered, or simply the affiliation provided.

PEER AND STEP-AHEAD MENTORS

Barbara Corday, professor and former chair of production of the prestigious film and television school at the University of Southern California (USC), has had a long and successful career in the entertainment business. She was nominated for an Emmy in 1981 for creating the drama series *American Dream*.

One of Barbara's most influential and longest-lasting mentoring relationships was with her former writing partner, Barbara Avedon (now deceased), with whom she created the highly successful and well-regarded TV show, *Cagney and Lacey*. Corday and Avedon initially worked together for the nonprofit organization Another Mother for Peace when Corday volunteered to do public relations work for them. Her relationship with Barbara Avedon began as a friendship of equals in the volunteer arena; however, in the professional world of television writing, Avedon was clearly the pro and Corday the novice. In the context of writing, Avedon acted as a step-ahead mentor to Corday. Later, as Corday's skills developed and she received credit and recognition, their relationship evolved again and they ended where they began—as peers and friends:

> Barbara was a professional writer and had been writing for television for a number of years—she had worked on shows like *Bewitched* and *Father Knows Best*—when she and I decided to start writing together. She was really taking on a junior person who had no credits whatsoever and there was no real reason why she should have done this except that we had become very close in Another Mother for Peace. I had an idea for a television show, and she said, "Well, I don't want to do it by myself. I would only be interested in doing it if you wanted to do it with me. It's your idea and you are passionate about it—let's do it together."

The two Barbaras found that they had many important things in common, such as similar political views, family situations, and subsequent personal and professional life transitions (including getting married, having a child, being divorced, and so on). As Corday explained in describing how their relationship evolved to become peers and friends:

> We had a nine-year writing partnership. Being partners with somebody who you have become so close to and become even closer with over the years is an incredibly special thing. We knew every morning when we woke up we were going to see each other and be talking about life, our kids, our husbands, and our world. I think all that came out in our writing. *Cagney and Lacey* was about wanting to do a show about women partners. And the fact that they were cops really was an accommodation to drama. You know, we would have been just as happy to do a show about two women in a bathroom talking all day. We were telling the stories that we wanted to tell because this was what was interesting to us.
>
> It was an enormously important relationship for me because not only did I have an older woman who was my best friend and my confidant but she really taught me how to write for television. The single biggest lesson that you can learn about writing for film and television is that you show, you don't tell.

Barbara was very savvy in managing her career in the sense that no matter what organization she worked for, she always had a mentor in that same organization. She started with Barbara Avedon as her step-ahead mentor and they evolved to become peers and friends.

Later she found that several of her bosses in her next jobs could also be effective mentors for her. Barbara Corday is a terrific example of someone who uses power mentoring, because she has a wide network of different types of mentors (Marcy Carsey, executive producer of *That '70s Show, Roseanne,* and *Cosby,* and Frank Biondi, former CEO of Universal). Moreover, she has used an additive approach to her network, since she has tended to stay in touch with former mentors even after moving on to another organization. Staying in touch with her network of former mentors has served her well in her position of influence at USC, where she has been able to draw on her connections and clout to benefit USC's highly respected film school.

There are a number of important benefits and challenges to peer and step-ahead mentoring relationships. One of the greatest benefits is that both step-ahead and peer mentors can effectively empathize with their protégés because they have recently encountered or are currently encountering the same sorts of career challenges and issues. Also, because of the equalization of status, these mentoring relationships have the potential to evolve into long-lasting friendships characterized by a high degree of trust and intimacy. However, these types of relationships can be challenging, since the mentor and protégé peers sometimes find themselves competing with one another on subsequent career moves. Therefore, an individual who relies on peer mentoring alone may find it helpful to follow Corday's example and seek out other peers and bosses as mentors as well.

MENTORS OF THE MOMENT

These are analogous to situational friendships. Many of us have had the experience of living in a neighborhood and becoming friends with our neighbors. While you are living near each another the relationships are important, and you spend a great deal of time together. Also, there is a certain amount of trust and intimacy, because you may exchange house keys, care for each other's pets and children, and in general become enmeshed in each other's lives due to shared proximity. However, after you leave the neighborhood, the friendship dissolves, not acrimoniously, but simply out of a lack of common interests or time on both sides. *Mentors of the moment* are a lot like these neighbors. Mentors of the moment often have a great deal of impact on their protégés, but they are primarily situational. They can be found in work situations that are short lived and project based, such as in the development and production of a film. They are often context specific and may be bound by the time individuals are brought together to work on a project.

Martha Coolidge, first female president of the Director's Guild of America (DGA) and director of *The Prince & Me* starring Julia Stiles (2004), described several people she called "mentors of the moment" who were very helpful to her throughout her directing career. These individuals included Peter Bogdanovich (director of, among other films, *The Last Picture Show* in 1971 and *The Cat's Meow* in 2001), Francis Ford Coppola (*The Godfather Trilogy* in 1972, 1974, and 1990, and *The RainMaker* in 1997, among others), and Robert Wise (*The Sound of Music* in 1965 and *Star Trek* in 1979, and others). Each of these men was very helpful to Martha during a particular film project, but while she has continued to maintain good relationships with them, she no longer considers them to be ongoing mentors for her. Coolidge shared the following reflections about what she learned from one of her mentors of the moment, Francis Ford Coppola:

> I learned that you should never be afraid of talent, never be afraid of hiring talented people. Never be afraid of hiring people who might even be more talented than you. I think it is a flaw if someone scares you and you think that they might overwhelm you, you don't hire them. Francis wasn't ever afraid of that. And look at the great work he's done—you always go for the best.
>
> When you hire a composer or whoever, you don't aim low just to keep yourself in a comfort level. It's very important that you get chills yourself from that person and that they can come up with ideas you never thought of.

Martha mentioned that Robert Wise inspired her to give back, and she has actively done that throughout her career, mentoring others and supporting the DGA mentoring program. She sees herself as a conscious role model and is a frequent speaker to encourage other women filmmakers.

Another film director, Lesli Linka Glatter, had the fortune to have rewarding similar experiences with her mentors of the moment along the way in her career. Her early career started with an Academy Award nomination for a short film she directed in 1984 called *Tales of Meeting and Parting*. As an extremely successful television director early in her career, she had the opportunity to work with such directing giants as Steven Spielberg (director of close to 50 films, including *Schindler's List* in 1993, *Raiders of the Lost Ark* in 1981, *Jaws* in 1975), Clint Eastwood (director of nearly 30 films, including *Million Dollar Baby* in 2004, *Mystic River* in 2003, and *Unforgiven* in 1992), and David Lynch (nearly 25 films, including *Mulholland Drive* in 2001 and the popular television show *Twin Peaks* from the 1980s). Lesli spoke very highly of the important lessons she learned from two of her mentors:

> Steven Spielberg had a show at the time called *Amazing Stories*. So I went in and met with him and had a great meeting. He asked me to do one of the shows and I said, "Since I've only done one thing, can I come and hang out and apprentice with you before I do mine?" So though I had already been hired, I asked if I could mentor with him because I realized what I knew and what I didn't know.
>
> That was an incredible experience because I felt like that was my film school. I apprenticed with Steven, and then I apprenticed with Clint Eastwood, which was also an extraordinary experience. First of all, they're both very conscientious and excellent directors. But they couldn't be more different in terms of how they work, how they approach material. That was a seminal experience for a young director. I could see how everyone approaches the material in their own distinctive way and sees the world differently. No one is going to tell the same story the same way.

Mentors of the moment require that protégés develop a keen sense of mindfulness in terms of being open to these opportunities. Although encountering a truly legendary mentor of the moment like Francis Ford Coppola may be a function of serendipity, being open to learning what you can—even if the interaction is brief—can make the difference between a life-changing mentoring moment and a missed opportunity. When you are in a competitive environment where time and resources are tight, mentors of the moment can provide you with invaluable support even if the relationship doesn't last forever, not unlike good neighbors who provide crucial friendship and assistance until they move away.

CONCLUSION

In this chapter, we introduced the various forms of power mentoring by elaborating on

- What power mentoring does
- What power mentoring looks like
- Where power mentoring lives

We also introduced the myriad forms power mentoring takes in the three industries we chose to investigate in this book. This introduction to the many innovative approaches to mentoring and their advantages and disadvantages can give both mentors and protégés new options to consider for their own career development. Moreover, an understanding of the particular nuances of power mentoring is very important for people attempting to enter this type of relationship.

We conclude with a summary of the key benefits relevant to each unique type of mentoring. We urge you to consider the following summary and determine what new type of mentoring relationships would be most beneficial for you to cultivate.

- *Traditional mentors* can
    Be useful in grooming for success if your interest is long term in a particular organization
    Provide a useful tool in developing the next generation of leaders

- A *boss mentor* can provide
    The chance to groom or be groomed as a successor (for the boss, this can be the ultimate way to gain a loyal cadre of supporters; for the protégé, it can be the easiest way to move ahead)
    The experience of going to work as a joy for both, with ongoing opportunities for learning

- *Reverse mentors* can
    Offer context-specific help like technical knowledge
    Give the younger generation political savvy and professional knowledge, and give the older generation fresh ideas and new skills

- An *e-mentor* can be great because

  You can communicate between London and Los Angeles at 2 a.m., since there are no limitations in time and space

  Judgments about appearance or group membership are suspended, because these attributes are less apparent than they would otherwise be

- A *group mentor* provides

  Access to busy executives that might otherwise be unavailable, and offers an efficient use of time

  An opportunity to develop valuable relationships with peers

- A *mentor for hire* can work well because

  You get what you pay for, in that the relationship can be efficient and task specific

  It can be a great way to develop your network of professional resources

- An *inspirational mentor* provides

  A vision, identity, and sense of purpose

  A standard of excellence to look up to and a litmus test of "What would so-and-so do in this situation?"

- A *family-member mentor* can offer

  Self-esteem from an early age

  The ultimate in love and loyalty

- A *barrier-busting mentor* can offer

  A fresh perspective on your industry or affiliation

  An opportunity to form nontraditional alliances, which can enhance your career opportunities down the line

- *Peer* and *step-ahead mentors* are useful because

  They may be the easiest and least stressful to connect with

  They can empathize with your life and work situation and provide an even and immediate exchange of benefits

- A *mentor of the moment* can be terrific because

  These mentors often appear just when you need them most, yet have the least time to develop the relationship

  Although short and sweet in terms of relationship duration, this type of mentoring can have an incredible impact

In the next chapter we explore in depth one of the key characteristics of a power mentoring relationship: *reciprocity*. Simply put, this
is the idea that both the mentor and protégé exchange valuable
benefits with each other. We take a "he said, she said" approach
and expose both the mentors' and protégés' reflections on what
they give and receive in their power mentoring relationships. We
also highlight how organizations can gain when they enable power
mentoring relationships to thrive.

CHAPTER THREE

MENTORING AS A TWO-WAY STREET
Benefits of Giving and Receiving

*Once upon a time, in a faraway land, Aladdin came
upon a battered lamp. The lamp was inscribed, "Ask and
it shall be given." When Aladdin rubbed the lamp, a
Genie emerged and in a booming voice proclaimed, "I am
here to answer all of your questions and help you obtain
all that you desire. Your wishes are my command."*
—ADAPTED FROM JACK CANFIELD AND MARK
HANSEN, *THE ALADDIN FACTOR*

Wouldn't it be nice if having a mentor was like having your own
personal Aladdin? Just rub the lantern and your personal mentor
genie would appear and then would grant you at least three career
wishes. What would you wish for? More money? Congenial
coworker relationships? Work that brings the acknowledgment and
recognition that you deserve? Or would you simply wish for greater
meaning in the sense that you feel your work makes a difference?
Well, the Gallup organization has found that these are some of the
most important things for managers today across various industries.[1]

Although we can't promise you a magic lantern with the req-
uisite genie, we can tell you that in the past 20 years researchers
have been busy assessing the various benefits protégés receive from
mentoring. In fact, all the "career wishes" just listed are related to
positive mentoring relationships. In the past, a great deal of
emphasis was placed on learning exactly what protégés derive from

mentoring. More recently we have seen a shift in this trend, with greater attention now given to what mentors—and even their organizations—gain as well. We suggest that being a mentor is not a purely altruistic act. In our interviews with power mentors and protégés, we found an enormous emphasis placed on the idea of exchanging mutual benefits—or what is known as *reciprocity*. The key to a sustained network of power mentoring relationships is that those involved must feel the relationship creates a win-win situation. In short, power mentoring relationships typically provide tangible benefits for both mentor and protégé—and their organazations.

GIVE-AND-TAKE IN POWER MENTORING RELATIONSHIPS

Without going into psychological explanations of human behavior in too much detail, we might consider why the idea of give-and-take or reciprocity makes sense for mentoring. The concept of reciprocity—part of a theory of behavior called *social exchange*—has been used to understand other two-person (or dyadic) relationships, such as those between bosses and employees or even between friends. Applied to mentoring, social exchange is simply the idea that mentors and protégés exchange valuable, albeit different, benefits with each other. Although what they exchange might be very different, the exchange has to be seen as equally valuable and reciprocal for both parties involved.

Consider as an example a reverse mentoring relationship in which a junior employee mentors a senior executive. When Jack Welch at GE first conceptualized this idea, it was seen as far-fetched by some and revolutionary by others. In a reverse mentoring situation, the junior employee might exchange her technical know-how for a senior employee's political savvy regarding organizational issues. As it has become a more accepted practice, the idea of exchange between both parties became the glue that kept these relationships together. Therefore, what they are exchanging might be very different, but both parties see the process of exchange as important. This idea of exchange and reciprocity was reiterated many times by our power mentors and protégés. In the following sections of the chapter, we provide an overview of the kinds of benefits power mentors and protégés exchange with each other and discuss what each group ultimately gains from the relationship.

WHAT DO POWER PROTÉGÉS GAIN?

There has been a great deal of research on what protégés gain from their mentoring relationships. In fact, typically when individuals consider a mentoring relationship, they usually think only about what's in it for the protégé. Our colleagues in academia have been hard at work compiling an impressive amount of research. Just for fun, recall the discussion from Chapter One and take the following true-or-false test:

- People with mentors make more money than those without mentors.   T/F
- People with mentors derive greater job and career satisfaction than those without mentors.   T/F
- People with mentors are promoted more than those without mentors.   T/F
- People with mentors have greater job mobility than those without mentors.   T/F
- People with mentors have better work-family balance than those without mentors.[2]   T/F

How did you do? If you answered "True" to all of these statements, you are ahead of the game by already understanding how important mentoring is for your career development and success. Many of these research findings are derived from traditional mentoring relationships; the question remains, To what extent do they apply to power mentoring? The good news is that the various forms of mentors introduced in the previous chapter—known collectively as power mentors—also offer the same range of benefits. So, if you can't find a traditional mentor, you can still enjoy these benefits by developing your own network of power mentors.

Although it is true that a protégé has a lot to gain from a mentoring relationship, it is also important to look at the other side of the relationship. That is, how does the mentor benefit?

WHAT DO POWER MENTORS GAIN?

Many people who mentor do so as a way to help others; however, in today's competitive work environment, mere altruism is not enough. Mentors often gain as much from their relationships as they put into them. An interesting study conducted a few years ago by Tammy Allen and her associates found that the reasons for mentoring could be categorized into other-focused reasons and self-focused reasons.[3] The other-focused reasons included goals such as wanting to pass on information to others, build a competent workforce, help others succeed in general or in their careers, benefit the organization, or help underrepresented groups such as women and minorities move through the organizational ranks. On the self-focused side, the reasons for mentoring included

- Gaining gratification in seeing others succeed or grow
- Freeing up time by mentoring protégés and getting them to take on projects
- Fulfilling a general need to work with others
- Acquiring new knowledge and insights
- Enjoying a feeling of pride
- Deriving satisfaction from influencing others
- Winning the protégés' respect
- Building support networks
- Getting possible payback some day from the protégés
- Enjoying the loyalty of the protégés

We bring some of these ideas alive by providing you with stories and examples from our power mentors' and protégés' experiences.

Road Map to This Chapter

In Chapters One and Two we introduced some of our interviewees. In this chapter you will be reintroduced to some individuals you met earlier, and will become acquainted with new power mentors and protégés as well. We asked our interviewees to reflect on what they gave to the mentoring relationship and what they gained in return, and in this chapter you'll become aware of the unique give-and-take so characteristic of power mentoring. It was fascinating to observe the similarities and differences in perspectives among our participants. Sometimes the mentors felt that they did not offer much mentoring or career guidance, whereas the protégés regaled us with countless examples of what their mentors had done for them. It was much easier for both mentors and protégés to articulate what they gained than what they offered to the other—highlighting the importance of hearing from both parties in the relationship. Much of what transpires in mentoring relationships may not be conscious on the part of one participant, but the benefits are readily apparent to the other. We conclude this chapter with an overall summary of benefits gained by the mentor, the protégé, and the organization.

As you reflect on these power mentoring relationships, we encourage you to keep in mind your own relationships, not only what you can gain from mentors, but also what you can offer. For those of you currently not in a mentor-protégé relationship, take stock of what you might need from a mentor in order to move ahead in your career and what you might offer a mentor in return. For mentors, think about your current relationships. Could you be asking more of your protégé so that you could benefit more from the relationship? If you are not sure of the reciprocal benefits of your current relationship, be sure to keep reading, because our power mentors and protégés will surely provide you with lots of great ideas!

MEET THE POWER MENTORS AND PROTÉGÉS: STORIES OF GIVE-AND-TAKE

In the following sections we provide you an introduction to some of our power mentors and protégés.

NBC UNIVERSAL'S CEO/GE VICE CHAIR BOB WRIGHT AND HIS PROTÉGÉS

You briefly met Bob Wright in Chapter One. He's an icon in American business, particularly in the fast-paced and competitive world of media. He was tapped as NBC's president and chief executive officer in 1986, was named chair and chief executive officer in 2001, and became chair and chief executive officer of NBC Universal in 2004. Over the years, he has been recognized by *Fortune, Hollywood Reporter, Premiere,* and *Vanity Fair* as one of the most influential and powerful leaders in media—no surprise considering his tenure and success in his position. He has presided over the evolution of NBC from a network broadcaster to a global media powerhouse, with leadership in broadcast and cable television, the production and syndication of television programming, motion pictures, Spanish language television, and theme parks.

Bob accepted the 2001 Excellence in Mentoring Award given by the National Mentoring Partnership Act for corporate leadership on behalf of NBC/GE. He was a protégé of the legendary Jack Welch, former CEO of GE; thus it makes sense that Wright would excel at developing talent through mentoring relationships.

Wright's protégés are illustrious and successful people in their own right. One is Pamela Thomas-Graham, chair of CNBC. As we mentioned earlier, Pamela seems to belie the myth that Superwoman doesn't exist. She has an amazing educational pedigree (she's a magna cum laude graduate of Harvard-Radcliffe and a former *Harvard Law Review* editor) and has an impressive list of work and personal accomplishments, including being recognized as the first black woman partner at McKinsey and Company. In addition to excelling in the work arena, she finds time to balance her personal life with a flourishing career as a best-selling mystery author. Pamela recently published the latest in a series of books titled *Orange Crushed: An Ivy League Mystery.* She was named one of *Fortune*'s "50 Most Powerful Black Executives in America" in 2000 and *Glamour* magazine's Woman of the Year in 2001.

In subsequent chapters you will learn more about how Bob Wright connected with his protégés, but here we focus on the reciprocity inherent in these relationships. Bob felt one of the most important things he gained from being a mentor was the satisfaction in watching other people develop: "I think you get a lot more than you give. You get a lot of satisfaction, at least I do. You watch people and their abilities grow. If their talent develops or it becomes more exposed, that's very satisfying. It's just a wonderful feeling, especially since you're generally working with people that you like in this role and people that you really do think have promise and abilities. So you're very excited about seeing them do well."

Bob certainly had the satisfaction of watching his protégés rise to difficult challenges, because he presented Pamela Thomas-Graham with the formidable task of staffing the CNBC dot-com organization; then, a year and half later, she had to completely dismantle it. Pamela reflected on the superb coaching and support she received from Bob during this process, and in turn, he expressed his admiration for her. So what does Pamela offer Bob in return? From her standpoint, she offers unique insight into her demographic group:

One of the things I've done here at CNBC is find some younger reporters from diverse backgrounds and given them anchoring roles that they might not have had if a different person had been running the business. One of those people is now actually graduating to go to work at the NBC network. So I feel good about the fact that we had this great person. He's of Hispanic origin. I like to think that that might not have happened if a different person had been in this role. And I think just because of who I am as a young black woman I have a different worldview about certain things. And I think that informs Bob's thinking and NBC's thinking about where talent can come from and brings them a different perspective.

The power mentoring lineage continues with Pamela both giving and receiving valuable—albeit different—types of support with her protégé, Lilach Asofsky. Lilach has flourished at CNBC as senior vice president of marketing and research. She is responsible for all customer experience and marketing efforts, and under her leadership, the number of registered users increased by 220 percent in an eight-month period.[4] What does Lilach offer Pamela? She offers loyalty and acts as a trusted confidant. In exchange, she gains insight into Pamela's unique brand of savvy and style. In Lilach's words:

> I can honestly tell you that I watch her in every meeting that I'm in with her and in every conversation, and I learn from her. I learn from her from a content standpoint. I think she makes me smarter because she's so savvy about politics and entertainment and current events. I also really benefit from her style. She has a way about her. She's just so savvy and poised but at the same time I think really comes across as down to earth and as an individual that you can speak to. I'm so impressed with the way she handles decision making, that she can make decisions that really take an iron stomach to make and most people wouldn't have that kind of iron, and she does it. And people will question it, and she doesn't back off. And most of the time I've seen them—and it may take a while—but they've been the right decisions. She's also inspirational. I've heard her speak many times about different causes, and I've heard her speak about mentoring. And I've heard her speak about her commitment to helping further the career of women and of minorities. And every time I hear her speak, I am blown away by how inspirational she is and how energetic she is.

I think in terms of what I give her, there are really two areas.
One is I think that I'm a good injector of energy and ideas. I think
I also give her a comfort level and a trust because she knows that
my loyalty is with her and that if I see something that's a concern,
I'll come to her immediately with the problem. She knows that
she'll never be surprised by something if I knew about it. And I
think that as a senior executive, you need to have people around
you that you feel comfortable with and that you trust. And I think
that I do provide that.

Bob's second protégé is another superstar—Paula Madison,
currently president and general manager of KNBC. It is said that
success is the best revenge, and Paula's early triumphs over adversity serve as sweet inspiration for anyone who has ever been told,
"No, you aren't good enough," or "You can't do that." She was the
youngest of three children of Jamaican immigrants, and her parents instilled in her an immigrant's determination to succeed.
When she told her high school guidance counselor that she
intended to go to Radcliffe or Vassar, the woman laughed. "Not just
a chuckle, but a robust laugh. 'Paula,' she said, 'people like you
don't go to schools like that.'"

Paula went on to received a prestigious Vassar scholarship and
begin her fast-track career as a print reporter. She has a long string
of distinctions marking her as the "first" and "best"—for example,
she was the first African American woman to become general manager at a network-owned station in a top-five market. She has also
taken a dual role as the regional general manager for the two
NBC/Telemundo television stations in Los Angeles (KVEA and
KWHY). For all of her accomplishments, Paula has been awarded
the Ellis Island Medal of Honor (1999) and was selected as one of
New York's 100 Top Minority Executives (1998) by Crain's New York.

Paula reflected on a memorable meeting with Bob when he
convened a task force on diversity; she also spoke of the give-and-
take inherent in their relationship. What Bob especially valued
were the style and voice that Paula brought to NBC. The following
exchange highlights the importance of candor, of clarifying expectations, and of being straightforward about what can be offered.
Paula recalled:

I remember asking Bob if he was prepared for what this task force
was likely to address. I said, "Let's pretend for a moment that

there's a rock. Under this rock there are maggots. No one knows that there are maggots under the rock because the rock is in place. And everything from above looks fine. But when you lift that rock up and you turn it over and you see all the maggots underneath, you have a couple of choices. One is either you clean it up—get the maggots out, and have nice, good, rich wholesome soil under there. And then you put the rock back, but you know that from above the rock to below ground everything's good. Or you look at—you lift the rock and you see maggots, and you try to put the rock back in place. But the problem is that you've already dislodged it, so it really won't go back in place quite the way it had been." And I said, "So here's what I want to know, Bob. What I want to know is if this task force is the force that lifts this rock." I said, "I'm not willing to look beneath the rock and just put it back and pat it down and hope that okay, well, let's move it over and everything's good." And so Bob smiled at me, and he said, "I absolutely want you to accomplish what we want to accomplish when we lift that rock up." Then I said, "Okay, Bob, good. I'm on your team."

In turn, Bob reflected on Paula's confidence in their first meetings. Bob and Paula both remembered the time during the course of their mentoring relationship when Paula distinguished herself as leader to Bob and helped him in difficult times with the Hispanic community in Los Angeles. As Paula recalled:

In the fall of '99 Kweisi Mfume (CEO and president) of the NAACP criticized the four broadcast networks for not having enough diversity in prime time. And there were meetings going on behind the scenes, which really were not turning out to be very productive. By then the NAACP's position had grown to a coalition. So it was Hispanics, African Americans, Asian-Pacific Americans, and Native Americans. And Bob left it to me to negotiate an agreement. And at that time, I was news director. And I'm thinking to myself, okay, this is on behalf of the entire company. So I said to Bob, "Look, I'm going to start this negotiation, but I need to be in touch with you so that I can get your approval." And he said, "Nope. You know what to do. I trust you to get it done." At which point I think my knees almost gave out. Because on the one hand, yes, absolutely, I have confidence. And on the other hand, in an arena . . . I've not walked into before, to have my boss say to me, "You are the ambassador." He said, "I'll be available in case you need me." He said, "But you can get this done."

Bob reflected that Paula handled the situation beautifully, and she became someone he made a point of helping. As he put it, "I tried my best after that to help her. And she went from being the head of the news here in New York to the head of the operation in Los Angeles. And she's somebody I try to stay with and make sure that she's learning quickly."

From this lineage of important mentoring relationships, we see the important lessons and benefits that flow both ways, not only within the relationships, but throughout the organization as well. Even though we have probably uncovered only part of the Bob Wright mentoring lineage, it is obvious that all those involved in these relationships gained unique and important benefits.

Plugging into these important mentoring relationships in organizations is a fantastic method of accessing the informal network bound up with the real work of many organizations. Even trying to plug into these networks from time to time, maybe outside of a mentoring relationship, will give you valuable information about the organization and ways to move your career forward. In some ways these mentoring lineages can be viewed as important components of social capital that allow organizations to achieve their goals through the relationships people have that are outside of normal reporting relationships. People with high levels of social capital, who network effectively in organizations, make more money and are seen as the most effective performers.[5]

Through his mentoring relationships, Bob gained both important perspectives and employees who contribute to NBC's success. In turn, the different perspectives and innovative ideas that many of Bob's protégés brought to NBC affected the careers of others throughout the organization and the customers they served. In sum, the benefits made evident by Wright and his protégés include

- Satisfaction in watching people develop
- New perspectives, such as insight into a different demographic group or a personal brand of style or political savvy
- Trust and loyalty
- Development of confidants
- Excellent job performance

U.S. TREASURER ROSARIO MARIN AND HER PROTÉGÉ

In Chapters One and Two, we introduced you to Rosario Marin, who at the time of our interview was the 41st U.S. Treasurer in the George W. Bush administration. Marin currently serves as an appointee to California Governor Arnold Schwarzenegger's Integrated Waste Management Board. Earlier, you also met Marin's protégé—Araceli Gonzalez, small business owner and rising star in the Republican Party.

In Chapter Two, we introduced you to the unwavering, unconditional support that Rosario provided to Araceli Gonzalez early in Gonzalez's career, during the crisis when she discovered corruption among her colleagues in the Cudahy, California, city council. Later in Araceli's career, Rosario also helped her think through whether to run for the California State Senate. Marin said that when Araceli was contemplating running for office, she used the same tactics with Araceli that her own mentors had used with her: "I tried to help clarify what the questions were that she needed to answer. I can guide the questioning versus providing the answer. I see Araceli as fearless—she is willing to take on a Goliath for the good of the community." Once Araceli made the decision to run, Rosario also made calls behind the scenes to help her with her election bid.

But what did Araceli offer Rosario in return? Araceli was quite modest in her assessment of her role in helping Rosario, yet her actions spoke louder than words. Araceli helped to nominate Rosario for the Remarkable Woman Award from the National Association of Women Business Owners. Also, she was a loyal supporter and acted as a gatekeeper for Rosario when she was in Washington. She had access to her private line and cell phone number and made sure that important information got through to her. In 2004, Rosario mounted a campaign to run against Democratic incumbent Barbara Boxer for U.S. Senator, and Araceli was one of the main organizers and supporters behind this effort.

Much has been written about the difficulty of getting and keeping political office, whether at the local, state, or federal level. Obviously, mentoring benefits protégés who receive public support from an incumbent, and if the protégé wins, the mentor can act as a confidant to share methods for success within a job for which training is difficult to come by. Although political mentoring may differ somewhat by state, we think it holds important lessons for both political and nonpolitical careers. The evidence suggests that this type of mentoring is not without risks, especially when it involves making a public endorsement of a protégé or mentor. David Dreier, U.S. Representative (R-CA), tells the story of a candidate he supported through a public scandal. His unwavering support for this politician temporarily hurt David's reputation and underscored to him how supporting another person publicly can be risky. On the other hand, mentoring can be especially important for careers in which training and development are virtually nonexistent; in these situations, the guiding hand of someone who has been there before is invaluable.

Another aspect of mentoring unique to politics is the idea of mentoring across party lines. We were particularly impressed by both Marin and Dreier for mentoring across party lines because their ultimate goal was to provide the best political representation for their constituents, whatever it took. Mentoring relationships involving political appointees like Condoleezza Rice (said to have been mentored by Brent Scowcroft, National Security Advisor to George Bush Sr.) probably have more similarity to organizational mentoring relationships, but also provide important lessons for mentors and protégés about the immense benefits both can gain.

Rosario Marin and her protégés present a great example of the importance of complementary skills and of how mentoring across boundaries can be so beneficial for both parties. Think about the boundaries that exist in your own profession or organization and how helpful an ally or even just candid insight could be in working across these boundaries. In sum, a number of important benefits were evident in the relationship between Marin and her protégés:

- Tremendous joy in helping others accomplish their goals
- New contacts gained
- Help in meeting work goals such as running a campaign
- Development of a trusted gatekeeper
- Recognition
- Specific strategies on how to act, dress, and assert yourself in a new environment

CISCO'S FORMER CFO LARRY CARTER
AND PROTÉGÉ PATTY ARCHIBECK

In Chapter Two, you met Patty Archibeck, senior manager, Executive Communications; her boss mentor, Larry Carter, former CFO, Cisco; and her step-ahead mentor, Debra Martucci, vice president of Information Technology at Synopsys. Patty had a lot to say about what she gives and what she gets from her relationships with Larry and Debra—two very different relationships. Larry is a boss mentor and has a direct say over Patty's future with Cisco. In contrast, Debra provides a much-needed perspective outside of Cisco and a window into another technology company.

Due to the differences in these relationships, what Patty offers Larry and what she provides to Debra are very, very different. For Larry, she plays the role of trusted advisor and confidant, and provides him with unrelentingly candid feedback. Patty feels, and Larry confirmed, that she is a person Larry can relax with and exhibit his sense of humor to. In short, they trust each other implicitly. As for Debra, Patty is careful to follow her advice, show her appreciation, and be worthy of her tutelage. She gives Debra a chance to reflect on her role as a prominent woman in technology and lets her know she is making a difference in Patty's life. Here are Patty's reflections on what she provides to Larry in their relationship:

> For Larry, I think I'm a trusted advisor in a lot of ways. He can bounce ideas off of me, and he knows I will be honest about my responses. A lot of what our relationship is about is me giving him honest feedback. So if he's in a room—he's a very respected person, so for someone in the audience to say that your presentation wasn't good, that would never happen. They say, "We're so happy you're here. You did the best ever." And he looks to me to give the honest advice. I watch him present all the time, so I see where he improves and where he doesn't improve, so I give him honest feedback.

In a different vein, Patty speculated on what she offers Debra: "With Debra I would say that with me she feels that she has someone whom she is impacting. And to have someone like me who is a female that hungry for success, and to be able to impact me is I think a nice feeling. She's very excited to meet me. When we're in the aerobics class, she will tell the whole class that we're going to breakfast for our mentoring thing."

So looking at the other side of the dyad, what does Larry think he gets out of the relationship with Patty? Carter feels that he learns strategies for improvement that can be used organization-wide. Here are his words:

> I get a lot out of it in the sense that I learn areas of improvement that I need to do for the organization as a whole or for specific groups. So sometimes things will come up that I realize we don't have enough training in a certain area or I'm pushing some parts of the organization too hard, and they are not staffed properly. So people are working overtime that I didn't even know about. Or there are pockets in the organization, people who are very unhappy with their manager, and we have a management problem that I need to go deal with in a nice way [so] that nobody knows that somebody brought it to my attention. So I get a lot of good feedback about how to do my job more effectively. And it's also personally rewarding to see people grow in their careers.

What does Larry feel he offers Patty? He reflected as follows: "I coached her on developing executive presence. It is not just how you look or dress. It is also a state of mind that you develop. So you think like an executive. You behave like one. You look at somebody like John Chambers (CEO of Cisco) and talk to him like you are an equal. It is about developing confidence in yourself and feeling comfortable around people of stature."

What did Patty feel she gained from each of her mentoring relationships? She spoke of presenting the same dilemma to both Larry and Debra and being struck by the similarities as well as the differences in their advice. Here's her take on what she gained from Larry:

> I remember talking to Larry about some transitions that were happening around my peers. It didn't involve him, and I was kind of picking his brain as to how he was perceiving it from the outside and what would be a good plan of action. He gave me some real insight and told me to remember what my career goals are, stay out of the controversy, and be a leader. He totally refocused me. What I learned from him is leaders don't get flustered. The basis of what's

right and wrong stays the same no matter what is going on around you. Larry is like a duck. His feet may be paddling like hell, but on the surface he is just cruising.

Debra provided a little different perspective on the same situation. According to Patty:

> I think the scenario where there was stuff going on among my peers was definitely perplexing for me because it was creating a rift in the team that I worked on. I presented it to Debra as well. Her perspective was very similar to Larry's except she said one thing that may be more of a female characteristic. She said if you have peers that you respect and you can go through the situation together, that might be worthwhile. I think that might be more of a female characteristic to gather together with your peers. It was similar advice but a little different perspective, and so both were very helpful to me.

The relationships that Patty has with Debra and Larry both benefit her career, but in slightly different ways. The different perspectives and advice that she gains from her mentors highlight the importance of the network approach to mentoring. Debra gives Patty "sisterhood," a female perspective, and emotional support along with a refreshing glimpse of life outside Cisco. Because of their shared gender and interest in fitness, they can enjoy a level of commonality and locker-room bonding that Larry and Patty can never have. Larry, on the other hand, with his high status and close relationship with John Chambers (Cisco's CEO), can help Patty smash through the glass ceiling and make inroads into the rarefied air of the executive elite. Debra and Larry are happy to be an integral part of Patty's career, because they both mentioned that Patty gives as good as she gets.

In sum, the benefits obtained through these relationships were:

- Trusted advice
- Candid feedback
- Appreciation
- Opportunity for self-reflection
- Learning about areas of the organization that could be improved
- Coaching, such as on executive presence

TV DIRECTOR MARC BUCKLAND
AND HIS PROTÉGÉ, LAURA J. MEDINA

Consider the give-and-take between TV director Marc Buckland and his protégé, budding director Laura J. Medina. Laura J. Medina was chosen as one of the 12 most promising women and minority members for the Single Camera Director's Prep Program offered by the Directors Guild of America (DGA). Participants in this program receive mentoring and instruction from the industry's most highly acclaimed one-hour drama directors. Laura received recognition for her early work addressing women's issues in film and came to directing with a solid background in production.

As part of this program, Laura was given a choice of mentors. One, Rod Holcomb, is a highly successful TV director with a long career of notable TV pilots (and shows and movies) including *The Education of Max Bickford, ER,* and *China Beach.* As a mentor he has been incredibly generous and giving of himself, his time, and his knowledge, and continues to do so. She also picked Marc Buckland because of his great work and reputation. Marc has a long string of "A list" TV series directing credits to his name and is highly regarded in the industry for his work on hit shows like *NYPD Blue, The West Wing, Felicity,* and many others. A former associate producer and protégé of eminent producer Steven Bochco, Marc has learned from the best. He was honored to receive a 2002 Emmy Award nomination for outstanding director of a comedy series for his directing work on *Scrubs.* In 2001, he was a People's Choice Award Winner for Favorite Comedy (for *Ed*). More recently, Marc executive produced and directed the pilot for the *Medical Investigation* TV series. In an industry known for temper tantrums and screaming, Marc is notable for his good humor and ability to create a professional and enjoyable atmosphere on the set.

A heartwarming movie was released in 2000 called *Pay It Forward,* about a young boy, Trevor (Haley Joel Osment), who is inspired by his social studies teacher (Kevin Spacey) to do favors for those who can't reciprocate directly, but instead must pass a favor forward to others who need help. In the movie, Trevor gives a homeless man a place to sleep and shower; the man repays his favor with a kindness to a homeless woman, who passes her favor on to a young reporter—in the film, paying it forward soon spreads across the country.

This idea of paying it forward is akin to the Hindu idea of generating positive karma; it came up often in our conversations with mentors and protégés. We found that since power mentors had themselves been given assistance in their careers, they feel an obligation and a commitment to give back to others—in other words, to pay it forward. Marc Buckland told us that he gets a sense of gratification from helping someone like Laura, and views his assistance both as a tribute to and as a way of paying back those who were so helpful to him. In other words, from those who have been given much, much is expected. Here are Marc's reflections:

> I love that somebody can just follow along [that is, job shadow him while he is directing on the set] and get something from the non-sense. It makes me feel good. It makes me feel good to do it because so many people have opened doors for me. I'm not saying I'm this altruistic person (because it's pretty consuming doing what we do when we do it [directing a TV show])—but to whatever extent I can open the doors for people it's great. In a way I believe that there's enough to go around. And I know I've been really lucky to have the opportunities I've had. If there was something I could do to help her [Laura] get an episode of a show I would be nothing but thrilled. When you feel really lucky in your life it would be horrible not to help other people. I've been so lucky that I'd have to be a real schmuck not to help others.

Marc feels good about helping Laura out of a global sense of obligation to give to others; however, he definitely benefits from the relationship as well. He mentioned that it is very helpful for him to have access to Laura's informed and yet unbiased opinion when he is on the set. Often, people on a set or the various stakeholders have very different agendas for what they want or need from the director. The actors may want to make sure they look gorgeous, the producers want to make sure the project is profitable and stays within budget, and the line producer wants to make sure the shoot proceeds in a timely fashion. In this sense, in addition to having to be creative and shoot his vision, a director like Marc must constantly manage a formidable set of competing expectations. Therefore, when Laura shadows Marc on the set and he solicits her opinion, it is one of Marc's few opportunities to gain an opinion that has only his best interest in mind. Laura is very cognizant that she can be helpful to Marc in that way. In her own words: "I give him my honest opinion about what he was doing [that is, about his performance in directing and the look of the daily shots]. It was genuine and I thought he needs people to say things to him too. And so I give him my opinion. I'm completely outside of the process, whereas everyone else is vested in some way or another."

What does Laura gain from the relationship? She talked at length about some of the technical skills she learned from Marc. She had transitioned from working on movies for nearly 20 years to aspiring to direct TV shows. She noted that "Marc is the most focused and organized director I have ever seen. In television the time pressure is so much greater than in film. He knows exactly what he wants and pretty much gets it. I really like watching his manner with people. He leads very well but does it with a light touch so everybody likes him. And also he is very funny."

Marc and Laura's relationship provides insight into the workings of a formal mentoring program in an industry that is somewhat unfamiliar to many: television directing. From outside the industry, directing may appear to require primarily technical skills, but in the course of our interviews you could see how there are many interpersonal facets to the job. The surprising importance of these nontechnical parts of the job has implications for other, ostensibly technological occupations for which interpersonal skills are usually considered an afterthought. Laura was able to go "behind the curtain" and observe the difference between a good technical director and one that gets called back to work time after time because he or she brings a great set of skills that impresses the producers, cast, and crew.

Even though their relationship was a formal mentor pairing through the DGA, maybe somewhat to Marc's surprise it was not unidirectional. He felt he also gained from Laura's presence on the set, specifically in thinking of shots in different ways because she brought an outside perspective. In our interviews with television directors for another project, many of the questions we asked got them thinking more carefully about the techniques they use on the set to motivate others. Through the act of articulating one's strategies to others, self-learning is an important outcome.[6]

In addition to self-learning, benefits that were highlighted in this relationship that also apply to other mentoring relationships include

- A chance to pay it forward
- Candid feedback
- Shared agenda and interests
- New technical knowledge about content and process

DISNEY PRESIDENT ANNE SWEENEY AND HER PROTÉGÉS

Meet Anne Sweeney—in 2004 named the "Most Powerful Woman in Entertainment" by *The Hollywood Reporter,* one of the "50 Most Powerful Women in Business" by *Fortune,* and one of the "World's 100 Most Powerful Women" by *Forbes* magazine. She is not just a survivor, but a thriver in the extremely competitive and mercurial world of entertainment media. Anne joined the team at the Walt Disney Corporation in 1996 as the president of the Disney Channel and executive vice president of Disney/ABC Cable Networks. In 2004, in addition to her already considerable leadership responsibilities, she was named co-chairman, Media Networks, the Walt Disney Company, and president, Disney-ABC Television Group, a role in which she is responsible for all of Disney's nonsports, cable, satellite, and broadcast properties, and which includes overseeing the programming of the ABC Television Network. How does someone as busy and as focused as she is have the time or inclination to mentor? Again, it is because of the value she perceives in these relationships, not only in what she offers, which is a great deal, but in what she gets back from these relationships.

You will meet two of Anne's protégés. First, we look at the relationship between Anne and Kathleen Von der Ahe, whom Anne was formally assigned to be a mentor to as part of Disney's high-potential mentoring program for women and people of color. Since 1999 Kathleen has been vice president of Affiliate Relations at ABC. In this role, Kathleen managed and redefined relations between ABC and its affiliates. What Anne offered to her protégés was considerable. She provided Kathleen with a tremendous female role model, insight into Disney at the higher echelons, and critical advice at a time when Kathleen was at an important work-family balance juncture. Anne reflected on the reciprocal nature of her mentoring relationship with Kathleen. She felt that she received encouragement as well as new ideas and inspiration from Kathleen. As Anne said:

I think the greatest thing we give each other is encouragement. We're living in a company right now that is as challenged as every other media company out there. And we're very aware of it. And we are both very interested in solving problems, making it better, moving the stock price and creating shareholder value.

So I think that knowing that I'm talking to someone in this mentoring relationship who's interested in the big idea here is very, very important to me. I think if it were just about helping me get to my next step, it would be a heck of a lot less interesting.

Kathleen came over for a meeting one day. And I was just having the worst week of the worst month of the worst year, and I can't remember whether it was the five-year plan or it was some kind of big corporate thing but I was drowning in it at the time. Kathleen told me about something she had done to let people be more informed about what was going on with the network and what she had set up. And I sat there getting really inspired. And I realized— get out of her way, Anne. You know, listen to Kathleen. This is what she did to get people moving forward. And you realize that if you really embrace the idea of mentorship and this program, you really have to go into it as the two-way street and be open to whatever information is coming your way in whatever form. I decided she took such a fresh perspective on an old issue. And it just inspired me to do the same.

Kathleen also talked about what she gained from Anne as well as what she gave back. In her opinion she was able to provide Anne with insight into a different area of the business. Indeed, this insight must have been really helpful because Anne was promoted to president, Disney-ABC Television Group, overseeing all of ABC: "I think I have been able to give Anne a little bit more insight on the ABC Television Network in terms of how things get done, possibly some issues that we deal with here in Affiliate Relations. I think she's probably realized the position that I'm in and the importance of really knowing the Network. Because I am dealing with ABC News, ABC Sports, ABC Primetime, ABC Sales, Compensation and Legal issues. It's perhaps broadened her understanding of our department." Kathleen went on to reflect on what she gained from Anne: "In terms of what she's given me, I think she's really given me some confidence in myself. And made me realize that she's a wonderful example of what I would like to be one day. She's just a very well-rounded and ethical executive. She's really made me believe that I can make a difference."

Next, we look at the relationship between Anne and her informal protégé, Diane Robina. Diane Robina is the executive vice president and general manager of The New TNN. In this role, Diane led the rebranding of the network and is responsible for its day-to-day management, including programming, marketing, and promotional strategies. Anne and Diane met when Anne hired Diane at Nickelodeon, and even though their organizational affiliations made them competitors, their relationship has stood the tests of geography and time.

Anne was originally a boss mentor to Diane; over the years they transitioned into becoming lasting friends, even though they live and work on different coasts. What benefits do Anne and Diane exchange with each other? Diane reflected on what she gets in her relationship with Anne: "From Anne, I get a friendship from someone who is in similar shoes that I am in. So we can understand a lot of the ups and downs of life in general because we have similarities. The main thing I think I get is a friendship in someone who you can sit down with and say, 'Oh, my God, what am I supposed to do now?'" Diane went on to speculate on what she offers Anne in return: "We have kids that are the same age, so we have similar pressures. I would also hope that she takes part in my successes and gets satisfaction in that respect. Even though our companies are extremely competitive, we can still maintain our friendship."

Anne Sweeney is an extraordinary mentor, and what she receives in return has been and undoubtedly will continue to be useful in her career. Anne knows that cultivating these relationships has put her where she is today. For example, she participates in a formal mentoring program and in doing so learned more about other parts of her organization from her protégés. She has also benefited enormously from the mentoring she received from the industry's best, including Rupert Murdoch, Geraldyne Laybourne, and Fred Silverman, the programming genius who worked at all three networks. Moreover, Anne's protégés, and in turn their protégés, are plugged into a powerful lineage, like those working within the powerful Bob Wright lineage at NBC. Tapping into the success strategies of powerful individuals is an invaluable benefit for would-be protégés, and mentors such as Anne can take pride in turn in what those they mentor accomplish for the organization and the industry. In sum, here are some of the mentoring benefits suggested by the experiences of Anne and her protégés:

- Exposure to excellent role models
- Friendship
- Enhanced self-confidence
- New insight into different levels or areas of the business or organization
- Critical work-family advice
- Encouragement and inspiration
- New ideas and a fresh perspective
- Contagious energy

IBM's SENIOR VP LINDA SANFORD AND HER MENTORING NETWORK

In Chapter Two, we introduced you to Linda Sanford, senior vice president at IBM, and to some of her past and current mentors, including senior vice president Nick Donofrio. Like Anne Sweeney, Linda has been mentored by some of the most influential people in her industry, so it makes sense that she is an excellent mentor to others. She has a large number of active mentoring relationships, both formal and informal, but she identified three people in particular as being some of her closest connections. Sanford's three protégés featured here—all at IBM—are Joan Buzzallino, vice president of Human Resources; Martha Morris, vice president of Global Services Procurement; and Charles Lickel, vice president of Software and Storage Development.

Martha Morris is a long-term IBM employee; her ascension up the ranks has been through a series of line positions. First joining IBM in 1981, she has held a number of top management positions for IBM all over the world. Her areas of special emphasis include issues of manufacturing competitiveness, diversity, education, and strengthening IBM's leadership in the global marketplace. Joan Buzzallino represents the classic upwardly mobile IBM employee, because she has spent nearly her entire career—spanning more than 30 years—at IBM and has been successfully promoted and lauded for her management skills. Since 2003 she has served as vice president, Human Resources for Enterprise on Demand Transformation, the next phase of e-business. We discuss Linda's exchange of benefits with Martha and Joan here and provide more information about Charles later in this chapter, when we discuss organizational benefits.

All three of Linda's protégés had similar things to say about what they learned from her, because she is an excellent teacher, connector, nurturer, and listener. In particular, Martha said one of the most valuable things she gained from Linda was access to her as a person and to someone at her level, as well as the ability to watch and learn. In Martha's words: "I get access to someone who's on the Top 20 List of the most influential women in the country. And that's amazing. And someone who you respect in that role that didn't get there by climbing over people and leaving a lot of broken glass. And I get to watch her and ask questions. She's a role model that I can also use as I talk to the folks I mentor or if I have roundtables, particularly with women, in the various plants." Martha also reflected on what she gives to Linda in return: "What she gets is a loyal employee that if she said, 'Martha, I want you to come do this again for me and take this,' I'd do it in a second. She gets a better IBMer in me because she has spent some time with me. And so she's made me better."

Joan Buzzallino talked about gaining the benefit of working with senior executives. Also, Joan and Linda have a peer mentoring relationship. Here is what Joan felt she got from her relationship with Linda:

> What I get is the benefit of Linda's experience in dealing with senior executives and her skill with dealing at that level. For me right now that's important. She does it so much it's intuitive to her. Right now with Linda as my mentor I have a sounding board. If I want to try to get something forward or have an idea she just will give me that added perspective. And that's what I need right now from a business standpoint. And so she's helped me be much more productive within the HR community because I have the benefit of the support of senior line management. And also that is a penalty-free sounding board who takes an interest to make sure that I've covered all the bases. So she's a coach. Not so much a career coach in terms of job and skill, but more about taking me to the next level.

In return, Joan acts as a confidant and sounding board for Linda:

> I think what I do for her is she uses me as a sounding board. Linda
> has a great gut. But sometimes she is so collaborative that she will
> move away from her gut. So I rein her back in sometimes and keep
> her true to herself. It's funny because at our level it's a different
> kind of relationship. But yet she'll know when to test. And then I'll
> bring her back and say, "Wait a minute. You know, they're taking
> you down a different path. You were right where you wanted to be."
> I might say, "You've been collaborative enough. You know, cut it
> and do that." That's why in picking mentoring relationships you've
> got to have people that complement each other, not necessarily be
> the same.

Finally, we turn to Linda's perspective. What does she feel she
gains?

> A lot. I think a lot more than I've been giving, actually. They can
> give me honest feedback and a fresh perspective. These relation-
> ships allow me to test ideas and thoughts on someone else as well. I
> can test what I'm instinctively feeling and see if it's real or some
> thoughts about things we might be thinking about doing and have
> somebody to bounce some of those ideas off of and get some real
> honest feedback. So that's why I think mentoring is really a two-way
> street, whether it's with Charles or Martha or Joan or with my next-
> generation reverse mentor.

In a tightly knit community such as IBM, mentoring relationships are very valuable for many different reasons. First, as we mentioned earlier, they serve as a way of increasing one's social capital
and making connections that help accomplish organizational
goals. Second, these relationships can be a valuable means of motivating individuals and of building two-way trust among organizational members. For example, in discussing her relationship with
Linda Sanford, Martha Morris noted that because of the trust they
had built and the mentoring Linda provides, Martha motivates her
group to do its best for Linda.

Linda Sanford exemplifies a mentor who truly understands the
importance of mentoring within her corporation. She mentors
many people and derives different benefits from each relationship.
Even more important, she cultivates a dedicated workforce she can

count on. The following is a summary of benefits derived from the mentoring experiences of Sanford and her protégés:

- Access to higher echelons
- Loyalty and trust
- Availability of a sounding board
- Help in saying no when needed
- Honest feedback
- Fresh perspectives

U.S. REPRESENTATIVE HILDA SOLIS AND HER PROTÉGÉS

Let's take a look at an interesting trio of mentoring relationships. In the previous chapter, we briefly introduced you to U.S. Representative Hilda Solis (D-CA) and California State Assembly Member Judy Chu (Dem.) as examples of mentoring across barriers. Solis was the first woman to win the John F. Kennedy Profile in Courage Award for her fight to move environmental waste sites out of the communities she represented in Southern California.[7] Congresswoman Solis serves on the powerful House Energy and Commerce Committee and was the first Latina to serve on this committee. Her political priorities encompass environmental protection, health care improvement, and the rights of working families. When speaking about what she feels needs to be done on an even larger scale, she makes it quite clear that giving back and being other-focused is why she both mentors those close to her and serves as a role model to others. Solis not only tries to ensure the success of those she mentors, but she volunteers to give talks to Latina high school students interested in college, serving as what she hopes is an inspirational mentor.

It is no wonder that Hilda Solis became involved in a mentoring relationship with California State Assembly Member Judy Chu. Since the beginning of her professional career, Dr. Judy Chu has dedicated her life to public service. In her illustrious career she has served on a local school board for three years, been a member of the Monterey Park City Council for 13 years, and served as mayor of Monterey Park three times. Judy and Hilda share a passion for many of the same issues, because Judy also has made significant inroads in protecting the environment, has served as an advocate for health care reform, and focuses on serving the underrepresented. She was recognized by the *California Journal* as one of California's top new legislators.

As a benefit of their mentoring relationship, both Judy and Hilda emphasized the importance of coordinating their efforts on causes of interest to them, which has enabled them to share resources. In Judy's words:

> We always check in with Hilda and coordinate our activities. For instance, we had a grant-writing workshop together. We cosponsored it. We invited all the community-based organizations and anybody who was interested in grant writing. We had federal, state, and private people there. I was amazed at the turnout; we must have had at least 200 people there. It was just a gigantic turnout for a grant-writing workshop. But actually we coordinate on a lot of things. For instance, we are coordinating on a campaign office now. But also, for instance, somebody may call over there and somebody's speaking Chinese. Then we'll talk to them. Or if somebody calls here and it's an immigration problem, then we'll refer them over there.

Hilda also talked about the benefits of working in partnership with Judy: "I worked very closely with her when she was on city council when I was in the Senate. We helped to provide funds for a lot of projects, community expansion of the senior center, expansion of the library, and other public work projects that benefit the community. So we were able to work together. And we're still doing that. We are good examples of how good things can happen when you coalesce."

Hilda and Judy have one other important thing in common: they both serve as mentors to up-and-coming politician Sharon Martinez, former mayor of Monterey Park. Sharon counts herself fortunate to be mentored by both of these extraordinary women. Sharon brings the sensibilities of a small business owner to her role as politician. She is founder and president of SMART Temporary Personnel Services, specializing in clerical, bilingual, and promotional staffing. This company employs more than 100 people daily, with gross annual revenues of more than $2 million.

Sharon spoke passionately and at length about what she gained from her mentors, Hilda Solis and Judy Chu. She received coaching early on about how to raise money for her campaign, was sustained by Hilda's encouragement when her opponent sent nasty letters about her, and benefited from Hilda's support and political endorsement. From Judy she gained an understanding of the political process, an endorsement, and a positive role model. In return, Sharon felt that she offered the following to Solis and Chu:

> I think a lot of what I give is my positive energy. I try to always have a positive attitude, especially when I'm with Hilda. I feel she's such a great person in my life. And also I try to give her a sense of what's happening at home when she's on the Hill [Capitol Hill in Washington, D.C.]. And I always give Hilda and Judy my loyalty. That will always be there and forever. I've gone through thick and thin with that loyalty because there were a lot of people that were upset when I supported Judy. You had a Latino running against her, but yet Judy was good for the city. There were a lot of people mad at me. I heard a lot about it.

This group of legislators shows the importance of productive mentoring relationships. Solis, Chu, and Martinez are well regarded by their constituents for fighting for what is best for their communities. They chose to ignore the typical ethnic divides that characterize their districts to tackle issues such as education, minority rights, and pollution. By pooling their strengths, they have become a formidable group engaging in power mentoring. Their relationships characterize what is typically called *step-ahead mentoring*. Solis began the process, Judy Chu has followed one step behind her, and Sharon Martinez is one step behind Chu. The advantage of a step-ahead mentor, as we pointed out in the previous chapter, is that the protégé has a mentor with a very recent perspective on how to navigate his or her career. Regardless of the form their mentoring took, for our three legislators the reciprocal benefits have been immense and show the importance of mentoring support. The benefits described here include

- Fundraising assistance
- Political strategizing
- Public support and encouragement
- Access to complementary resources
- Positive energy
- Career coaching

GENERAL LEE BUTLER AND HIS PROTÉGÉ, BRIGADIER GENERAL DONALD PETTIT

We turn now to a fascinating mentor-protégé pair from the highest echelons of the military: General Lee Butler and his protégé, Brigadier General Donald Pettit. General Butler had a distinguished career in the military between 1961 and 1994; as commander of the U.S. Nuclear Forces from 1991 to 1994, he led the efforts to dismantle the U.S. nuclear arsenal. In this role, he was responsible for the operational safety and security of the arsenal as well as for preparations to deploy nuclear weapons. During his tenure he became horrified at the "chilling ballet" we engaged in with the former Soviet Union in regard to nuclear weapons and had an insight that led to a moral imperative to dismantle the U.S. nuclear arsenal. During his three-year tenure, he canceled $40 billion worth of strategic nuclear modernization programs and reduced the nuclear warplanes by 75 percent. Featured in Michael Collopy's book *Architects of Peace* as one of the 50 top world leaders in peace (along with luminaries such as Mother Teresa, Mikhail Gorbachev, and the Dalai Lama of Tibet), Lee Butler has a lot to say about peace, politics, and mentoring.[8]

Lee counts himself fortunate to have had several influential mentors and what he calls "angels" in his career, including General George Brown (chair of the Joint Chiefs of Staff in the 1970s), General Russ Dougherty (commander of the Strategic Air Command from 1974 to 1977), and General Colin Powell (Secretary of State from 2000 to 2004). Although Lee was effusive about what he learned from his mentors, he was perhaps even more eloquent when he spoke of his relationship with his former protégé, General Donald Pettit. Lee served as a boss mentor to Pettit during their tenure together in the 1980s, when Lee was deputy director of Air Force Operations and Don was his executive assistant.

Brigadier General Pettit, in his last assignment, served as commander, 45th Space Wing, and director, Eastern Range, Patrick Air Force Base, Florida.[9] Additionally, he was Deputy Department of Defense Manager for Manned Space Flight Support. As commander, the general oversaw the preparation and launching of U.S. government and commercial satellites from Cape Canaveral Air Force Station, Florida, and granted final approval for all launches on the Eastern Range. Lee reflected on the type of exchange inherent in his relationship with Don:

The role that Don came to play for me is another dimension of a mentor-protégé relationship that I think is rather rare. But when that relationship is operating at perfection, I think that it is its highest dimension, and that is Don became the guardian of my conscience.

> There are a lot of ways to fire people. There are ways to let people know that their career might not be going great. There's the dealing with the difficult personality. All these personal issues that come into play and land right on the boss's desk. Don was my principal sounding board for these kinds of things. And we had a clear moral compass always do and say the right thing. Never put a tough job off on someone else. Be brutally objective in your assessments but compassionate in the consequences.

General Lee Butler said that Don helped him stay true to his ideals by playing the role of "truth teller" in his life:

> As Don watched me operate day to day with my staff and in other presentations he was always attentive. One of his purposes was to tell me the moment that he saw me stray in any way from the proper path. It was nothing any more than, "Hey, boss, you might want to rethink that." So he played a very, very powerful role in helping me to always be true to the things that I believe in with regard to having an organization succeed and how to stay within the boundaries of my own value system. The responsibility of the mentor is to nurture the relationship and make that possible. Because you can shut that door forever with one curt word or angry glance.

Don felt the exchange of benefits went both ways and talked a bit more about how he offered feedback: "It goes both ways. And I've always believed we all put our pants on the same. However, I remained mindful of the fact that he was a General and I was at that time, a Major (working for him). So I made an effort to and hopefully did provide my comments to General Butler with distinguished reverence to him and to his position. Fortunately for me, General Butler encouraged my feedback and discussed/shared his thoughts openly with me—this relationship allowed me to grow personally and professionally and I will be forever grateful. Because we had this relationship, when I just thought something was going wrong, it allowed me to be pretty vocal if I felt I had to be. But normally with him you didn't need to be very vocal, you just had to rationally show him there's another side to something that should be considered or a different point of view—invariably, he would always make the right decision."

This set of interviews showed the intense reciprocity of benefits characteristic of successful mentoring relationships. Lee Butler focused on the high-level benefits he received from his protégés that almost took the form of another conscience. In this day and age, many high-level executives could use a person who might challenge them around ethical issues. The type of close mentoring we saw in this relationship between Lee and Don may be somewhat unique to the life-and-death decisions faced by military personnel. Formal and hierarchical relationships may spawn close and trusting relationships that may have a different feel from mentoring relationships in other, more informal organizations. This doesn't mean that close relationships cannot be developed in other types of organizations, but these relationships may take longer to develop or may be expected to focus on less pivotal decisions. In sum, the benefits ascribed to this formidable mentoring pair pertain to the roles of

- Guardian of conscience
- Sounding board
- Truth teller
- Career coach

SUMMARY OF BENEFITS FOR PROTÉGÉS AND MENTORS

Our interviews, drawing from both sides of the mentoring dyad, showed us how many successful mentors and protégés have relationships that are characterized by an important give-and-take. In this chapter, we have presented you with a snapshot of the two-way, reciprocal benefits gained by many of our interviewees. You may have already started to notice similar themes and benefits in your own mentoring relationships.

We conducted a complete analysis of all 50 of our interviews and created a comprehensive list of benefits gained by protégés, mentors, and organizations. Next, we took our list and compared it to the considerable body of research that already exists on mainly traditional mentoring benefits. We found that our list of benefits from our power mentoring interviewees and those from past research on traditional mentoring were very similar. This means that power mentoring confers many of the same benefits as traditional mentoring and can be just as beneficial to your career as traditional mentoring. Incidentally, you might wonder if the benefits we discuss in this chapter apply if you are not as far along in your career as many of our interviewees are. Let us reassure you that the answer is a resounding *Yes*. Past research has found that the various benefits of mentoring have been well documented among workers at all stages of their careers in a variety of organizations, industries, and professions.

WHAT DO POWER PROTÉGÉS GAIN?

In sum, what do protégés gain from their power mentoring relationships? At the beginning of the chapter we touched on research findings on the benefits of traditional mentoring, then we shared stories illuminating what our power mentors and protégés gain. Now we provide an overall conclusion that integrates past research with our findings. Exhibit 3.1 contains a summary of what we know from earlier research as well as our current findings on how protégés benefit from their mentoring relationships.[10]

EXHIBIT 3.1 PROTÉGÉ BENEFITS

Career Support	Personal/Emotional Support
Promotion opportunities	Self-efficacy at work
Job mobility	Interpersonal growth
Pay raises	Sponsorship and protection
Job involvement	Advocacy
Career and job success	Friendship and social interactions
Organizational commitment	Counseling and listening
Job- and career-related feedback	Support and confirmation
Challenging assignments	Acceptance
Access to resources/information/ people	
Exposure and visibility	

WHAT DO POWER MENTORS GAIN?

At the beginning of the chapter, we briefly considered why people mentor others, discussing both self- and other-focused motives. Here we provide you with an overall integration of past research along with our findings on what power mentors gain. Take a look at the list in Exhibit 3.2 and consider what applies to your mentoring relationship.

How can you develop your power mentoring relationships so that they provide maximum benefits to both parties? Begin by assessing what you want from a particular mentoring relationship as well as what you have to offer. As a protégé, think not only about what your mentor can do for you, but also about what you can do for your mentor. As a mentor, think about the added benefits you could get from your mentoring relationship and what more you might give. We provide you with many more specific ideas on how to do this in future chapters, particularly in Chapter Seven. In the next section of this chapter, we examine what organizations stand to gain from effective mentoring relationships.

WHAT DO ORGANIZATIONS GAIN?

Consider the following example from IBM. Lou Gerstner came to IBM with a mission to transform Big Blue and engineer a badly needed comeback. How he did it is another story (see *Who Says Elephants Can't Dance?*); what is relevant here is how he made mentoring and diversity a core part of IBM's culture.[11] Each of our five IBM interviewees estimated that they had anywhere from 10 to 50 protégés, some formal and some informal. They estimated spending 10–20 percent of their time on mentoring, even at the very senior levels. In fact, mentoring is a key part of the criteria on which senior management is evaluated.

Every IBM interviewee with whom we spoke referred to the mentoring they received from Lou Gerstner either directly, as in the case of Linda Sanford and Nick Donofrio, or indirectly, as filtered through Linda to her three protégés. When we asked Linda and Nick what they tried to pass on to their protégés, they said it was the maxim, "Be yourself, be your best self, be your true self." While this might sound a bit trite, what is interesting is how this represents a change from typical IBM culture—and how the

EXHIBIT 3.2   MENTOR BENEFITS

Career Support	Personal/Emotional Support
Recognition as a developer of others	Rejuvenation
Recognition as a leader	Personal satisfaction
Reputation enhancement	Increase in knowledge, empathy, and skills relating to diverse groups
Increased influence and power	Greater collegiality
Expanded network	Friendship
Career satisfaction	Sense of pride and personal satisfaction
Career and job motivation	Support and confirmation
Improved management and leadership skills	Respect and empowerment
Improved job performance	Greater confidence
Job-related feedback	Interpersonal skill development
Assistance in doing job	Satisfaction in role as mentor
Insight into different roles or areas of the organization or profession	Transmission of knowledge, skills, and values
Challenge and stimulation	Excitement and inspiration
Visibility and exposure	Greater consciousness of what you are doing by teaching another

maxim was translated into some pretty dramatic behaviors. Pre-Gerstner, the maxim might have been, "Be like us," and "Be yourself only if it is like us." This kind of implicit message kept gay employee and Sanford protégé Charles Lickel in the closet for 16 years.

Charles Lickel, who described himself as an extremely shy executive, had typically worked 70 hours or more a week at IBM for 16 years when he decided to confide his secret to his mentor, Linda Sanford. This moment of self-disclosure and ultimate trust became a defining moment for both of them. Not only did it draw Linda and Charles closer together, resulting in a long relationship through which she was able to give him some painful but necessary constructive performance criticism, but it also gave Charles a career boost.

With Linda's encouragement, he wrote a letter to Lou Gerstner offering his assistance in the newly formed diversity caucus. Lou named him cochair of the gay and lesbian caucus; as a result, Charles has been nationally recognized as one of the 25 most influential gay and lesbian executives in the country, and IBM enjoys a reputation as an excellent work environment for gay and lesbian employees. Charles is vice president of Software and Storage Development and is responsible for a 2,500-person organization that drives IBM's worldwide storage systems solutions. When you consider that gays and lesbians make up 10–15 percent of our workforce, tapping into this population is a shrewd move that can yield significant recruiting opportunities.

Past research has provided a great deal of compelling evidence that organizations benefit from providing an environment where mentoring can flourish. As the previous example shows, the benefits for organizations include improved recruitment and attraction of talented employees. As an organization becomes known as one that develops people, its reputation is enhanced in the professional community, making it much easier for the company to win the war on talent and attract the best and brightest.

Another benefit is greater organizational productivity. In fact, in some of our past research we discovered that effective mentoring relates to greater organizational commitment and better citizenship behavior. In workplaces like IBM, where mentoring flourishes, we typically find a greater esprit de corps, and overall better workplace communication and relations with employees. Mentoring can help to orient new employees and bridge the gap between training and learning. There is even some evidence that mentoring can help employees adapt readily to change.

CONCLUSION

To reiterate, in this chapter we presented examples of the reciprocal or two-way nature of mentoring relationships. We focused on both the mentor's and the protégé's perspectives to highlight the many things each can gain. In the next chapter we delve deeper into the mind of the mentor in mentoring relationships. If you are a mentor, you will find out what type of mentor you are and what you look for in a worthwhile protégé. As protégés, you will see the styles of mentoring that best fit your particular career development goals, and you will become acquainted with the types of tests and challenges mentors may pose to you in your developing relationship. Most important, by the end of this book you will learn specific strategies and be guided through a step-by-step process that will enable you to take advantage of all the potential benefits that we discuss.

Chapter Four

The Mind of the Mentor

*You had what it takes to get into my office. Now do you
have what it takes to stay? . . . You are either inside the
game or out. Money never sleeps. . . . I've showed you how
the game works. Now astonish me. . . . I am going to make
you rich. . . . Greed captures our evolutionary spirit.
Greed is good.*
—As told to Bud Fox by Gordon Gecco in
the film WALL STREET

Twenty years ago, Oliver Stone's film *Wall Street* provided a telling
commentary on life in corporate America during an era of get-rich
quick schemes, hostile takeovers, mergers, and acquisitions.
Although the characters' clothing and hairstyles might be a bit
dated, *Wall Street* as a morality tale is timeless. Moreover, the depic-
tion of the young stockbroker, Bud Fox (played by Charlie Sheen),
pursuing the billionaire businessman, Gordon Gecco (Michael
Douglas), is a terrific example of how a protégé can win a mentor,
get inside the mind of the mentor, and then learn valuable lessons
about himself through the mentor's betrayal.

In 1985, Hollywood provided us with a fictional example of an
unethical mentor. In 2005, Hollywood has provided us with a real-
life example of Gecco's polar opposite—the enormously respected
and well-liked Ron Meyer, president and chief operating officer
(COO) of NBC/Universal. In that role he is responsible for Universal Pictures, Focus Features, and Universal Parks and Resorts.
Everything Meyer touches seems to turn to gold. Prior to his reign
at Universal, Meyer was one of the original founders of the Creative Artists Agency (CAA); along with Michael Ovitz, he built CAA

into one of Hollywood's most successful talent agencies. Ron is well known not only for his business acumen but also for being a developer of talent. Richard Lovett, president of CAA, Stacy Snider, Universal Pictures chair, and Nikki Rocco, Universal Pictures distribution chief, all credit Meyer with being an important mentor in their career journeys. So, what's in it for someone like Ron to be a mentor, or for their organizations?

Many mentors see mentoring as just part of their jobs. Often supervisors or managers make it a priority on their own to develop their employees' skills and abilities, while sometimes they are formally tasked with that responsibility. Although most organizations recognize mentoring as a valuable method of informal and formal development for high-potential employees, effective mentoring can increase the total number of qualified employees by providing direct contact with more experienced employees. Not only do these mentors help enhance their protégés' technical or management skills in their current positions, they also expose the protégés to the values, skill requirements, and strategies of upper management. While it is no secret that mentors in traditional mentoring relationships are expected to devote a great deal of time and expertise to the development of competent employees for the organization, many, as they reach the upper levels of their careers, are in fact very eager to share their knowledge with the next generation of up-and-coming employees. The practice of giving talented people room and resources to develop, a strategy employed by Universal's Ron Meyer at the top, is contagious and, if practiced well, becomes part of the culture of the entire organization.

In Chapter Two, we described the many forms that power mentoring relationships can take. Behind each of those types of mentors (mentors of the moment, boss mentors, reverse mentors, and so on), there lies a set of expectations about how the mentoring relationship will unfold and the particular role of the mentor and the protégé. Moreover, an important distinction between power mentoring and traditional relationships is that most power mentors feel that they get as much out of the relationship as they put in (reciprocity). As mentioned in Chapter Three, in power mentoring relationships, mentors recognize that mentoring benefits go beyond those of a typical employee development opportunity or merely a situation in which mentors feel proud of their good deeds.

In this chapter, we take these ideas further by exploring in depth the philosophies people hold about what it means to be a mentor. Why is it important to examine mentoring philosophies? Think about it this way. People have their own ideas about what makes a good parent. Should a parent provide structure and discipline for the children? Or rather act as a supportive friend? People also have different conceptions of the ideal marriage. Will the two individuals collaborate in a partnership with equal responsibilities and an equal division of labor? Or will one person take the job of running the household and the other be a breadwinner?

The parenting and marriage models each of us subscribes to affect the ways we interact with our children or our partners. Our ideas or philosophies about these relationships determine our expectations for the kind of behavior we hope to see. The idea of mental models captures this notion of conceptions that guide our actions: A *mental model* is a philosophy or set of attitudes we hold with respect to a particular issue; the model includes underlying assumptions about the way the world works, about how the issue affects other people, and about how society might respond to or be affected by the issue. We tend to accept information that confirms our mental models, and we disregard incongruous information.[1]

Just as we do about parenting or marriage, many of us hold a general idea or mental model of what a mentor is supposed to do, whether the mentor is part of a formal or informal relationship. The same holds true for the nature of the mentoring relationship. Our ideas dictate who is expected to do what in the relationship, what happens as the relationship unfolds, and what kinds of support the mentor might provide to the protégé. Further, this notion affects whether we feel the mentoring relationship has been successful. For example, imagine a protégé who views a mentor as someone akin to a superhero—in other words, as a person who will rush in and save protégés who are making career mistakes. Now let's think about what happens in that same relationship when the mentor thinks of herself as more of a hands-off teacher, who provides protégés with general lessons but lets them learn from their mistakes. The incompatibility in this relationship becomes readily apparent and most likely will lead to dissatisfaction with the relationship for both people involved.

The overall purpose of this chapter is to explore the inner workings of the mind of the mentor. After we delve into the mind of the mentor to uncover some common mental models from our study, we also look at

- The characteristics of a perfect protégé in the eyes of the mentor
- The purpose and nature of the possible tests and challenges that they might pose to protégés
- The ways the mentoring relationship can develop successfully

Getting inside the minds of our power mentors is likely to answer many questions about your existing or hoped-for mentoring relationships.

MENTAL MODELS: THE PHILOSOPHIES OF MENTORING

In our exploration of power mentoring relationships, we uncovered a set of mental models that describe how the mentors we studied conceptualized mentoring. We highlight four of these models in this section—those of the corporate citizen, pragmatic mentor, global citizen, and master mentor. These philosophies explain why the mentors chose to be involved in mentoring relationships in the first place, but go further in that they also shed light on the mentors' expectations of the power mentoring experience. We summarize the various reasons for mentoring by giving specific examples of the various mentoring philosophies. Our discussion is not exhaustive; we've merely tried to capture key aspects of the mentoring relationships that were shared with us. Of course, you may encounter other types of mentoring models or even hybrid models (those combining features of two or more models). The important concept to remember is that uncovering what the mentor thinks he or she should be doing in the relationship makes a world of difference in affecting the shared expectations of mentor and protégé in the relationship.

CORPORATE CITIZEN

Individuals whose mentoring philosophy emphasizes the idea of the *corporate citizen* view mentoring as a way of ensuring that the corporation's next generation of leadership is ready to take the reins of the organization, and as a method of informal training so

that individuals can flourish in the organization. In some organizations, this type of mentoring for development or training is initiated by a mentor, whereas in others, the impetus comes from
programmatic efforts initiated by human resource departments or
upper management. The bottom line for the protégé, however, is
the same in either case. Mentors with this philosophy consider
mentoring as just part of what a person does to be a good corporate citizen.

As former president of Disney Channel Worldwide and now
Disney Media Networks and president of Disney-ABC Television
Group, Anne Sweeney has had an opportunity to be involved in
mentoring relationships from both sides. She worked at Nickelodeon, the premiere children's cable network for twelve years
and was chairman and CEO of FX Networks, where she learned
much from close collaborations with former boss mentors like
Geraldine Laybourne, currently chair and CEO of Oxygen Network and Rupert Murdoch, chairman and CEO of News Corporation. Anne has also mentored a number of individuals herself.
These interactions have given her considerable insight into the
forms mentoring can take and have allowed her to develop her
own set of expectations as to how she would interact with a protégé. At the time we spoke with her, she was involved in a formal
mentoring relationship with Kathleen Von der Ahe from ABC Affiliate Relations. The relationship seemed shaped by the corporate-
citizen model.

When we spoke, however, it was obvious that even though
Sweeney was mentoring in the mode of a good corporate citizen,
she took it much further than a typical relationship. She understood that even in the context of a formal mentoring relationship
like this, mentoring works as a two-way street. Anne also explained
why mentoring, as part of corporate citizenship, needs to become
more personal. She emphasized that people give their advice and
time for a reason, and that it's important for protégés to listen to
that advice. In the following example, she talked about the benefits she enjoyed by being mentored by Fred Silverman, the television programming guru:

> I think you have to be very unselfish about the mentoring relation-
> ship. And if it doesn't fit into 3:00 to 4:00 on Monday, once a
> month, it should grow into the kind of relationship which, if you

don't speak for months or a year or you speak every week, you still are able to maintain the same level of trust, the same level of communication. It is important that you recognize the value of the relationship in that regard.

I remember when we were launching a comedy network at MTV Networks in 1989, and Fred Silverman, who's the legendary broadcast programmer, was a consultant. And Fred came in, and I was head of acquisitions. I was out there buying product—millions of dollars of product. And he sat down, and he said, "Okay. Well, it's a comedy network." And he pointed at me, and he said, "Okay, you're going to go out, and you're going to tell me where everything from the Beach Blanket movies are to the old black-and-white comedies. I want to know where you're going to find Texaco Star Theater to *M*A*S*H*." So I worked like a dog getting to know all this information. How could I not do this? I told myself, "How many times in your life do you get to work with Fred Silverman? This guy is the original triple threat. He led programming at all three networks. His programming taste was spectacular and smart. He was a risk taker. I could learn from this guy." What is interesting is that it doesn't matter if we don't talk for six months or six days, the relationship is still there. Now when I've been in some of my toughest programming moments, really trying to think through the positioning of the network or, for example, should this show go in this direction, and if so why . . . he's always been a wonderful sounding board for me.

Therefore, while Anne realized that many of her mentoring relationships began as part of a corporate initiative, or as part of a boss-subordinate relationship, she transitioned those relationships into real relationships that were sustained over time. This is how power mentoring relationships of the corporate type seem to evolve, as opposed to ending once the individuals depart from the company. These are often lifelong mentoring relationships that develop from formal relationships into something bigger and self-sustaining.

In summary, the corporate-citizen philosophy dictates the general nature of mentoring relationships in which mentors are committed to mentoring for the good of their organizations. For some mentors, the relationship may stop at that point: fulfilling an organizational need. But in some cases, though not all, the mentor's model of the relationship expands. We argue that even though

Anne's mentoring began as part of corporate citizenry, she deepened some of her mentoring relationships to include more personal connections, mutual benefits, and, in many cases, relationship longevity. Protégés may find some shortcomings in the corporate-citizen model of a mentoring relationship if they are looking for something deeper. The mentors may be reproducing the highly structured types of mentoring relationships they have been in previously, or they may not have received specific training to help guide the relationship.

This is not to say that a corporate-citizenship mental model is lacking. Mentors with this philosophy can provide valuable career advice, especially on how to get ahead in a particular organization. However, if the protégés make it clear that they hope for more, the relationship may turn into something even more mutually beneficial.

PRAGMATIC MENTOR

A second group of mentors approached their mentoring relationships very pragmatically. When asked about the nature of mentoring, they focused on what they did for their protégés as a transaction—in other words, as an exchange for benefits they might receive. Because of this pragmatic outlook, these mentors tended to see their power mentoring relationships as egalitarian. Rather than taking a cold and calculating approach that asks, "What's in it for me?" they thought in terms of the reciprocal benefits the two parties would receive.

Many involved in these pragmatic relationships understood that protégés and mentors give each other different things. For example, Ron Dellums, former U.S. Congressman from California, found that mentoring was a great way to preserve his own legacy, grooming the person who would take on his passions and issues and continue to move them forward. Through years of mentoring his protégé Charles Stevenson, in his role as his boss, Dellums was honing Stevenson's skills, but at the same time ensuring that Dellums would have someone to keep his initiatives alive. As Dellums put it:

> I think you should always prepare for your replacement. For example, when I retired in 1998, I talked Charles into leaving with me.

"Come with me," I told him, "and let's take a chance. I think that there's a whole other world out there, and we will continue to do well." Well, I take Charles with me everywhere I go. If I'm meeting with the president of the United States, if I can get him in, he's in. If I meet with the president of the World Bank, if I'm going to the WHO [World Health Organization], when I went to see Kofi Annan at the UN. . . . I take Charles everywhere I go. And my point to him is, "When I'm talking, listen, observe, learn." I want someone to know as much as I know. You know, there are a lot of people who are intimidated by other people having knowledge; I'm not intimidated by that. I think that is important. So I told Charles, "Look, you know, I'm in my sixties. I don't know how long I'll be around here, but you've got a lot longer to work, and when the time comes for me to walk away, or whatever happens, I want you to be a repository of all that knowledge and all that information. I want you to know what I know so that you can continue to go."

While we would not characterize Dellums's entire mentoring philosophy as pragmatic, when it came to talking about grooming his successor, the approach he described seemed very pragmatic. Dixie Garr, vice president of Customer Success Engineering at Cisco Systems, also presented some pragmatic views on mentoring relationships. She tends to make these views quite clear to protégés or potential protégés, as noted here:

I'll often speak at a function, and people will come up and say, "Would you be my mentor?" My answer will be probably be no if they are talking about a, "Let's just chat and have fun" type of relationship. To me, if you have a goal and you need help with that, and we have measures of success, whatever that is, I'm willing to help, but I don't have time to just be friends. So my answer to those folks is always, "If you have a specific thing that you want to accomplish, and a specific goal and things that you want . . . or need help with . . . that I can be of value helping you think it through, I am happy to do that, but 'Let's sing Kum ba yah' is not my thing." There is a young man who used to work for me but has moved to another team. For example, he and I had a mentoring session two weeks ago, and he called up and said, "You know, Dixie, I need to talk to you." He knows my style. He said, "Here's the situation. Here's what we need. What do you think?" I do that a lot. I am very results/target/goal oriented. And I like for the person to know what success looks like and what it is. If you can't tell me what it is that we're after and what the outcome is that we're after, you probably haven't thought it through enough for it to be a real goal.

As a very high-level African American woman in corporate America, Dixie has numerous people seeking her advice. Her pragmatic style allows her to help those who are strongly focused on their careers. Further, Dixie talked about the specific rewards she has received from mentoring, again showing her assessment of the pragmatic benefits in the relationship:

> The reward is that you're a better leader and perceived as a better leader, and you get to know what the heck is going on. Because, let's face it, you get to know the feared tip of the iceberg, and by the time an issue or a situation bubbles up to you through official channels, it's already gone through all the coffee bars, down the street, around the corner, and been camped outside your door for a week. So, when you spend this time, you get to know much earlier what's going on, what needs your attention, and kind of the mood of the team. So from that perspective, I'm rewarded. And sometimes people come in and just say, "You know, I just really appreciate your coaching." And that's a reward. None of us gets enough appreciation. Thank your mentor.

Pragmatic mentors are those who are very upfront about what they want to give, and gain, from a mentoring relationship. That level of clarity is good for protégés who know what they want.

GLOBAL CITIZEN

A number of our mentors saw mentoring as a duty to society or the world in general, as opposed to simply their own organization or industry. We mentioned generativity (the concern for the next generation) as an important reason for mentoring in Chapter Two. How does this model of mentoring affect the way someone mentors? We found that mentors with this mental model or philosophy of mentoring aimed to provide a broad set of life lessons to their protégés, rather than concentrating on what needs to be done to get ahead in any particular job. These mentors focused on the long term, the big picture, and on how they could give of themselves across many different contexts to impart to others the lessons they have learned in life.

In some respects, Dixie Garr saw her desire to mentor as a way to give back to society on a broad scale: "Speaking and motivating are a passion with me. Because, even though it sounds corny, but you affect so many lives, and you have, what I call, impact per minute. That's how I measure my life, in impact per minute."

Mitch Koss is a producer for Channel One News, which features stories on breaking news and in-depth issues that affect the world, the nation, and specifically, America's teenagers. Channel One News is seen by public and private secondary school students in 48 states and the District of Columbia, reaching 12,000 American middle, junior, and high schools and representing more than 8 million students and 400,000 educators.[2] Since its first broadcast in 1990, Channel One News has garnered more than 150 news and educational programming honors, including the prestigious George Foster Peabody Award. That level of integrity is what Mitch brought from previous jobs at the *MacNeil/Lehrer NewsHour* and as a producer of documentaries for PBS. Through Channel One he also produced a documentary series for MTV, as well as segments for ABC News, CNN, and the WB. He has written for the *Los Angeles Times* and other newspapers.

Mitch's global-citizen approach to mentoring parallels his approach to news stories. He has worked with a number of young people, including Anderson Cooper, a reporter and rising on-air personality for CNN who has his own show, *360*, and Lisa Ling, former cohost of ABC's *The View* and currently host and reporter for *National Geographic Explorer*. Channel One's on-air reporters tend to come to the network fresh out of high school or college, or, as in Lisa Ling's case, still as a high school student. Mitch imbues these young people with his passion for telling the story. He recalls working with Anderson Cooper and making a conscious choice that the news stories they were producing were going to be "real" for a discerning high school audience:

> The first person they assigned me to work with substantially was a guy named Anderson Cooper, a 25-year-old kid in '93. And at that point he's 25, I'm 39, and I realize I can either share with him everything I've learned in this industry, in which case he would hate me and the audience would hate us, or I can say, "Okay, partner, what do you want to do?" And I chose the latter of course because Anderson wasn't looking for someone to teach him, he was looking for someone to help him figure something out that no one

knew, namely a new approach to television journalism. Anderson was a terrific punk and phenomenally brave and very confident in being different. And the high quality of his innovations made it easier to recognize another revolutionary, even younger punk, Lisa Ling, when I was assigned to work with her a year and a half later. Lisa's ambitions further raised the level of risk in being associated with her because not only did she want to be a serious foreign correspondent at an extremely young age, she was interested in covering abstract issues—the impact of globalization in the developing world—that were then mainly the domain of the *New York Times'* Thomas Friedman. So she was not only risking her life in far off lands, she was risking being in way over her head. Yet Lisa went ahead and made this edgy, funny, visceral sort of new television on issues that college professors were just becoming cognizant of—we even had a documentary Mini-Series on globalization on the Los Angeles PBS station. And if you go back and look at her stuff today, you see that her coverage pretty accurately presaged the world that we now find ourselves in.

For those of you not familiar with Channel One, the stories are not what you might remember from your school newspaper. These are hard-hitting reports. One early example by Lisa Ling and Mitch Koss concerned what was happening in Afghanistan in the early 1990s. Mitch says he was amazed by Lisa's poise in her reporting. They again worked together on stories about Russia and China. In each of these instances, Mitch focused on inculcating high-quality reporting techniques in his young protégés. Why? What was his motivation for mentoring? In his case it was his belief in a general dedication to effective journalism. He probably also saw the experience as an apprenticeship, where the young reporters were learning the craft by his side. In terms of the forms of mentoring we discussed in Chapter Two, for Lisa and Anderson, Mitch could be considered a barrier-busting mentor. He helped them take their craft to new levels that they might not have reached without him, at least at so young an age. Mitch and Lisa's teaming resulted in their creating award-winning PBS documentaries in addition to their innovative work for Channel One. Mitch brought a selfless dedication to the craft that helped Lisa grow as a reporter. When asked about her experiences with Mitch, Lisa recalled:

He is perhaps the most selfless, brilliant, giving, pure individual. He is someone who had worked in the field of journalism almost all of his life, and could have probably pursued it to the highest executive level, but he has instead chosen to stay essentially as a reporter/producer and go into the field. Most people eventually seek out kind of cushy behind-the-desk jobs. The guy is 20 years older than me, he's almost 50, and he is still out there producing. When we were working together, and he introduced me to many of the people he had worked for at *MacNeil/Lehrer,* at PBS, at *National Geographic,* and what was so incredible about him was it was never, "I have this documentary," it was, "My colleague Lisa and I . . ." He also had such a powerful impact on me because he included me, and that gave me so much confidence because here is this prestigious, award-winning filmmaker, documentary filmmaker/journalist who had taken me under his wing and included me in such a way that my work is recognized as much as his.

Mentors who mentor with a global-citizen philosophy often have a passion for their craft as it relates to larger societal issues. This passion may make them a fairly demanding mentor. In many ways this is beneficial for protégés who are young, in the early learning mode in their careers, and do not quite know what skills and knowledge are most important to succeed. Although all effective mentors can enhance an individual's self-confidence as Mitch did for Lisa, mentors with a global-citizen philosophy not only provide many of the typical mentoring benefits, they do so in the greater service of their craft and to serve a higher calling. In Mitch's case, the higher calling was journalistic excellence. In addition, mentors of the global-citizen type emphasize sharing the creative process and credit for the work they do with their protégés. Both mentor and protégé benefit enormously from this type of relationship.

MASTER MENTOR

At IBM, Fran Allen worked in the area of programming languages for nearly 45 years. She was the first woman IBM Fellow at the Thomas J. Watson Research Lab, IBM's highest technical honor, and she has done much to give back to women in computing. In tracing her relationship with IBM, she remembered reading a recruitment brochure titled *My Fair Ladies*—enticing women technologists to join IBM—as she completed her master's degree at the University of Michigan.

Today the enticements remain; in fact, IBM sponsors many programs to encourage young women in the sciences. At the 2000 Women in Technology Convention, Lou Gerstner, IBM board chair at the time, spoke to the conference about the need for IBM to nurture its technical women. "We're in a battle for technical talent right now," he said. "It's not strictly about money, it's about opportunity. It's about what we do to create the right kind of culture— where they know ideas are valued and acted on. Go mentor our young talent."[3] Gerstner was not merely paying lip service to the idea, but in fact IBM had begun a variety of programs under its "Global Women Leaders Task Force: Creating the Climate to Win" in 1995 to specifically target women and minorities for leadership development, both nationally and globally.[4]

Lou Gerstner is not the only one who realizes the importance of mentoring at IBM; Fran Allen's commitment to mentoring has resulted in an award that bears her name—the Frances E. Allen IBM Women in Technology Mentoring Award, of which she was the first recipient. Her commitment is also evidenced in her work on the advisory boards of numerous organizations, such as the National Academy of Engineering, the Association for Computing Machinery (ACM), and the American Academy of Arts and Sciences. Fran is what we call a *master mentor*. It is her mission to get more women involved in computing within her profession. We consider her a master mentor because of her intense involvement in mentoring, which at IBM is recognized as being beneficial to the bottom line. Fran's own philosophy of mentoring comes from having mentored many people throughout her career. This is what she shared with us:

> I try to connect with the individual as a person. It also means a huge amount of listening. And I think it's less about talking than it is about listening. And sometimes by just listening and getting people to say—people have someone to express what their issues are, what their goals are, and whom they can trust and just providing a sympathetic ear so that they can just talk very openly about it. And very often I suspected that verbalizing it and getting small amounts of feedback helps them clarify it with themselves. And ultimately I think that that's very important because I keep thinking, well, one of the most important things for people is to understand what they're good at and what they really want. And one can't tell somebody. You can reinforce them in many ways and say, "Well, you're very good at something."

From her remarks, Fran demonstrates a very individualized perspective on mentoring. (She also utilizes many of the forms of mentoring discussed in Chapter Two: group, boss, inspirational, and even some reverse mentoring.) Obviously in mentoring so many people over the years, she has realized that any one style of mentoring or advice giving will not work well for everyone.

Understanding protégés as individuals goes a long way toward creating a productive mentoring relationship. In some circles, the distinction between coaching and mentoring has begun to blur. We believe, however, that a clear distinction exists. By definition, people who exclusively coach are not mentors. Coaching is one of the many supportive behaviors a mentor can use in the course of mentoring. Coaches are usually hired to train an individual, often with respect to interpersonal management or decision-making skills. Also, a boss could coach subordinates to improve their handling of a certain aspect of their job. We view mentoring as more of a comprehensive relationship that addresses many aspects of one's career, including career strategies. Coaching is less comprehensive in its approach and often is subject specific.

Through Fran's numerous mentoring relationships during her 45 years at IBM, and her involvement in organizations that provide mentoring, she has found that another important component of mentoring is connecting individuals to the right people who can help them. This could be called *delegated mentoring*. This makes sense in a highly technical industry such as computers, where it is doubtful that one mentor would be able to give an individual all the technical assistance he or she would need: "Most of the people I mentor are people whose goals are to be successful technically. And for some of them, I don't know their field well. But in this laboratory—it's a very large laboratory—I make a lot of connections for these people because I'm exposed to a lot of what's going on. So I can say, 'Oh, that's a terrific idea, have you talked to you know who?' Or I can help them understand what it means to be successful technically, and how to achieve that kind of success."

Within IBM, the mentoring systems were created by top management and by Fran over the years. IBM has one of the most comprehensive mentoring systems in corporate America today. A mentor who holds the philosophy of master mentoring utilizes his or her extensive professional connections to help protégés find the type of mentoring that will be most useful.

SUMMARY: A MENTOR'S MINDSET

We have highlighted some of the different mentoring philosophies that we uncovered in our research. From these examples, it is obvious that mentors vary widely in what they think a mentor should do and why they should do it. As either a mentor or a protégé, it is important to take time to uncover these philosophies or mental models about mentoring, because they have specific implications for furthering the relationship. How do you find out your own mentoring philosophy, or, as a protégé, your potential mentor's philosophy? We introduced four general types of mentoring philosophies we found in our research: corporate citizen, pragmatic mentor, global citizen, and master mentor. As noted, this list is not exhaustive; lots of other models of mentoring exist. We do not claim that any one model is better than another; each has its own unique style and benefits. To illuminate your preferred model as a mentor, ask yourself what you think your role as mentor should be. Or as a protégé, ask yourself what you hope to get out of a potential mentoring relationship. Posing these kinds of questions helps reveal the mind of the mentor and sets the stage for what follows.

THE MENTOR'S ATTRACTION TO THE PROTÉGÉ

What initially attracts power mentors to their protégés? Past research in mentoring and attraction has drawn largely from social psychological theories and found a great deal of evidence supporting the adage that "birds of a feather flock together"; in other words, it has underscored the importance of similarity. Surface-level similarity based on demographic characteristics such as age, gender, and race has been found to be important when mentors form initial impressions of their protégés. It is interesting, however, that more recent research suggests that deeper levels of similarity in terms of values, attitudes, and goals are more important in producing attraction than demographic similarity is.[5] Paradoxically, another adage, "Opposites attract," also applied to our interviewees' experiences. Two additional reasons mentors found themselves attracted to their protégés had to do with either compelling personal characteristics or the protégé's demonstrated performance or potential.

ACTUAL OR PERCEIVED SIMILARITY

Much academic ink has been devoted to addressing how demographic factors such as gender and race affect mentor and protégé attraction toward one another. One line of research has argued that because people are often attracted to those like themselves, and because those in positions of power in organizations have tended to be white men, women and minorities are at a disadvantage in attracting powerful mentors.[6] However, one study showed that *perceived* similarity, rather than actual similarity of demographic characteristics, attracts mentors and protégés to one another.[7] With respect to gender, the research is not as clear. Women benefit from having either male or female mentors. However, in organizations where men in powerful positions outnumber women, male mentors provide more benefits.[8]

What we found in our study mirrored previous research. A comment from Debra Martucci (who works at Synopsys and whose background is described in Chapter Two) encapsulates the feelings generally reported about cross-gender mentoring: "I think that it is always the first tendency for women to feel more comfortable with a woman mentor. . . . Maybe it's like your gynecologist! However, I have found I have been more successful with men mentors in general. They have been very helpful to me. Also, I have mentored some men, and what I find is that there is a difference between men and women, whether we want to accept that or not. And usually with the women, it's helping them manage their emotions."

In terms of discussing cross-race mentoring, we found that interviewees were often cautious in discussing their experiences, with a few notable exceptions. Martha Coolidge, Ron Dellums, Dixie Garr, Judith Gwathmey, Ron Kirk, Paula Madison, Rosario Marin, Hilda Solis, Pamela Thomas-Graham, and Henry Yuen all shared the distinction of being "the first and best" in their fields. Martha Coolidge, for example, was the first female president of the Directors Guild of America (DGA), and Pamela Thomas-Graham was the first African American woman partner at McKinsey. Because of this distinction, these interviewees and others in similar "first and best" positions were extremely sensitive to the need to be role models and mentors for others, taking this responsibility very seriously in addition to performing their day-to-day high-level jobs with excellence.

The awareness of their unique positions also leads these individuals to act in ways that help their organizations increase diversity.
For example, Paula Madison, in addition to her considerable duties
as president of KNBC in Los Angeles, had undertaken the job of vice
president of diversity and senior vice president of diversity for NBC
from 2000 to 2002, reporting directly to CEO Bob Wright, as we
mentioned in Chapter Three. Dixie Garr had an experience with
diversity in her organization that illustrates the effects of this awareness: "I went to a partner conference, and there were 5,000 partners,
500 Cisco employees, 50 Cisco executives at this conference, and I
was the only black woman in the room. I came home. I called John
[Chambers, CEO of Cisco] and I said, 'John, you won't believe
what's happened to me.' And I gave him the statistics. I said, 'John,
we've got to get me some company here.'"

Experiences like these have caused Dixie to reach out not only
to protégés at Cisco but much more broadly as well. She has
become a highly sought-after national motivational speaker. Like
Dixie, many of our power mentors who had the distinction of being
"first and best" have transformed themselves into "supermentors"
and champions, using their positions to influence diversity-related
policies and strategies in their organizations far beyond their role
as mentors to individuals.

Clearly, perceived similarity is critical in attracting and keeping
a mentor's attention. So how can a protégé interested in gaining a
mentor's attention capitalize on this fact? The best way to do so is
to get to know a potential mentor and figure out what you have in
common. For example, Rosario Marin related that what she saw in
her protégé, Araceli, was her ability to be fearless, which was an
important trait they shared. Another mentor, Larry Carter, said of
his protégé (Patty Archibeck) that he was attracted to her sense of
humor—something he also valued in himself, particularly as a way
of coping with stress. Mentors often spoke of shared goals, values,
practices, and business beliefs as being instrumental in the initial
attraction stages of getting to know their protégé. We come back to
this topic again in Chapter Six when we discuss the importance of
gender and ethnicity in deepening mentoring relationships.

COMPLEMENTARY SKILLS OR PERSPECTIVES

Although we just spent a lot of time convincing you that it is important for a protégé to find points of similarity between themselves

and a mentor, now we want to convince you that opposites attract as well! Many of our extremely successful mentors were surprisingly humble in their own assessment of their abilities. Many saw clearly that they needed protégés who were enough like them so they would have some common ground to build on, but they also realized that protégés who had complementary skills or perspectives were enormously helpful as well. For example, Henry Yuen described the following experience with his colleague and peer mentor, Elsie Leung (then CFO of Gemstar):

> I negotiated a deal with Microsoft, one of the biggest license agreements. It involved $50 million and many years of payment going forward. I remember I first arrived at a tentative agreement. I came back to brief Elsie (she was the CFO). And she would not sign off. She said that this would have given the company's future away. We had an incredible argument because I had already given my word, I thought. And I got her to fly up with me to Seattle to say no. In the end, we negotiated an agreement that we felt very comfortable with and probably saved the company. I think the unwavering standard-setting was something that I greatly admired in her.

A COMPELLING CHARACTERISTIC OR SKILL

An additional reason that power mentors became attracted to their protégés was that they perceived the protégé to have a unique quality or compelling personal characteristic that they admired. For example, Anne Sweeney (president of ABC Television Network) described Kathleen Von der Ahe (vice president, ABC) as "effervescent. She has a bright light in her eyes. What struck me first was that this woman exuded the feeling she could do anything." While the specific personal characteristic at issue varied from one mentor-protégé pair to another, regardless of what it was, it had to be something the mentor admired.

DEMONSTRATED POTENTIAL OR PERFORMANCE

Power mentors such as Bob Wright (CEO of NBC) and Ron Meyer (president and COO of Universal Studios) were attracted to protégés who distinguished themselves by their exemplary reputations, or by a demonstration of their excellent performance or potential. As Bob stated, "Every place that I have been, I've always been drawn to certain people that I thought had significant potential or ability that might not come out on its own without some help." Bob went on to discuss his protégé Paula Madison (president of KNBC): "As I got to know her I realized that she had a tremendously positive sense about things. She was so good at getting things done that I really became a big fan of hers." Ron Meyer shared a similar recollection about Nikki Rocco, president of Universal Pictures Distribution: "I always had great admiration for her. I thought she was smart and knew her business. And when I saw an opportunity I promoted her to President of Distribution at Universal Pictures. She was the first woman—and remains the only woman—in the entertainment business to hold that job."

WILLINGNESS TO LEARN

The demonstrated potential of many of the protégés attracted the attention of their mentors. The mentors admired the protégés personally and felt they held great professional promise. Some protégés showed a willingness to learn that was very attractive to their mentors. As Barbara Corday put it, "I guess the first things that come to my mind are enthusiasm, passion, willingness to learn, not a complainer. Somebody who puts out to the community an upbeat attitude that expresses how I like to run my business."

Bethany Rooney, another woman in entertainment—a television director—mentioned that it was crucial for novice directors to be open to learning: "I would like them to be open to the learning possibilities. I would like them to be willing to put in the time to do the shadowing, and I would like them to be really patient because if they're patient, sometimes opportunities present themselves where the mentor can go, 'Oh, here's an opportunity where I see I can help you.'"

One study in fact found that a protégé's willingness to learn was a key attribute from the standpoint of many potential mentors. The study also found that the mentor's own motivations affected what he or she looked for in the protégé. For example, mentors who were very interested in enhancing their own reputations looked for very capable protégés, whereas mentors less interested in their own reputations found willingness to learn to be more important.[9]

In sum, a distillation of our research and other studies suggests five main reasons mentors take an interest in their protégés. In protégés they are attracted to, mentors see a

1. Perceived similarity to themselves
2. Complementary skill or perspective
3. Compelling characteristic or skill
4. Demonstrated potential or performance
5. Willingness to learn

These elements seemed very important in determining a mentor's first impressions. In the next section of the chapter we build on these ideas by delving more deeply into what makes an ideal protégé from the mentor's point of view.

THE PERFECT PROTÉGÉ

Is there a power mentoring secret to becoming the perfect protégé? The answer is . . . yes and no. Let's assume "yes" as we examine the common themes that were consistently reiterated by our power mentors and protégés. Past books on mentoring, how-to mentoring manuals, and even academic articles are quick to provide lists to eager would-be protégés. Usually these lists are written by mentors or mentoring experts, or represent a compilation of mentor ideas that, while valid, are also one-sided (that is, usually from the mentor's perspective). Imagine trying to uncover the secrets to finding the perfect spouse but only gathering data from all of the husbands in the world, rather than husbands *and* wives. This would be an incomplete list, since a marriage is not a list of someone's qualities but a dynamic relationship between two people. Valuable information can be gained from surveying both parties involved in the relationship. The fact that we gathered information from both mentors and protégés makes the following discussion unique.

We conducted a thorough search of the literature to uncover what makes a perfect protégé and found that most of what is frequently cited dates back 20 years. In 1984, Michael Zey conducted interviews with 150 executives in Fortune 500 companies as well as smaller firms, and from this material created a list of criteria that the ideal protégé meets.[10] The mentors in Zey's study looked for the following 10 qualities in their protégés: (1) intelligence, (2) ambition, (3) desire and ability to accept power and risk, (4) ability to perform the mentor's job, (5) loyalty, (6) similar perceptions of work and organization, (7) commitment to the organization, (8) organizational savvy, (9) positive perceptions of the protégé by the organization, and (10) ability to establish alliances.

Zey's criteria for the ideal protégé have some very interesting similarities to and differences from our list. In terms of similarity, both groups of mentors valued three identical characteristics in their protégés: intelligence, ambition, and a willingness to take risks. These attributes are consistent with what we value in our corporate leaders today, so it is not surprising that these attributes have remained constant among mentoring relationships as well.

Perhaps more telling than the similarities are the changes that have occurred over the past 20 years. Our list of characteristics comprising the perfect protégé includes not only the first three attributes mentioned (intelligence, ambition, and a willingness to take risks), but seven additional ones. These are as follows: (4) initiative, (5) energy, (6) trustworthiness, (7) integrity, (8) high emotional intelligence, (9) optimism, and (10) complementary skills. It seems clear that mentors' ideas of the perfect protégé are shaped by the environment and values of the times.

Zey's list clearly pertains to traditional mentoring, because 7 out of 10 of his characteristics seem to presume shared organizational membership and upward mobility within the same organization. Zey identified the ability to perform a mentor's job as a critical protégé attribute, indicating that this is likely a classic hierarchical relationship, in which the protégé is being groomed to be the mentor's successor or at least to move up to higher levels in the organization. This characteristic was not mentioned even once by our power mentors. Instead, we heard many examples of more global qualities such as initiative and energy. This may be a sign of our times, because in one episode of NBC's *The Apprentice,* when Donald Trump was asked what he looks for in a young executive or protégé, he said, "Energy and stamina."

We found it particularly interesting that the 1984 mentors' emphasis on loyalty and organizational commitment was replaced in 2004 by an emphasis on trustworthiness. This is indicative of today's tendency toward boundaryless careers and mobility, discussed in Chapter One. Because knowledge workers and particularly senior executives experience relatively short tenures within their respective organizations (the range is three to nine years for a CEO[11]), the emphasis is less on loyalty to an organization than on loyalty to an industry or profession. Perhaps because organizational commitment and loyalty are at an all-time low, trust has become more salient to mentors and protégés. In fact, trust between mentors and protégés was such a resounding theme in our research that we devote a significant portion of Chapter Five to this idea.

In 1984, mentors valued organizational savvy, positive perceptions of the protégé by the organization, and the ability to establish alliances. In 2004, mentors valued more global and portable attributes, such as emotional intelligence, integrity, and optimism. This is not surprising, because research on emotional intelligence—popularized by Daniel Goleman's best-selling books, *Emotional Intelligence* and *Working with Emotional Intelligence*—shows that interpersonal competence or emotional intelligence (EQ) may be even more important for organizational success than IQ.[12] This is reflected in the concepts related to EQ mentioned frequently by mentors, including the importance of the protégé being a good listener and being able to give feedback effectively. The importance of integrity mentioned by the 2004 mentors may be a reaction to the recent spate of corporate and government scandals. Finally, we heard from many of our 2004 mentors about the importance of optimism on the part of the protégé; many of them mentioned the desirability of an "upbeat attitude," "positive outlook," and "no complaining." Indeed, there is a surge of popularity of optimism studies in organizational psychology, and researchers have found that optimism is an important predictor of career satisfaction and success.

The other characteristics mentioned by Zey, such as similar perceptions of work and organization, commitment to the organization, organizational savvy, positive perceptions of the protégé by the organization, and the ability to establish organizational alliances, all related to the assumption that the role of a mentor is to groom a protégé for succession purposes and organizational success. While this may still be very important in some mentoring relationships, today's power mentors offer an expanded perspective.

Perhaps the most important difference of all leads to a new theory or paradigm shift related to mentoring. In 1984, the ideal protégé had a perception of work similar to that of his or her mentor. In 2004, we found the opposite. While similarity in terms of values and goals was very important, we found that mentors and protégés thoughtfully sought out mentoring relationships with people different from themselves. As noted in our earlier discussion of attraction, there was tremendous energy from both mentors and protégés around the idea of complementary skills and diverse perspectives. As Henry Yuen of Gemstar articulated so well, "I look for complementary skills, complementary approaches and sometimes even complementary ways of handling a problem. You want to have as much diversity as possible. We have to share moral and business values but have diverse or complementary approaches. If you want to build an organization all over again, I would look for those similarities: a sense of value, both moral and business, and look for diversity in skill sets and style and approach."

Joan Buzzallino captured the idea of a complementary theory of mentoring very well in the following comparison of herself with her IBM mentor, Linda Sanford: "Linda came from a technical discipline; I came from a sales background and then in HR. Linda was clearly an assimilator. I'd be sitting there talking to her, and she'd be assimilating everything and forming ideas. I'd say, 'I've got to watch her and just [notice] how disciplined she sits there and absorbs all the information.' She is much more of a visionary. I mean, she can just not only assimilate all this information, but really think it out and beyond, where I am much more of a tactical person."

In sum, the answer to the question of what makes the perfect protégé is simply that "it depends." It depends on the industry, the project, the mentor's expectations, and many other variables. In short, it depends on the unique dynamic between the protégé and the mentor. The attributes that the perfect protégé can offer depend especially on the complementary skills the mentor may be looking for. In other words, if you want to be the perfect protégé, figure out what the mentor doesn't have and then see if you can fill that need. Fortunately, there is no one-size-fits-all protégé model, and more than anything we were struck by the wide variety of traits that mentors found important in their protégés. More often than not, the perfect mentor-protégé match involved an ideal "fit," taking into account the complementary characteristics of both parties rather than a one-size-fits-all perspective. As in most marriages, we found little evidence of mentor "soul mates"—instead we saw wise careerists at the top of their game who relied on a diverse network of mentors for various aspects of their career development.

No matter how similar or different mentors and protégés were, mentors often recounted the importance of tests and challenges in determining whether the mentor relationship would get off the ground and eventually deepen.

TESTS AND CHALLENGES

> The ultimate measure of a man is not where he stands in moments of comfort, but where he stands at times of challenge and controversy.
> —Martin Luther King Jr.

Our power mentors posed a number of tests and challenges to their protégés. It is interesting to note that many of these tests and challenges were remembered very vividly by the protégés, yet sometimes not at all by the mentors. This indicates that the mentors may have been posing the tests and challenges unconsciously; alternatively, the protégés may have perceived challenges where none actually existed. Some of these tests did occur consciously at the beginning of the relationship, as ways to "weed out" unsuitable potential protégés, whereas others occurred later and led the mentoring relationship to deepen, transition, or terminate. Tests and challenges are important for both mentors and protégés to know about, because they help protégés gain a unique glimpse into what power mentors may want and need. If you are already a mentor or are considering becoming a mentor, you may find these ideas to be useful in your interactions with potential protégés. In this section, we provide a description and examples of the various tests and challenges discussed by our mentors. We conclude each subsection with a list of assessment questions that you will find helpful, whether you are interested in getting started or in deepening your mentoring relationship.

Also, it is important to mention that several of our interviewees initially felt uncomfortable with the idea of testing their protégés.[13] As Judith Gwathmey, CEO/president and chief scientific officer of Gwathmey, a biotech firm, stated, "The world tests you enough, I don't test my protégés—I prepare them." However, on further consideration, most of the mentors and protégés realized that testing was an integral part of the relationship, even if only in the initial stages.

INITIAL TESTS AND CHALLENGES

Most interpersonal relationships involve some testing. Also, because the power mentors we spoke to were top leaders in their respective industries and thus are highly sought after, they needed to develop litmus tests for evaluating the myriad requests for their time and attention. To pass initial hurdles of this kind, protégés need to follow some basic strategies:

1. *Have a plan.* First and foremost, when a protégé approaches a potential mentor, it is important for the protégé to have and be able to communicate to the prospective mentor a goal and a plan of action for their future career. This idea was well articulated by Linda Sanford and Nikki Rocco and was echoed again and again by our other power mentors, who stated that the key test questions are

- What do you want to do—what is your ultimate goal?
- What do you see yourself doing at the peak of your career?

2. *Bring something to exchange.* Debra Martucci added a second idea, which relates to the idea of social exchange—the expectation that both the protégé and the mentor should gain something valuable from their relationship. The following passage captures her typical thoughts when she is approached by someone who wants her to be his or her mentor:

> I weed them out on a basis of two things: "Can I actually help them?" and "Do they really need me?" I mean, I've had women bluntly ask me, "Could I take you to lunch? I'd love an opportunity to talk to you about my career." And I've had to, in the nicest, gentlest way say, "No." You know, it just didn't have that feel. I don't think I'm the right person to fulfill that need. And it may be selfish, but I didn't see what I would get from it. So I think there is a bit of mental filtering that I go through.

As part of their career plan, would-be protégés should be able to show how the mentoring relationship would benefit the mentors, too.

3. *Make a good first impression.* There is an entire body of literature related to the idea of impression management and job inter-

views. Practical wisdom maintains that an interviewer often makes a decision about a job candidate in the first five minutes of the interview.[14] Cisco's former CFO, Larry Carter, would likely agree with this assessment. He says he looks for several important non-verbal characteristics, including good eye contact, attentive body language, and clear communication in terms of how questions are phrased, when he evaluates a potential protégé. Larry related the following story to illustrate those points: "I had one lady [a potential protégé] who rocked [in her chair], and it drove me nuts. She was sitting there talking and rocking—drove me crazy. So, in a private session as she was explaining a work problem, just in a nice way, I just leaned over and held the chair and said, 'I just want to make sure I can listen to everything.'"

Larry also suggests that the use of appropriate self-disclosure can be helpful in enhancing communication and trust. He went on to describe an experience where self-disclosure served as an important tool for developing trust with a protégé: "I had one experience with a fellow who was talking about his son having a learning disorder. Well, it turns out that I have a son who has a learning disorder, too, so all of a sudden we had something in common, and we shared about what was his son's problem and I shared what mine was and what we did and what he did, and all of a sudden we bonded because we had something in common. This builds trust, and if you don't have trust you are going to waste a lot of time."

Also related to the idea of impression management is something that Larry says he looks for in a potential protégé. It is their capacity to manifest or acquire that "special something," which he refers to as "executive presence":

> Executive presence is not just how you dress or how you look, but it's something about a state of mind that you develop. So you think like an executive. You behave like one. You can look somebody like John Chambers in the eye and talk to him just like you are an equal. You don't have to talk up to him. So this is a little bit of psychology. Develop confidence in yourself and have the ability to communicate, and feel comfortable around people of stature. I call this executive presence.

4. *Communicate positively and with passion.* Debra Martucci emphasized what *not* to do in the following example. She also

stressed that protégés should make sure they are clear about what a potential mentor can do for them and vice versa:

> The quality of the person and their motivation is important. I tune out very quickly with anyone who starts to use, "I'm a woman, it's all against me." I have a real struggle with that, and hence that would be a quality or a characteristic that I would not want to be involved with. And I find that more and more I'm not here to change the world for everyone, and it may not be always a fair world, but you know I do believe in equity. I do believe in the ability to be acknowledged for the talents that you have and not for how you dress or what gender you are. So I think when I see the passion in a person, that they want that for themselves and for their organization and for what they can give, then I think I connect very much with them. So that would probably be one that I would use that is sort of a litmus test.

QUESTIONS TO ASK IN NEW MENTORING RELATIONSHIPS

1. Does the protégé have a goal?
   - What are the protégé's goals, and are they aligned with what the mentor is willing and able to provide?
   - What ideas does the protégé have in terms of where they want to be at the peak of their career?

2. Can this be a win-win relationship?
   - What will the mentor gain from the relationship?
   - What are the specific ways the mentor can be of assistance to the protégé?

3. What do your first impressions say about the protégé?
   - How does the protégé's nonverbal communication style (for example, eye contact, body language, and energy) check out?
   - Does the protégé have—or do they have the potential to develop—that "special something" or executive presence?

4. Is this protégé a winner or a whiner?
   - Does the protégé describe problems and challenges in their career and job constructively (that is, without whining or slamming other people)?

TESTS AND CHALLENGES THAT DEEPEN THE MENTORING RELATIONSHIP

In mythology, would-be heroes and suitors are typically asked to pass a test, such as slaying a dragon, before they can achieve a desired goal, such as marrying the princess. Sometimes it works the same way in mentoring. We found that often mentors require that protégés perform certain tasks before the mentor agrees to continue the mentoring relationship. On most first tests, the protégé's failure to perform successfully usually hurts the protégé only in the sense of a lost opportunity. For the mentor, the first test generally represents only a loss of time. Congresswoman Hilda Solis (D-CA) is often deluged with requests for mentoring and assistance from up-and-coming politicians. She posed the following first test to her protégé, Sharon Martinez, now Council Member, City of Monterey Park, California. As Martinez described it:

> Hilda began by asking me, "What's your budget?" She said, "I need you to raise this much money by this date." That was my test. She said, "You come back, and when you tell me you've raised $10,000, then we'll talk again." And she told me exactly how you do it. She said, "You call all your friends. You make a list of 100 people who may give you $100. You make another list of another 50 people who may give you $200. And make a list and do that. And come back, and when you've done that and you've got your $10,000, then let's talk again."

The next test posed by the mentor can have direct work implications and serious repercussions, both for the mentor and for the protégé. Typically, these tests are about a mentor giving a protégé a serious work challenge, providing the protégé with a big break or opportunity, or publicly aligning himself or herself with the protégé. If the protégé performs well, the mentoring relationship deepens and often results in more trust, greater respect on both sides, and more professional opportunities. Bob Wright and Pamela Thomas-Graham both recalled one example in this regard. As Pamela related:

> I think there were challenging times in terms of the cycle of our dot-com company (CNBC.com). Because we had to build it up very fast in 1999, and then pretty much over the course of the latter part of 2000 into 2001 we basically had to take it back apart. This meant

hiring and then laying off or reassigning people in a very short time period. Now, that was not a deliberate test that was set for me, but it was certainly very challenging. And I think I learned a lot from Bob in terms of being able to manage both the growth period as well as the downsizing period.

In recalling this incident, Bob Wright also described additional challenges: "After this, Pamela went on to become head of CNBC, which was an existing organization at the beginning of a big downturn for financial services companies. So that was a very different challenge and different set of relationships. Even harder, she had to reduce the cost to the organization to deal with failing revenues and establish herself as a leader."

In fact, we found that often power mentors and protégés were successful in their careers because of their propensity to take risks. However, sometimes no matter how big a risk taker the protégé is, the risk they have taken doesn't pan out. What happens when the mentor poses a challenge, provides a big break, or aligns himself or herself with a protégé and then the opportunity backfires? How the mentor and protégé recover from the protégé's failure is the true test of relationship resiliency. Marc Buckland reminisced about working with his mentor (who could be considered a mentor of the moment—a common phenomenon in Hollywood), executive producer Steven Bochco (creator and producer of *NYPD Blue*, *Murder One*, and *LA Law*):

> Every time that I would go off to direct an episode, the last thing Steven would say after our meeting was, "Don't f**k it up." And I think he still says that to everyone. You know, he's kidding, but he's not. Well, in Steven's company, if the director comes in and f**ks it up, you don't usually get invited back. And that's just because Steven wants to maintain a certain level of quality in his work. But, I must say, Steven endured and supported my learning curve. I know the first episodes I did were . . . I certainly was a young, new director who had a lot to learn. After my first show I did for him, I do remember that he gave me the note to really keep an eye on the actors because perhaps I was so concerned about covering a scene and staging a scene that I may have not been focused enough on the shape of a scene, the performance and all that.

Even though Steven Bochco had tremendously high standards, it is notable that he took the time to give Marc Buckland a chance to develop his skills. This risk has paid off for both, because Marc is now an extremely successful television director in his own right. His directing credits include *Ed, Scrubs, Felicity, The West Wing,* and *NYPD Blue.*

On the other hand, U.S. Representative David Dreier (R-CA) relates the following story of mentoring a protégé (in what one could consider a barrier-buster relationship) who failed, causing serious repercussions for Dreier:

> Congressman Jay Kim was the first Korean American to run for and be elected to the Congress as a Republican, and I was very excited and enthused about that. He got into real trouble and was defeated in his election because he was convicted of campaign finance misdemeanors. I had really taken to this guy and I supported him to the end because he said to me that he was not guilty, he loved this country and all that. He looked me in the eye and asked me to support him, and I agreed. Well, I was politically attacked, and there were letters to the editor in the newspapers out in California saying, "David Dreier must be a crook because he is supporting this crook." I have one of the most pristine records. I mean, nobody has ever questioned my ethical standards and credibility. When I mentor someone I'm intensely loyal, and I mean, I supported this guy until the very end. And a lot of people backed away from him; and I didn't. And I don't know if that was a fault on my part or not, but anyway, I did it. I paid a price, as it did give some fodder to my political opponents that I had mentored this guy, but I seem to have withstood it.

Although David bounced back based on the strength of his own record and reputation, clearly the mentoring relationship was over. It seems likely that when a protégé fails as miserably as Jay did, the mentor might be reluctant to mentor others in the future.

Another story from the entertainment world relates to well-known producer Gale Anne Hurd (*Terminator*) and Roger Corman (Hollywood's top "B" movie producer, with more than 300 titles since 1954). Corman is known not only for being prolific but also for giving some of Hollywood's greatest their starts. Gale Anne Hurd is one of Corman's former protégés, and she recalled the tests she encountered from Roger early in her career:

> Everything with Roger was a test. His philosophy was sink or swim. Roger would task me with three or four different things at once. And one was casting a film, another was location scouting, and a

third was arranging for a production company to be set up in a foreign country. All this was to be done when he was out of the country. And I'd never done any location scouting before. So I went to a number of different locations; I took some notes, I didn't think to take a Polaroid camera. I didn't think to put it all down on the board so I could share it with him. I had it all in my head, and so when Roger came back, everything else was pretty much done, but, you know, he said, "Well, so what are the locations?" And I said, "Well, I found this, and I found this." And he said, "Well, where are the photos?" I said, "Well, I didn't take any photos." And we had a big falling out, and then I was very defensive about it because I wasn't used to failing at something. I was devastated. And it took me a while to realize that the only way that you learn sometimes is by either by making mistakes or by asking someone, you know, how they have done it, and in some cases if you don't get the right answer, pooling a number of people and see if everyone has reached the same conclusion.

Gale went on to relate the story of quitting in a fit of frustration. However, she also had the courage to return to Roger and ask to be reinstated. He gladly welcomed her back. Although her failing was difficult for both of them, ultimately it resulted in a better working relationship because she learned how to do her job more effectively and he trusted her skills.

Trust is a tremendously important theme that mentors and protégés spent a great deal of time discussing in our study. The theme of one popular test is "Can I trust the protégé to tell the truth to me, and reciprocally, can he or she be a trustworthy confidant for me?" It is said that it is lonely at the top, and often power mentors tended to solicit feedback from and confide in their protégés. Sometimes testing comes in the form of soliciting opinions or advice, where mentors and protégés use each other as sounding boards and confidants. Marc Buckland, director (*Ed*), shares the following story about testing his protégé, Laura J. Medina:

The only way I would test her is sometimes I would ask her after a certain take what she thought. And that wasn't so much to test to see if she had the right answer or the wrong answer. It was more to get the sense of her sensibilities. I've let her watch cuts of all the shows. And I was always interested in hearing what she liked and didn't like. And a lot of that was for selfish reasons, too, because

I'm a big believer in fresh eyes, somebody who I think is smart, okay, why didn't you like that? How can I fix that? Or what did you like?

Perhaps one of the most crucial tests of all in determining whether the relationship can deepen is simply whether the protégé acts on the mentor's advice. As Dixie Garr, put it, "My biggest test is, 'Are you willing to do the work? I'm willing to put in time, but you've got to be willing to put in time and effort too.' So if I ask somebody to think about some idea or put together this plan, and they don't come back, I am so through."

Kathleen Von der Ahe related the following story about advice given to her by her mentor, Anne Sweeney. Later, when we interviewed Sweeney, she reiterated the story and was most impressed with the way Kathleen had followed through with her advice. In Kathleen's words:

> I had a real tough month professionally. The Network performance was just horrible. The affiliates were just not happy. It was a very depressing time for me. It's like why am I getting up this morning? I had one of my meetings with Anne that afternoon. I said to her, "I kind of feel like I'm stagnant right now. I need something to sink my teeth into and feel good about." And so she said to me, "Kathleen, what you need to do is set yourself goals." And so she shared a story with me about some goals that she set for herself. And about a week later I had a meeting with my team, and I said, "We are going to start conference calls every morning for the next two months. And we're going to do a sales meeting with every one of our 43 TV stations. And we're going to give them a sales pitch about our May Sweep plans."

Kathleen's story underscores how she passed the challenge Anne put to her. The test deepened their relationship in a couple of ways, because Kathleen risked telling Anne about challenges she was having at work, which is often difficult to admit to another, and Kathleen met the test by following Anne's advice in setting specific goals in order to overcome these challenges.

The final set of challenges relates to getting to know the protégé as a whole person. These might involve observing them in social situations, judging if they are fun, and observing how they react under pressure. The depth of the relationship can depend on how the protégé responds in social settings or outside the boundaries of work. Bob Wright mentioned this: "I always try to find or look up people in social environments if I can, because you do see other sides of people. Or maybe you don't see another side, you see the same person. But some people are different. And sometimes it's tension, and sometimes it's just you get more of a chance to see their personality and their interests."

Mentors may also test protégés by either putting them into a pressure-filled situation or observing how they respond under pressure. Patty Archibeck and Larry Carter both discussed observing one another under pressure. Patty related a story of how they work together in tense situations when she talked about what happened during a very important presentation:

> When I feel Larry's eyes on me [in tense situations] I just go calm. An example would be on a presentation I remember where he came in, and there's was a change that needed to be made, and he was supposed to be on stage in like two seconds, and he wanted a slide moved or something like that. He was literally walking up onstage after he told me, so I said, "Okay, your cue is that you don't start speaking onstage until you see me in the back of the room," because then the presentation is closed back up. So I ran back to the graphics person, and they made the change. And I walked to the back of the room and he looked at me and smiled and just started.

In working together, Patty learned how to respond when Larry put her on the spot, and Larry learned that he could depend on her time after time when he challenged Patty. Although making a last-minute change in a presentation looks trivial, this situation shows that they knew they could depend on one another whatever challenge was presented. This type of trust is the result of an ongoing cycle of tests that the protégé passes, and it eventually deepens the mentoring relationship.

TESTS THAT DEEPEN THE MENTORING RELATIONSHIP

1. Can the protégé "put their money where their mouth is"?
   - When the mentor gave the protégé their first assignment, did the protégé do it, and if so, how well? Typically, failing

at the first assignment hurts only the protégé; the only
loss to the mentor is time spent giving the advice or suggestion.

2. Will this protégé help me or hurt me?
   - How well did the protégé handle the first challenge that
     had direct work implications or repercussions for the
     mentor's career? The next challenge is more serious,
     since the protégé's failure can have serious work or reputa-
     tion repercussions for the mentor. This challenge is often
     job related and really ties the protégé to the mentor's rep-
     utation.

3. To err is human, to forgive divine . . . if you learned something.
   - How did the protégé deal with failure, and how did the
     mentor and protégé overcome this stumbling block?
   - What happens to the relationship when the protégé embar-
     rasses the mentor or damages the mentor's reputation?

4. Can I trust this protégé to tell me the truth and really hear me?
   - How well does the protégé provide useful opinions, advice,
     and/or feedback to the mentor?
   - Did the protégé prove to be a trustworthy confidant to the
     mentor?

5. Is the protégé doing the work, and does he or she appreciate
   the mentor?
   - Is the protégé continuing to act on the mentor's sugges-
     tions?
   - Is the protégé communicating to the mentor on how he
     or she acted on suggestions, corrections, or advice?
   - Is the protégé communicating appreciation of the
     mentor?

6. What's this protégé *really* like, as a whole person, and do I like
   him or her?
   - How does the protégé behave in social settings, and how
     comfortable are the mentor and protégé with each other
     outside of work?
   - How does the protégé respond under pressure, and how
     does that help the mentor?
   - Is the protégé fun to be around?

CONCLUSION

In this chapter we examined the important factors, from the mentor's perspective, that affect the nature of the mentoring relationship. The chapter underscored the need for mentors to explore their own philosophy of mentoring by asking themselves a series of questions:

- Why do I want to mentor others? In other words, what's in it for me?
- What is the protégé's role in setting the tone of the relationship?
- What do I expect from the protégé in this relationship?

Protégés should ask themselves similar questions about potential mentors in order to understand the mentor's philosophy. In addition, protégés should explore their own expectations for the relationship and their assumptions about their perfect mentor.

Mentors noted a wide range of attributes that are attractive in a protégé. Sometimes the success of a relationship boils down to a question of chemistry, and if such chemistry is not present, then it is important to find a relationship that holds other promise. Generally, though, the five main reasons for attraction included:

1. Perceived similarity, not necessarily based on demographic similarity
2. Complementary skills or perspectives
3. A compelling characteristic or skill
4. Demonstrated potential or performance
5. Willingness to learn

We also discussed important characteristics of the "perfect" protégé from the point of view of the many mentors we interviewed. These characteristics give would-be protégés a comprehensive list of skills that are important to a power mentor. For a protégé, leaving the attraction to chance is not an effective way to attract a power mentor. Successful protégés should work to perfect the following abilities:

1. Intelligence
2. Ambition
3. Desire and ability to accept power and risk
4. Initiative
5. Energy
6. Trustworthiness
7. Integrity
8. High emotional intelligence
9. Optimism
10. Complementary skills

From the mentor's perspective, the relationship often begins with a series of tests and challenges. The mentor gives a potential protégé a small assignment to determine whether the protégé has the qualities the mentor is looking for, or as we said earlier, to screen out unsuitable protégés. The tests often tell the mentor whether the protégé is skilled, trustworthy, and/or optimistic, or any other of the characteristics that may be desirable to that mentor. As the mentoring relationship deepens, the tests and challenges often become more numerous and complex, and we argue that, in power mentoring relationships, these events are important in determining the intensity of the relationship and its outcomes.

This chapter has provided guidelines that can help both protégés and mentors come to a better understanding of the mentors' expectations and behavior in a developing mentoring relationship. In the next chapter, we investigate protégés' motivations for entering into mentoring relationships and what they hope to gain.

CHAPTER FIVE

THE PROTÉGÉ'S PERSPECTIVE
How to Get and Keep a Power Mentor

Lefty encouraged me about my future in the mob. The thing is, Donnie, you gotta keep your nose clean. You gotta be a good earner and don't get into trouble, don't offend, don't insult anybody, and you're gonna be a made guy someday. Now, the only thing is, they might give you a contract to go out and whack somebody. But don't worry about it. Like I told you, I'll show you how. You got the makings, Donnie. You handle yourself right, keep your nose clean, keep on the good side of people, I'll propose you for membership.
—JOSEPH D. PISTONE WITH RICHARD WOODLEY,
    DONNIE BRASCO

It might seem a bit strange to find the advice of a mob boss in a business book. However, as unsavory as the nature of the relationship is between mobster Lefty and his budding protégé, Federal Bureau of Investigation (FBI) undercover agent Donnie Brasco, much can be learned about the dynamics of mentor-protégé pairs from this relationship. The account provided by FBI agent Joseph Pistone (his alias was Donnie Brasco) of his undercover assignment to infiltrate the Mafia makes for fascinating reading. Pistone was one of the FBI's most successful infiltrators ever; his testimony resulted in more than 200 indictments and 100 convictions of organized crime figures in the United States. The close personal mentoring relationship that Pistone established with Lefty, his mob mentor, made it all possible. Of course, in the end, Pistone/Brasco betrayed his mentor, so from Lefty's perspective, the mentoring relationship ended rather badly. However, while it lasted, it was extremely beneficial for both. Lefty was a compulsive gambler and was chronically short of cash—Donnie Brasco was able to keep cash flowing to Lefty through his excellent skills in thievery and relationship building, which reflected well on Lefty and enhanced his reputation among the other wiseguys in the mob.

One of the most important steps protégés can take to find a worthwhile mentor, after first acknowledging that they can't make it on their own, is to take stock of the many real advantages a mentor can bring to a protégé's career. Protégés must also carefully determine what specific benefits appeal to them. For example, Donnie Brasco needed someone to introduce him to the Mafia's inner circle and make explicit the underworld norms. Once protégés have those factors mapped out, it then becomes easier to find that mentor who will work with them to help them get the most out of their careers. Protégés use different strategies to find the mentor of their dreams. Many actively seek out important relationships to further their careers or to find good advice and support for their next career decision. Donnie did extensive background research on his targeted would-be mentor and approached Lefty with a win-win approach to the relationship. While you may not have the resources available to you that the FBI does, you can still learn as much as you can about a possible mentor using conventional means (such as the Internet and professional recommendations) and think about what you might offer to a mentor.

In Chapter Four we explored the mind of the mentor, specifically uncovering not only the mental models mentors hold in typical mentoring relationships, but also the characteristics they look for in the perfect protégé. In the current chapter we focus on the mentoring relationship from the perspective of the protégé and address the question of how to get and keep a power mentor. We begin by emphasizing the importance of being willing to initiate the relationship and getting clear about what attracts you to a potential mentor. Then we consider various characteristics that will make you successful as a protégé. Finally, we present specific strategies to attract and target a power mentor. This chapter is not only for protégés, however. If you are a mentor, you will find valuable ideas in the following pages as well, particularly if you are looking for goal-oriented, trustworthy protégés who will work to their full capacity.

INITIATION AND ATTRACTION

One of the key characteristics of a power mentoring relationship is the high level of initiative shown by the protégé in establishing the relationship. The majority of the mentoring relationships discussed by our interviewees were either protégé initiated or mutually initiated. In fact, only five relationships were initiated primarily by the mentor—usually because the mentor was hiring or connecting with the protégé based on a referral. So clearly the burden of responsibility in connecting with a mentor rests on the protégé, which, in many ways, can be very empowering for a protégé. From the mentor's perspective, this can be enlightening, because one of the best sources of potential protégés is referrals from others who were previous protégés. Also, it seems that it is relatively easy for mentors to attract high-quality protégés, because it is a matter of getting involved in one's profession and becoming visible. As a protégé, think about what you can offer a potential mentor, even if it is just your sincere admiration. Are there any risks involved in initiating the relationship? Sure, rejection is possible. And unfortunately, the rejection will feel personal, although in many situations, the potential mentor may merely be overloaded with work. Be courageous and take the risk of approaching a mentor you're interested in. It doesn't hurt to ask, and if nothing else, your potential mentor will likely be flattered. To make it easier on yourself, you might want to take the first step via e-mail and/or get someone else to provide an introduction.

In Chapter Four we discussed what attracted mentors to their protégés; we now consider the opposite perspective—what attracted the protégés in our study to their mentors? Not surprisingly, perhaps, many of the elements that attracted mentors to their protégés were identical to those that attracted protégés to their mentors, including perceptions of similarity in important areas (for example, a shared passion for a cause or similar values). Also, protégés often spoke of being attracted to a mentor because the mentor had a skill or type of experience that the protégé did not have but wanted to obtain. Most of the protégés had strong expectations of learning something valuable from their power mentors. Usually the mentor was someone the protégé respected and aspired to be like; thus the protégé found a way to form a relationship with that mentor, either through working with them or becoming part of their circle. Many of our protégés spoke of the importance of their first impressions of their mentors; these impressions were in themselves pivotal lessons and set the tone for the future relationship.

Recall General Lee Butler from Chapter Three. He shares his recollection of his first impression of his mentor, Colin Powell (Secretary of State in the first administration of George W. Bush):

> The first time that I saw Colin Powell was shortly after he had been named to be the Chairman of the Joint Chiefs of Staff, October of 1989. It was General Powell's first morning staff meeting as Chairman. There was a group of at least 50 people in the room. I didn't know Powell personally and I didn't know much about him. There was a time-honored ritual played out in each staff meeting. As the Chairman approached the door of the conference room, a non-commissioned officer would announce in a great voice, "Ladies and gentlemen, the Chairman of the Joint Chiefs of Staff (in this case), General Colin Powell." The words seemed to echo up and down the corridor that General Powell had passed. On hearing this announcement, he stopped and said, "Now that was splendid. In fact, that was so well done I doubt that anyone here will ever forget who I am. So I don't think we'll need to do that again."
>
> Second, after he sat down he said, "Let's just use this as a place where we can talk and exchange information." He then started at the right-hand side of the table, went around and he called on every person, by the name that they preferred, not just rank and last name, and not by just the first name. Just think of the work that he had to do—photographs, memorization, getting it all together. And so at that point I knew I was dealing with someone very, very special. I had the highest regard for General Powell, and yes, he is a wonderful mentor, and I'm sure he played a strong hand in my subsequent promotion to become commander of the nuclear forces. It was our personal relationship that allowed me to make historic, sweeping changes in the structure of those forces during my period in office.

In this chapter, we make explicit a key element of power mentoring relationships, which is how a protégé such as General Butler can become a confidant to his or her mentor. In this case, General Powell was appointed as General Butler's superior, and they forged a relationship based on mutual trust, stemming in turn from shared work ideals and values.

DEVELOPING TRUST IN THE MENTORING RELATIONSHIP

Those who trust us, educate us.
—T. S. Eliot

Trust is integral to the mentoring relationship. Mentors and protégés share secrets of their success, stories about their failures, and often reveal many details of their lives. Not only must protégés learn to trust someone else, they in turn must *be* trustworthy. In this section we focus on stories from the protégés that describe how they developed trust with their mentors. Being trustworthy is one of the most crucial things that protégés can do for their mentors. In other words, trust is the fundamental currency exchanged in many mentoring relationships.

Over and over again, our power protégés and mentors spoke emotionally, often glowingly, and sometimes painfully of the importance of trust with each other. There has been some past research on the importance of trust in mentoring, but surprisingly the work in this area has been very sparse. (We discuss some of the related literature on trust in the next chapter.) We found trust to be a crucial aspect of the development of power mentoring relationships, particularly from the perspective of the protégés. Trust in power mentoring relationships is about both attitude and behavior. It is about attitude in terms of shared values and a deep understanding of the other. It is about behavior in terms of giving and receiving difficult feedback, sharing secrets, and proving loyalty in word and deed. Trust is also about positive work outcomes, because mentors and protégés alike described how trust enabled them to develop a synchronicity or rhythm to their work together.

TRUST IS ABOUT SHARED VALUES

For many of our power protégés and mentors, trust and its ensuing behaviors arose from a foundation of shared values and similar perspectives. Often, protégés can sense this right away, but ultimately trust develops over time. Pamela Thomas-Graham reflected on the trust between her and her mentor, Bob Wright: "We had a very good rapport on our first interview, so we found enough similarities and enough similar worldviews that our impulse was to have a more trust-based relationship right from the start. However, trust is ultimately a function of time and experiences, right? You have to go through a few things and see how someone reacts. And then it just takes a little time."

Trust also can grow out of shared values and similar styles in the process of doing business. We had the great fortune to interview Kay Koplovitz, an amazing entrepreneur who saw the future market for sports TV and became the first woman founder and president of a network television station, USA Network. After running the organization for 21 years, she now advises large numbers of women starting their own entrepreneurial ventures. She talked about someone she considers a mentor, Bob Rosencrans (currently of Columbia Partners and on the board of directors of firms such as C-SPAN), for whom she worked briefly at a cable company, UA Columbia. Kay and Bob shared ideas of what could be done with the new medium of sports cable broadcasting, and he also shared her passion for the possibilities of satellite communications. Their shared values were centered around their attitudes toward negotiation and business dealings:

> I learned most observing the way he saw business and treated people in business relationships. Bob is very easygoing and relaxed about his business. His business thought process was always to simplify the business proposition and to make it easy in many ways for people to say yes.
>
> I learned from Bob that both parties, or multiple parties, in a negotiation all need to take away something that they needed to take away. Leave a little bit on the table for the other guy. Some people negotiate as, "I win, you lose"—that's the only way they ever deal. To understand that the health of a person or company you're

doing business with is important for you in the long run because you need healthy customers, and you need healthy relationships, was good positioning for me to learn early on. Consequently, I think it's now my own predisposition. I learned the value of the plain vanilla deal, in the sense that you make the deal proposition easy to understand, easy to say yes to. And one that would be beneficial to you. Don't put a lot of complicated trimmings onto a negotiation that are unnecessary. It just prolongs the discussion and sometime complicates it beyond comprehension to people.

Although the examples from Pamela Thomas-Graham and Kay Koplovitz focus on different types of shared values, nonetheless, these commonalities helped the mentoring pairs form trusting bonds with their respective mentors.

TRUST IS ABOUT GIVING AND RECEIVING DIFFICULT FEEDBACK

Most of our protégés spoke positively about trust in their mentors. In fact, trust was a vital currency of exchange between protégés and mentors, because a number of power protégés mentioned that they provided value to their mentor by acting as trusted confidant and truth teller. Therefore, an essential element of a successful power mentoring relationship is giving and receiving difficult feedback and accepting the level of risk that accompanies it. This might seem particularly challenging for protégés to do, because they are frequently in a position of less status and power than their mentor, but it is their willingness to do it, skillfully and truthfully, that makes them valuable to their mentor. Often, they become trusted confidants to their mentors.

The experience of Pamela Thomas-Graham and Bob Wright presents a particularly compelling example of trust and how it develops through a process of telling the truth to each other. In the words of Pamela Thomas-Graham:

One way that I built trust with Bob early on is through receiving coaching from him about succeeding at a series of meetings. There's a budget cycle that happens every fall. And my first fall at NBC there was a pretty intense round of meetings with Jack Welch and the senior GE management about budgets and business plans. That was fairly intimidating for a newcomer as I was new to the company and to my management role. Bob was great about work-ing with me to get me ready for those meetings, in terms of posi-tioning me to be successful. He was willing to go over the presentations with me several times and beat up on them and send me back to do them again. By the time the presentation actually came, I was totally ready. There's a way that you can make a presen-tation better that increases the confidence of the speaker and then there's a way that you can do it that makes them feel like, oh my god, I can't do this. He's very good at improving on something but doing it in a way that makes you feel like yeah, I can do this.

Just as Pamela received critical feedback from Bob and grace-fully accepted his suggestions, in return she was also called on to tell the truth and give difficult feedback to him and her other men-tor, Jack Welch. In the following passage, Pamela reflected on the feedback she had to deliver to Jack and Bob during the height of the dot-com fever:

I think a lot of people believed that the trees would just grow to the sky around the Internet, that these businesses would just grow for-ever. And I think the reason, frankly, that I'm in my current role is because I really trusted Bob and had a lot of confidence in his lead-ership and so I was able to say to Jack, "You know, this is what this business can and can't be. This is how much money we can make from this. But we can't make twice that. And it's not going to be the next big thing." And I think being able to say that and not being unrealistic about what the prospects were was important. The rea-son I was able to do that is because I had a lot of trust and confi-dence in Bob in knowing that saying this was not going to get me fired. I think it's an important part of the GE culture that telling the truth about what a business can be is rewarded.

TRUST IS ABOUT LOYALTY IN THE FACE OF ADVERSITY

Several of our protégés related compelling stories of trust being manifested as loyalty, particularly during times of adversity. The fol-lowing is a particularly fascinating example from Congresswoman Hilda Solis's two protégés, Judy Chu and Sharon Martinez. As we discussed in Chapter Two, Hilda Solis and Judy Chu had a barrier-busting mentoring relationship across ethnic lines. As is typical in power mentoring, Solis shared her network with Martinez, and Judy Chu became a mentor for Sharon as well. Sharon Martinez made a successful bid for city council member in Monterey Park, California, and in 2003 was elected mayor. These three politicians commented on the high level of trust and regard they have for each other. We hear first from Judy Chu, reflecting on the loyalty shown by her mentor, Congresswoman Solis, during a difficult campaign for the California State Assembly:

> You really find out a lot about people when you're running these very hard campaigns. And there are so many moments where there's some kind of tough vote. One of the biggest moments in my campaign was when I was up for the labor endorsement [the Los Angeles County Federation of Labor]. Hilda is considered an absolute hero in the labor movement. And so her pushing behind the scenes really meant a lot with the labor community. And it's things like that that make you know that that person is not just talk. Another defining moment with Hilda is when she endorsed me. That was difficult because there was a Latino male running. And the natural inclination would be for her to go with the Latino male. In fact there was a lot of pressure for her to go with him. But by that time she and I had forged quite a relationship over this number of years. And I'd helped her a lot. She'd helped me a lot, things like that. And we had a lot of trust between the two of us. I know she took a lot of heat for it.

The loyalty and trust between Chu and Solis extended to Sharon Martinez, an up-and-coming politician. In the following anecdote, we hear Sharon Martinez explaining why she did not immediately run for an Assembly seat as an example of her loyalty to both of her mentors, Judy Chu and Hilda Solis:

> I will give you an example of how Judy is my mentor and of my loyalty and my trust toward her. In March 2001, she went for reelection to the Monterey Park City Council. In June, she won an Assembly seat. So in March, that seat was open and people said I should run. I didn't do it. I said, you know why, my turn will come. There were two seats that were available, but I'd still be going against Judy Chu. I think this is one of the things that Hilda has taught me is that you wait your turn, and it will be your turn. Wait. And obviously it happened. And Judy, obviously in June won the Assembly seat, so I took over in November.
>
> Hilda and I are the same in our loyalty to each other and how important it is to us. But the trust issue, the loyalty, especially since

being an elected official, it's almost like you're in a minefield, and you need to be very careful because you never know. And the unfortunate thing . . . there are a lot of people who tend to turn on you, but I know Hilda would never [do that], nor would I ever turn on her. Even if it drags me along. I doubt that would happen, but I would go to the end for her, and I know she would do that for me, whatever the cause was.

Adversity was manifested a little differently in the world of journalism, but also was a true test of trust being forged under fire. Lisa Ling noted that trust was essential to overcoming moments of adversity as she reflected on her mentoring relationship with Mitch Koss:

> We have been in situations that most ordinary people [wouldn't be], which is the two of us would be on the front lines of many different contentious situations, like in Afghanistan, Cambodia, Colombia, and so on, and if we didn't trust each other, then we would really suffer. I know that if anyone ever physically tried to hurt me in those environments, he would be there. When we were in Japan, we were getting chased by this six-foot, seven-inch Japanese Yakuza [organized crime gangster]. Mitchell was shooting, and this guy came up and he started wrestling with Mitchell for the camera; they got into a physical confrontation, and I got right in there, and I started peeling his fingers off the camera. It's just this instinct that I have that I knew that he would do the same for me under that situation, so I'd better get in there and try to fight this six-foot, seven-inch Yakuza. We eventually pulled away from the guy, the two of us against him so we got away. But it was scary.

TRUST IS ABOUT BEING PERSONAL

Fans of the hit TV show *The Apprentice* know that one of The Donald's maxims is "It's not personal—it's business." This cliché was debunked by the experiences of our power mentors and protégés. In fact, for the development of trust one might say it's business and it's very personal. Trust is about secret stuff, sacred stuff, and locker-room bonding. It's about being vulnerable and knowing enough about the other to inflict damage but never doing it.

Lilach Asofsky, senior vice president of Marketing and Research at CNBC, reflected on receiving personal support from her mentor, Pamela Thomas-Graham, when she shared the news of her first pregnancy with her. As one of the few high-level women at CNBC, Lilach had some trepidation about telling her boss and colleagues about her pregnancy, for fear of a negative reaction in this traditional male-dominated environment. However, when she confided in Pamela she found that her concerns were greatly alleviated:

> When I first told her that I was pregnant she really shared in my joy. I was concerned about the conversation with my supervisor and letting him know about my pregnancy and she was really helpful with that. I can think back to several conversations that we've had since then that have helped—mother-to-mother conversations where she is already a much more savvy parent than I am and has been doing it for a lot longer. And it is comforting because I trust her and I really respect her. . . . If I ask her a question, I take her response with a different feel than if somebody else were to just tell me. I know how smart she is and I really trust her response.

Female bonding was evidenced in the relationship between Debra Martucci and Patty Archibeck as well. Their relationship began in a more personal fashion and then evolved into a power mentoring relationship. As mentioned earlier, Debra was Patty's 6:00 a.m. step-aerobics instructor, and they began their relationship over a shared interest in a good workout and then informal postexercise locker-room chatting. The forced intimacy of a locker room speeds the development of trust and mutual regard. Patty's mentor, Debra, reflected on the development of trust out of a more personal relationship with one another:

> In the locker room where all of us are getting ready for work, we really use that locker room as sort of a forum to share some of what's going on, both good and bad. And I noticed with Patty she was going through [a period] where she was looking at changing jobs. This was back when the whole dot-com nightmare in Silicon Valley was going on. And so that's what we did—a few breakfasts where we were able to just get away from the group and the locker-room environment and just sort of talk a little and share a little. And she was going through changes there prior to moving to the U.K. and her wedding. I mostly tried to just help her through the thought process. I think that's the biggest thing that a mentor does. The last thing I think a mentor should do is tell you what to do, right? Because you can't ever tell people what to do, but I think

helping them feel comfortable to think it through out loud is very beneficial. I do fairly well thinking out loud. It's clearer for me as I can I let the inner turmoil and the inner voices go.

Another aspect of trust being personal relates to the idea that trust is ultimately about being vulnerable to the other person. The more vulnerable one is, the more damage they can potentially inflict on the other. The relationship between former U.S. Treasurer Rosario Marin and her former mentor, California Governor Pete Wilson, exemplifies this very well. Their relationship began in a personal way. Rosario Marin got her start in politics because she found it necessary to advocate for services for her son, Eric, who has Down syndrome. Marin was drawn to the Republican governor of California, because when she heard him speak about people with disabilities she felt his compassion. Marin went on to work for him as his liaison with the Latino community. She elaborated:

> I've always said that you can tell how much another person trusts you by the amount of damage you can inflict upon them. You see this at the White House in the sense that the people who can damage you the most are the people that are very close to you. Because they know your goods and your bads.
>
> When Governor Wilson spoke to the Latino community and I translated for him in Spanish, nobody on his team would even know what I was saying because they didn't speak Spanish. They just trusted me with the entire governor's agenda. I think that you will find loyalty's a huge issue. And I have learned that from both Governor Wilson and certainly President Bush as well.

TRUST IS ABOUT MUTUAL WORK PRODUCTIVITY

Trust translates into a productive working relationship, because the power mentors and protégés who truly trust each other find that they often develop a work rhythm together—a sense of synchronicity. It is about trusting a protégé enough to allow them to take risks and maybe even fail. It is about enhancing a protégé's self-esteem and trusting their opinions. It can even take the form of leaving someone alone to do their job.

Earlier in this chapter, we introduced you to General Lee Butler and his reflections about his mentor, General Colin Powell.

Now we examine the relationship between General Lee Butler and his protégé, Brigadier General Don Pettit, and the synchronicity they enjoyed in their work relationship that evolved out of their shared trust. Both Pettit and Butler reflected on an incident when they traveled to Russia to work together with the commander of the Russian nuclear forces. Here is Pettit's account:

> Admiral Crowe was the chairman of the Joint Chiefs of Staff at the time. And before he was leaving office, his counterpart from Russia and he agreed it would be a good idea if the two countries could reach an agreement that could potentially prevent their countries from inadvertently engaging in hostile activity with one another due to a mistake by one side or the other. General Butler got the task to develop this agreement. I think our relationship with each other had a lot to do with achieving a successful agreement, in a very efficient manner, because we could play off of each other and discuss strategies, and so forth, very openly and candidly. He would have gotten the task done with or without me, no doubt about it. But I think because of the confidence and the trust we'd built up over time, knowing each other's capabilities and how we were going to be managing things, it worked out a lot better.

Our power protégés, such as General Pettit, frequently reflected on decisions they made that involved very high stakes. Pamela Thomas-Graham, who described the high level of trust between her and her mentor, Bob Wright, spoke candidly about the way he allowed her to take risks and learn from both failure and success. Pamela articulated how Bob's trust enabled her to learn and how important this was for her and for other budding executives, particularly highly visible protégés of color:

> It comes back to what I said originally about Bob being willing to give people a lot of room. There have been a couple of times when I might have wanted to do something and he's said, "Well, I don't think I would do that if I were you. But you're running the business. You're responsible for the business. I'm telling you I wouldn't do it. But if you want to do it, go ahead." And quite frankly, there were a couple times when he was right and I did things that I shouldn't have done. And to the point about being able to recover from mistakes, these were things that were reversible. You know, we reversed them. He said, "You know, this is why I told you not to do that." And then it's done.

So I think that the ultimate way to build trust is to be able to stumble, to be able to make a mistake and to feel like the person helps you get back up, doesn't say, "I told you so," but just kind of says, "Okay, so the next time you'll know." And you keep moving. You know, that's ultimately how you build that kind of deep trust where you really feel like your interests are aligned with someone.

And we spoke about this a lot at McKinsey in terms of why it had taken so long for a woman or a person of color to become a partner. A lot of it was that in the past people would make mistakes and never really were able to recover from them, that there wasn't that mentor there or that group of mentors that could help the person recover.

Because everybody makes mistakes in their career. I mean, I think that's a given. I think the point is who's allowed to recover and who isn't allowed to recover and who bounces back quickly as opposed to who's kept in the doghouse. So the more that women and people of color are not kept in the doghouse, are allowed to just keep going or are allowed to trip but get back on stride, the more you're going to see women and people of color progressing. Because nobody is perfect. It's just a matter of how much . . . institutional support is there for people.

Nikki Rocco also reflected on how trust can lead to workplace productivity in terms of a wildly successful movie-marketing campaign early in her career:

There was an example and I remember it vividly because I was a nervous wreck, and this was 12 or 13 years ago. Tom Pollack said something to me about Marty Scorsese and something to do with the fact that we had a movie called *Cape Fear,* and he wanted me to go to New York, and he wanted me to take a look at the movie. And I said, "What?" And he said, "No, I trust your opinion. Sid Sheinberg is going into New York." I was senior vice president at that time. It was a turning point in my career because it was the first time that I ventured away from the pack, and I took the trip.

I watched the movie in a private screening room in Scorsese's building with Scheinberg and Michael Ovitz. And after that we went to lunch, and I had to give my opinion of what I thought, not of the film but what to do with it; how to release it. And that was almost a turning point in my career because as it turned out the picture was very successful. I don't want to take credit for it, but I certainly take credit for carving out the release, which was a very unusual release date and strategy. So I remember that vividly.

Trust is sometimes about leaving someone alone to shine. Martha Morris reflected on this approach by her then-boss, Linda Sanford: "Linda left me alone to do this job, which is her way of trusting me. I'd report to her every week, give her a report on it, you know, here's how manufacturing is doing. She'd read it. And she'd ask some questions. And you know, we talked about manufacturing in all our meetings and she . . . relied on me to make decisions. She did not question me as long as I was performing. That really brings out the best in people. So she does that by really trusting us."

SUMMARY: DEVELOPING TRUST

As we said at the beginning of this section, trust is an integral part of the mentoring relationship. It can be developed through various means, but as is often said, trust takes much time to build but much less time to lose. We highlighted the many stories of trust shared by the protégés in our study and provided insight into the special nature of their relationships. In the next section we discuss additional relationship-building techniques that are important for worthwhile mentoring relationships.

IDENTIFYING A POWER MENTOR

In general, to identify potential power mentors it is best to start by finding out who are the movers and shakers within your profession or industry. Recalling the differences between power mentors and traditional mentors discussed in Chapter One, we see that power mentors are often found in the protégé's own organization, yet they can also be found in a different organization or party. Remember that a traditional mentoring relationship can be a power mentoring relationship if augmented by additional mentors or other means.

Often, power mentors are part of a lineage of the power elite or the in-group of a given profession or industry. These people are relatively easy to identify, because their names come up frequently in conversations as expert "go to" people, and they are often in highly visible positions or poised to ascend to an influential position.

In fact, you can use the same methods to find power mentors for yourself that we used to identify power mentors for this book. Begin by looking at industry-specific lists to identify top people (for example, *Hollywood Reporter*'s top women in Hollywood) and then do some background research on people that look interesting. Try to connect with people who work in that industry who might know someone who knows your targeted mentor. Use the six degrees of separation and snowball techniques.[1] *Six degrees of separation* is the idea that everyone we want to connect with is only six people away from us, and that people we know can readily link us with others we want to know. In working to contact our interviewees, we found that often that link was even closer—often only three or four people away. Six degrees of separation works like this: Begin by identifying who your industry's most influential players are. Research or ask those you respect in the industry what they think. Next figure out if you know someone who might know someone who is linked to the person you are trying to reach. For example, if you were to look at multimedia conglomerates, you might start with the former head of GE—the iconic former CEO, Jack Welch. We found that Jack Welch mentored Bob Wright, who in turn mentors Pamela Thomas-Graham, who mentors Lilach Asofsky. While it might be difficult to get Jack Welch to be your mentor, you might find that getting to know someone at Lilach's level is easier. Then, once you have established contact with one of your sought-after people, ask them to refer you to another connection. Soon the number of your people in your network will grow exponentially or "snowball." This was a great method for contacting our many interviewees.

Louise Wannier, successful serial entrepreneur, founder of MyShape, Enfish, and Gemstar, talks about using the snowball technique for building her network of business contacts. She reflected on her time working at Gemstar with her then peer mentor, Henry Yuen (cofounder and former CEO of Gemstar; Louise was cofounder and former COO and CEO of Gemstar Europe): "When I started working on building Gemstar, I was introduced through one of the partners I knew at Ernst (now Ernst & Young) to the head of engineering at Dimension Cable, who in turn introduced me to the head of marketing at the *Los Angeles Times,* who in turn introduced me to the president of the *New York Times,* and so on. From there I discovered that the syndicates could help with these introductions and ended up doing a deal with United Feature, the syndicate that markets Peanuts and Garfield, to represent us to the bulk of the newspapers. It was through this serial networking that I was able to learn and absorb how the market functions and to structure the business relationships that would enable us to launch the company."

You met Dixie Garr in Chapter One. Later you will learn about the humorous way she connected with her protégé, Anthony Hayter, over a pastry at a professional event. Meeting at professional events is a great way for mentors and protégés to connect; other alternatives include working in the same organization, making contact during job interviews, encountering each other in educational settings, or being involved in an extracurricular activity (social causes, sports activities, and so on). Many protégés spoke of knowing about their mentor and admiring them from afar. A large number of our protégés made a conscious effort to follow their potential mentor's career, ultimately developing a relationship with that person when the opportunity arose. Former mayor Sharon Martinez (Monterey Park, California) had that kind of experience with her mentor, Congresswoman Hilda Solis (D-CA):

> I first met Hilda when she was running for Assembly in the late '80s. I had been following her career because I saw her at a forum at Rio Honda [College], and I said what a dynamic woman, what a great person, plus she wasn't too much older. She was for the same things that I was for, which is higher education, women's rights, and especially minority rights, and that was exactly what I was striving for in my own way. I didn't know how yet to get there, but at least I could start to see how by looking at her.

Surprisingly, there have been few articles that have attempted to uncover what protégé characteristics attract mentors. For example, one study showed that mentors were mostly attracted to a protégé's ability level, and much less so to the mentor's perception of the protégé's need for help.[2]

In the previous chapter we discussed the main characteristics that we uncovered related to mentor attraction. Moreover, we encountered repeated examples in which getting involved in one's professional community provided an excellent way for mentors and protégés to connect. However, more often than not, while the professional situation may have provided a meeting ground for the potential mentor and protégé, it usually fell to the protégé to make the first contact. Therefore, getting involved is an excellent first step toward meeting a potential power mentor, but a firm commitment to following up on potential contacts is critical as well.

CULTIVATING THE ART OF IMPRESSION MANAGEMENT

An important key to finding and connecting with those you want to work with is the art of *impression management.* Impression management is what it sounds like: a way to manage or control the impressions people have of you. A vast amount of research shows that people engage in many types of impression-management tactics.[3] Some impression management is explicitly concerned with the way others see us. Sometimes we engage in impression management to make ourselves seem to be something we are not, while at other times, we are more subtle and merely attempt to show our best side, as we might in the course of a job interview or a lunch with upper management in our organization. We also engage in impression management because as humans we try to present ourselves in the best light to our own evaluative self. In other words, we make up excuses, even to ourselves, for our shortcomings.[4] We take more credit for the good that happens to us and tend to dismiss our role in the bad that happens. An example of the quintessential impression manager comes from the character Eddie Haskell in the 1950s TV show, *Leave It to Beaver.* If you have seen reruns of the show, you will recall Haskell's syrupy sweet voice from time to time saying, "Gee Mrs. Cleaver, that's a lovely dress you're wearing." His impression management was necessary because he was much more mischievous than the Cleaver boys and didn't always create a favorable impression.

Given these explanations, impression management sounds like lying to oneself or others. We are not advocating lying. But we do ask that protégés think critically about the impression they make on others. Many people adopt the stance "I am what I am," or

"What you see is what you get," and spend little time trying to be anything else. If you can honestly say that your raw personality, behavior, and style are resulting in the opportunities and the right quality of people in your life, then impression management may not be necessary for you. But most of us can use some polishing around the edges to make good first impressions. People are quick to make judgments about a person's personality. That is the way our brains are wired, to predict whether other people are friend or foe or generally what to expect from them. After we assess our initial impression of someone, we spend time looking for information that confirms that initial impression and disregard information counter to it.

Politeness, engagement, interest in life, optimism, and so on are just a few of the characteristics that attract people to someone else. Showing a potential mentor your best self is not a lie. It takes effort to make sure you are demonstrating your more positive side, and it may require some practice. For example, if you know that you are nervous with certain types of people, you need to practice coming across more calmly. How a person comes across in that first meeting is under his or her control. Moreover, in some ways impression management is a positive step toward becoming what you would like to become: your best possible self. The more you practice how you would like to behave, the more likely that behavior is to eventually become part of you.

We heard a few stories of astute mentors who took the time to look past initial impressions to develop long-lasting relationships with their protégés. For example, Linda Sanford of IBM ended up questioning her first impression of her protégé, Charles Lickel:

> My initial impression was nice guy, but how strong a leader is he going to be? Fortunately, I try to spend time listening. Which too many people don't do anymore. And so people get an impression, and they don't take the time to really listen and understand somebody. And so I spent the time to really get to know Charles and spend one-on-one time with him where I could get to understand what makes him tick, what motivates him, what are his thought processes. I realized this guy is just immensely talented. And he is also very multidimensional. He is not just focused on the business results. He looks at all the various layers of delivering successful

projects. He looks at process underneath it. Where are they broken? Where are they working well? Do I have the talent? And then have I developed the culture? So he is a very thorough, multidimensional, extremely intelligent individual.

Linda made a conscious effort to get to know Charles instead of relying on first impressions. Both Charles and Linda were lucky that she took the time. Another mentor also talked about a slightly unfavorable opinion he had of his protégé. As he put it:

> She's very confident. And when I first met her, I was put off by her because she was just so sure of herself. And sometimes that that can be a turn-off to people as well as an asset.
>
> But as I got to know her, I realized that she really had tremendously positive senses about things. And I found working with her was quite a surprise. She was so good at getting things done that I became a really big fan of hers.

The preceding stories tell of mindful mentors, but also highlight the importance of initial impressions. Managing the impression the protégé makes on others is important, but is not the only way to connect with a mentor. In the next section, we discuss the role of goal setting and self-management in connecting with various types of power mentors.

DEVELOPING A GOAL-ORIENTED ATTITUDE

Goal setting has been shown to be an extremely consistent method of motivating people.[5] In fact, research has demonstrated that mentors are attracted to and provide higher-quality mentoring to those protégés who are goal directed.[6] Ron Meyer, president and COO of Universal Studios (his job includes management oversight of Universal Pictures, Focus Features, and Universal Parks and Resorts), discussed his early learning about goals and how he became convinced of the importance of meeting all of one's goals, rather than just some of them. He recalled how he learned this from one of his early mentors at CAA: "In the days when I was a messenger, I used to think that if someone gave you 10 things to do and you got 9 of them right, you had accomplished your tasks.

I learned that it is not acceptable, and I don't accept it to this day from people."

Many stories of goal setting came from mentors who encouraged goal setting as part of their mentoring relationships. From the mentor's perspective, we have an example from William Wulf, who works as a master mentor in his role as both a professor of engineering and also the president of the National Academy of Engineering. Wulf talked about how he sets clear expectations for the many graduate students he mentors and others he supervises:

> I carefully manage and set expectation levels. People will work their tails off to try and live up to the expectations of people whom they admire. And so my trick has always been to make sure that I don't set those expectations too high at the beginning so that they can't succeed, and not too low so that they don't grow.
>
> I can point at some very particular examples in the company where an individual was failing. They were just not doing well. And with some time, attention, expectation setting and getting them in the right job they began to succeed. And the benefit to the company was just enormous. It was just so much better to see these people who were now feeling good about themselves, and willing to work their absolute tail off for the company because they felt good about what they were accomplishing. I could have fired them and hired somebody else, but the net gain was so much higher this way.

Wulf's skillful use of expectations is an important strategy for all mentors to incorporate into their relationships with protégés. What can the protégé do? Sitting down with their mentor and discussing their expectations for the relationship would benefit both parties. Larry Carter from Cisco Systems related the following story when asked about the nature of his many mentoring relationships:

> Some of them are very formal. Some will bring their laptop, and they'll actually have put together a presentation. Here's what their goals were for the end of the year, here's how they've been doing, here are some accomplishments they have had, here's where they have had some difficulties, and so forth. Others just come in and just want to chat. I ask them basically how they are doing and what some of their key objectives were, and how do they feel like they've been doing. And I ask in what areas they think that I could help

more, or John [Chambers] could help, or others in the company. Then we end up, usually talking about their own personal career, and I try to counsel on things like . . . somebody might say, "Well, I'm thinking about my next . . . There's this opening. I'm really thinking about this job. What do you think about it?" And my answer, as opposed to thinking about that job, is "What is the next job you are thinking of?" I tell them, "Think about two jobs out because every move you make ought to be a move as a step to the next move. Right? So if you haven't thought it through, maybe you ought to do that."

I get them to think further out. More long term. Not that they have to stick by it, but it helps them gauge whether this next position is really the right position. Because if it's a stepping stone into another role that they're working toward, that's great. Or if it's just a place they think they can have fun and make a contribution, then that's fine too, but they ought to be thinking about two jobs out.

Larry finds highly motivated protégés who feel comfortable making their career goals known. However, going too far with goals and expectations can perhaps backfire. Another mentor, Nick Donofrio of IBM, relayed his preferences in his many mentoring relationships for an appropriate degree of goal setting:

If they ask, as long as they're willing to be flexible in interfacing with me, I'll be glad to spend time with them. Call me once, call me twice, come to see me. I had one person, who will remain nameless, who wanted me to sign a contract with him. And I just said, "You got the wrong person. You know, I do a lot of things, but I can't sign a contract with you." They were looking for, how much time will you give me and how often will you give it to me, and that's not what I mean by mentoring at all.

I mean, come see me. Come call on me. Send me an e-mail when you have a problem, when you need something. I'll respond to you as fast as I can. If you really want to have a career counseling session and you think I could be of value, I'll do that too.

Lilach Asofsky of CNBA told the story of a fairly goal-directed team member who wanted Lilach to mentor her. She described the experience as follows: "Somebody in my team that definitely is a mentee and who, as I hired her, made it clear to me that that was something that she very much valued in the relationship she'd had with a previous manager and that's something that she was hoping to find. I think that people see limitations in themselves much more frequently than you see limitations in them. And I have found throughout my career that if I give somebody a challenge that they would never take upon themselves, it becomes an epiphany. It liberates them and they go on to tremendous things."

Both Nick and Lilach showed that their goal-directed protégés were comfortable asking for what they wanted in the mentoring relationship. Nick pushed back a bit on the protégé who wanted to sign a contract, while Lilach wanted to focus on the challenges she could give to protégés and understood that the limitations some protégés set for themselves could be overcome though clear challenges.

Although anyone can set goals, it is the important technique of self-management that helps people manage their lives and accomplish goals in many different arenas. Self-management involves a set of behavioral and cognitive strategies one can use to manage life's challenges.[7] Behavioral strategies consist of ways of replacing ineffective behaviors with more effective behaviors. This approach involves rewarding oneself when a positive behavior is done. It might consist of taking yourself to a movie when you complete a difficult project, or treating yourself to a spa session when you make a sales target. It may also involve not allowing yourself a treat of some sort when you do not meet a goal you set. Self-management training teaches people many different skills for managing not only their thoughts and behaviors, but also their surrounding circumstances. For example, people are asked to brainstorm the types of situations that prevent them from completing their goals. They then are asked to devise ways to avoid those distracting situations, or to manage their environment more carefully.

In addition to managing one's behaviors, self-management is also about managing the cognitive processes that either enhance or distract from goal completion. For example, you can think of the many things you learned to do as a child to take boring tasks and make them seem more fun. Positive thoughts are very useful for facilitating goal completion, but in the face of adversity, many people have a difficult time avoiding thoughts of failure. Used in conjunction with goal setting, self-management techniques can also help a person engage in more positive thought processes.

The takeaway message from goal setting and self-management is that by utilizing these strategies, not only do you become clear about your own priorities, you help a mentor help you because you are clear about what you want out of the relationship. From the protégé's perspective in the mentoring relationship, what does it mean to be goal directed? In entering a relationship, a number of things should cross a potential protégé's mind, including what realistically one can get from the relationship. In our interviews, we found protégés who were very goal directed. Not all of them started out that way, but it was soon made very clear to them by their early mentors, or else by mentors later on, that setting and accomplishing goals was an important method of career advancement.

In summary, goals play an important role in the success of mentoring relationships, but one key to attaining goals is the process of self-management. First, protégés should be fairly clear about their career goals, especially about what they hope to accomplish later in their careers. Second, protégés should be clear about their reasons for seeking a mentor. Third, once they have established a mentoring relationship, they should work with their mentor to set specific goals for the relationship (if the mentor is receptive). And finally, a protégé might also want to consider goals related to the duration of the relationship. By referring back to the original reasons for initiating the relationship, the protégé can determine whether the current relationship is meeting his or her expectations.

Goals also come into play on the mentor's side of the relationship. Mentors may find that protégés vary in the degree to which they know what they want from the relationship. Extremely busy mentors will impose expectations, goals, and challenges to keep the relationship moving forward.

If you are interested in becoming a protégé, we hope that one of your very first goals at this point is to identify and connect with a power mentor. We turn to connection strategies in the next section.

FORMING CONNECTION STRATEGIES

In Chapter Two, we introduced the various types of power mentors. Here we provide specific suggestions for how to connect with the various types of power mentors. To begin, we suggest that you closely examine your circle of friends, acquaintances, and family members in your real home and work home. Take a look at Figure

5.1. This gives you a sense of all the possible circles of influence where a potential mentor might reside—or where others reside who could connect a protégé to that perfect mentor.

FAMILY

Is there someone in your immediate or extended family who can serve as a mentor for you? If you were fortunate enough to win the gene pool lottery, you may have a rich and successful parent or uncle who is happy to serve as a mentor for you (for example, Donald Trump and his father, Fred Trump). Of course, a family-member mentor does not have to be a Mr. Trump to be helpful to you. They just need to be successful in their own world. Kim Fisher, director of AudioBasket, described her experience with her first mentor—her mother:

> My mom was a mentor for me. She was a full-time mom for 22 years, had four kids, and then decided that she wanted to go back to work, and had been at IBM before she had kids but decided to get into market research. So she joined a sort of two-person team in market research. She worked her way up to becoming a project director. I had two models—my father, who worked all his life [at] IBM for 42 years, and then my mother, who kind of jumped in to do something, then after 10 years she said, "Okay, that was great, now what else am I going to do?" And now she's getting her real estate license. So, I just kind of saw that that was possible. That you could start a career and do something and then do something else. I saw what she was doing and how much she was excited by sort of doing these things all the time and loving it.

For many of us, our family of origin may not provide a rich source of mentors. In fact, because we tend to spend more time with our coworkers than with our family members, our work family may provide the best source of potential mentors.

BOSSES

Consider your next closest group of contacts—your work family. You may be one of the fortunate few who can actively cultivate your boss as your mentor. How do you transform a boss-subordinate relationship into a power mentoring relationship? First, by making

FIGURE 5.1   SOURCES OF MENTORS

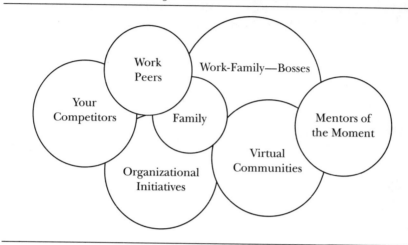

explicit your wishes and the potential benefits available to both of you. Think about what you can offer your boss as a protégé that is value added above and beyond what you offer as a subordinate.

Second, a boss mentoring relationship cannot be forced—the essential elements of mutual liking and respect must be present as a firm foundation to build on. Barbara Corday reflected on how she connected and what she learned from her boss mentor Marcy Carsey, cofounder of Carsey-Werner, who produced television shows such as the *Cosby Show, Roseanne, Grace Under Fire, 3rd Rock from the Sun,* and *That '70s Show,* and was the 2002 recipient of the Lucy Award from Women in Film. When Barbara Corday's writing and peer mentoring relationship with Barbara Avedon broke up, she found it necessary to get a job elsewhere, so she went to work at ABC:

> It was my first executive job. It was my first time obviously working at a network or anything like that. And it was my first time in nine years really working alone. And that was very scary. I walked in the door at ABC, and Marcy was in charge of prime time series. And I was officially working for her. Marcy had an extremely relaxed work style. She is a very unusual person. She's the least buttoned-up person of any executive I have ever worked with. I don't think I've ever

seen her in a suit or any of the things that you think of women executives in. And at that time she had a playpen in her office and she had just had her second child. And she used to bring him to work a lot. And this was extremely unusual in 1979. And I had a 10-year-old. And after a while my daughter started coming and doing homework at my office and felt very comfortable there. You knew all the other executives. And it was a very familial atmosphere, which was all Marcy's doing. Considering it was a corporate situation—networks are traditionally even more corporate than studios. And Marcy really was able to bring her own personal style to ABC in those days.

Obviously, Barbara was initially attracted to Marcy as a potential mentor because of their shared family values. For a working woman, encountering another working woman who at that time had the power to make family important was a fantastic find. Not only did Marcy hold similar values, as a boss she had many important mentor qualities. In other words, while some bosses mentor, not all do. Research shows that boss mentoring relationships are not available to all employees. In fact, only a select group of individuals have bosses who also work in a mentoring capacity.[8] Bosses who mentor spend time developing employees though successively more challenging assignments, and eventually develop a great loyalty to those employees who do succeed. Barbara described how Marcy encouraged her to take risks that sometimes could have led to failure. As Barbara recalled:

> Marcy was . . . a very important mentor to me because she really gave me the flexibility to fail. She was the first person who ever said to me [that] development is about failure. If you're lucky, you're going to get one show that's going to make it. The rest of it is just development. That's what the word *development* is. So you can't allow yourself to be tied up in knots about every single decision that you make. You have to be willing to fail.
>
> You have to be willing to put yourself out there. Because you're not going to get something different, new, unusual, interesting, exciting, whatever, unless you're willing to put yourself out there. The minute you start holding yourself back and self-censoring, this stuff is going to be all the same and all boring.
>
> And so that was a very, very key thing if you're in a development job in the entertainment business. It doesn't matter if you're in movies or television, that is an extremely key thing.

Risk taking is very important in creative environments; however, that doesn't mean that all bosses are comfortable with risky decisions, especially from all employees. Building a trusting relationship based on mutual respect between boss and subordinate through successful risk taking is just one of the ways a boss relationship turns into a mentoring relationship. Barbara also reflected on other lessons she learned from Marcy and passed on to others as she mentored:

> The second key thing that she taught me, which I have passed on to dozens of people who have worked for me over the years, is that you're only in the chair for a short time, that you're kind of a renter, you're not an owner. And that people are coming to you not because of you, but they're coming to you because of the position that you hold and that they're going to still be doing what they do when the next person is in that job. So you have to have a sense of yourself. You have to have a strong ego and a strong sense of self to realize that these people are not your best friends. This is your business situation. And no matter how many people take you to lunch or dinner or buy you things or send you flowers or give you basketball tickets or whatever, the minute you leave, they're going to be doing that to the next person. It's not about you, it's about the job.
>
> And that is an enormously important lesson. And truthfully it's an important lesson in any job. I mean, I'm the chair of this department. I have a hundred faculty working for me. And I have 600 students in my department. And they're in and out of here all day long. And I get to say yes and no to a lot of things, but believe me, next fall when I'm not in this job anymore, I'll be lucky to get a hello in the hall from the same people.

The question might be, Why did Marcy take the time to mentor Barbara in this manner? Marcy saw something in her that took a typical boss-subordinate relationship further into a relationship where Marcy took time to develop Barbara's skills. With similar intensity, Barbara was eager to learn the lessons Marcy offered. The readiness on both sides of the relationship allowed it to develop.

PEER GROUPS

It would also be helpful to examine your peer group and ascertain if there are members of the group who could offer you support or resources. Of course, it is important to consider the same exchange discussed earlier. What complementary skills or resources can you offer? If you can't find direct peers, then what about someone one step ahead?

Louise Wannier, serial entrepreneur, was in a peer mentoring relationship with Henry Yuen when they worked together to found Gemstar. They initially reconnected through Louise's father. Henry had been his graduate student some years earlier, and Louise had met him on a number of occasions. Reconnecting years later, they were immediately drawn to each other because of their complementary skills, and so they entered into a relationship as cofounders in Gemstar, along with four other cofounders, two of whom had also been fellow students at Caltech. Louise reflected on what they offered each other as peer mentors:

> I think we worked very well together partly because I wasn't afraid to say no to him, and he certainly wasn't afraid to say no to me. We would often argue and we always spoke very directly. When I felt strongly, I would say, "We need to do this." When we were negotiating, he was often the "bad cop" to my "good cop." At times I was frustrated because I didn't have the time in my role to sit and think through all of the permutations. I used to get frustrated because he would often send me very long memos, saying many of the things that he had been thinking about, and I would say and feel, "Well I haven't had the time to get there." But at the same time, his insights were tremendous, he had an incredible strategic mind, and while he would be pushing in certain directions, at the same time I would be experiencing and drawing my own conclusions directly from the market. So it was very much of a give-and-take. It was a very good working relationship. I think I pushed him to go to places he wouldn't have. I had more business exposure than he had at that point and offered contexts from that as well. I also reached out and helped to bring other key executives into the business.

ORGANIZATION-WIDE INITIATIVES

Your organization may offer access to mentors through formal one-on-one programs, group mentoring efforts, or reverse mentoring programs. Check with your human resources department to see if these are available, because human resources personnel are often tasked to develop formal mentoring programs in organizations. Not all mentoring programs are well advertised—sometimes you have to investigate how or whether you can become designated as high potential. Also, sometimes mentoring programs are part of a management development, executive leadership, or coaching program. You need to find out what the procedure is for getting involved in a program. Reverse mentoring and group mentoring are two forms of mentoring that are often part of organization-wide initiatives.

Recall reverse mentoring. As we mentioned previously, in 1999 GE's Jack Welch introduced an organization-wide initiative to his 600 top managers, urging them to learn about the Internet from younger workers in the organization. He encouraged them to use the technique of reverse mentoring to seek out this knowledge. Although no statistics are available on how many companies use reverse mentoring, a small sample of individuals involved in reverse mentoring relationships provides some hints; 41 percent say reverse mentoring is often used to spread technical knowledge from younger to older workers.[9] As the founder of the magazine *FastCompany* noted somewhat unflatteringly, "It's a situation where the 'old fogies' in an organization realize that by the time you're in your forties and fifties, you're not in touch with the future the same way the young twenty-somethings are. They come with fresh eyes, open minds, and instant links to the technology of our future."[10] Deloitte and Touche began a reverse mentoring program in 2001, which according to participants has provided much insight into what happens in the trenches in their organization. As one manager put it, "The big muckety-mucks sometimes lose connection with the crowd and forget what it's like to be out in the trenches."[11] Procter & Gamble is another company recognizing the benefits of reverse mentoring. Chief information officer (CIO) Steve David—who is "a 30-plus-year veteran of the company and a longtime mentoring advocate"—sought out a mentoring relationship with a younger staff scientist to understand more about how science affects the company's business decisions.[12] We also found out that IBM regards its reverse mentoring program as critical in acquainting top management with the younger generation's views on technology and the Internet. If you are a protégé in search of a mentor, you might ask whether your organization has a reverse mentoring program; if it does not, you could suggest that they begin one. As you can imagine, this is a great way for a young protégé to establish contact with an executive.

Other companies utilize company-sponsored programs that focus on group mentoring. We previously mentioned the efforts at Cisco, including lunches in which Larry Carter mentored groups of individuals. As a companywide initiative, more companies report attempts at using the technique. For example, the Chubb Group of Insurance Companies developed such a program in 2001. Another firm that has operated a group mentoring program with much success is Budco, a marketing services and distribution outsourcing company that works with General Motors and Disney. It appears that the specifics of group mentoring may vary from company to company, and a protégé should evaluate whether the goals and outcomes of the group mentoring program meet their career needs. To take advantage of group mentoring, of course you first need to determine if your company currently has a program. If not, proposing a program after doing a little research into what has worked well in other companies would be useful. For example, some group mentoring programs are composed of groups of peers mentors, others include individuals at various ranks, and still others feature mentoring efforts such as the "lunches with Larry" mentioned earlier, which allow employees to meet with a top-level executive to gain insight into the workings of the organization. According to one article, for the group setting to work, there must be a commitment to the program by management, clear expectations on the part of mentors and mentees, and explicit program objectives.[13]

VIRTUAL COMMUNITIES

If you are not fortunate enough to have direct access to mentors in your immediate circle, we encourage you to turn to virtual communities. There are a large number of established e-mentoring programs for such diverse jobs as nurse, educator, scientist, public relations professional, and academic. Chances are there is an e-mentor who would suit your needs. Check out your professional organizations and communities for leads on e-mentoring programs as well. You may also find it helpful to join chat rooms and listservs, which may lead you to individuals who can become spontaneously developed e-mentors. As we mentioned in Chapter Two, e-mentoring can offer many of the same advantages as face-to-face mentoring and even offers distinct advantages (for example, greater access, reduced costs, equalization of status, decreased emphasis on demographics, and a record of interactions).[14] Like some of our colleagues, we have given our students the assignment of connecting with an e-mentor for the past several years, and this assignment has been very successful and yielded many positive results.[15]

For examples of online mentoring programs, check out MentorNet (www.mentornet.org), which pairs women undergraduates and graduate students with professionals in science, technology, engineering, and math. MentorNet is a nonprofit organization whose mission is to further women's progress in scientific and technical fields through a dynamic, technology-supported mentoring program and to advance women and society by developing a diversified, expanded, and talented workforce. Since 1998, more than 23,000 individuals have participated in MentorNet's e-mentoring program. Many corporations—including Intel, Hewlett-Packard, and Microsoft—have found e-mentoring programs such as MentorNet to be beneficial. The mentors who participate develop important job-related skills and their relationships with their young protégés serve as a pipeline for future talent.[16] Another formal online mentoring program, the International Telementoring program, also found that their participating protégés reported improved self-confidence and motivation to succeed as a result of being e-mentored.[17]

A search of online communities may lead you to another type of mentoring we mentioned in Chapter Two: for-hire mentoring. If you are entrepreneurial, check out venture capital groups and incubators for good sources of mentors for hire. These individuals can provide all types of advice regarding start-up venture concerns, whether it be making connections with the right group to help an idea flourish or to review an existing business plan. Many of these organizations can take an entrepreneur through the entire process of getting a start-up venture up and running.

COMPETITORS

In addition to looking close to home and in the virtual world, look far away for potential sources of power mentors. Ask yourself whom among your main competitors you most admire and respect. Is there a person or group that you find yourself on the opposite side of the fence from, but with whom it would be helpful to form alliances—as Congresswoman Solis and Councilwoman Judy Chu did? Are there mentors across barriers who can be helpful to you? In today's volatile political environment, we often hear of the extreme partisanship that can create professional barriers and make it harder to get things done. U.S. Representative David Dreier, although a loyal Republican, spoke eloquently about the importance of finding a mentor across barriers in terms of his Democratic colleagues:

> I just ran into a Democratic colleague of mine, Grace Napolitano. She's also been a mentor to me. That's one of the things in relationships that you have with people. I like to learn from them. This is a woman whose husband died of alcoholism when he was 45. She grew up in abject poverty. A Mexican American woman in Brownsville, Texas, she came out to California and was elected the mayor of Norwalk, then served in the State Assembly, and now is a member of Congress. I like to learn from people who have backgrounds that are much different from mine. Completely different. So in many ways, you know I told her this too, I said, you know, you have a fascinating life perspective, which I don't have and would never have, so I consider it learning. At the same time, I have been able to help her, so it is really a two-way street too.

David actively sought out someone different from himself, and in some respects, a direct competitor, from a different political party. The strategy he used in connecting with Grace is one he has employed in many other situations in order to learn from others in Congress across political lines. He says he was never afraid to ask others for help. He remembers asking lots of questions when he got to Congress. He sought out the answers where he could even if it meant approaching competitors. Today he mentors others across party lines in the same way he was mentored. He feels that the benefits are immeasurable.

MENTORS OF THE MOMENT

Among the many ways to find a mentor, there is also the situation in which you and a potential mentor find one another for just a short period of time. Finding a mentor of the moment often has an element of serendipity. The key is to be mindful of mentoring moments or opportunities when they arise. Oprah Winfrey says,

"Luck is opportunity meets preparation; be ready when it happens." This obviously applies to mentors of the moment. Mentors of the moment often appear during short-term, intense work assignments—an opportunity will present itself to get to know someone or make an impression, and it take extra time or effort just when you think you can ill afford it, but do it anyway. Watch for these mentor-of-the-moment openings in your career—they can change your life!

Ron Kirk, former mayor of Dallas and former Democratic U.S. senatorial candidate from Texas, considers himself both lucky and smart. Lucky in that people offer to help him and smart because he knows when to accept their help. Here is a man who is one of the friendliest people you could ever meet. What is the payoff? People flock to his doors. Not because they want something, but because they want to give him something. Maybe these are people he has helped in the past, or he might help in the future. He told the story of becoming mayor of Dallas and immediately receiving unsolicited phone calls from the former mayor of Atlanta, Maynard H. Jackson, and Henry Cisneros, former Secretary of Housing and Urban Development in the Clinton administration. These individuals just wanted to give advice on some of the challenges he might face as mayor:

> Maynard would call me and just say, "How's it going? I was born in Dallas. I never dreamed I'd see this. But you can do this." And when I won, the Sunday after the election, the first phone call I got was from Maynard Jackson, congratulating me, but also saying, "Okay, you might as well accept—ain't nothing you can do about it. Just accept the fact no matter what you do, you ain't going to be black enough for everybody. No matter what you do, you know, you're not going to do enough." And then Henry Cisneros called me every day for two weeks. Every day. Henry Cisneros, who was a wildly popular mayor [of San Antonio], had already broken a barrier before I did [having been the first mayor of Hispanic descent in a major city]. I mean this guy's saying, "You realize you won by the same percentage as I did. Best I can tell, you got this percentage of the black vote and you got an opportunity"—but they had been there.

Ron Kirk did not have long-term relationships with these individuals, but as soon as he became mayor, he was offered lots of advice. He could have chosen to ignore the wisdom of these powerful individuals, but instead he understood that people who come into one's life from time to time offer many important lessons. As a protégé, he knew that these mentors were to be listened to, and he did just that.

INSPIRATIONAL MENTORS

And finally, we recommend that everyone find an inspirational mentor. Your potential pool of inspirational mentors is particularly broad, because it is not necessary to have a personal relationship with them. The best way to find an inspirational mentor is to read, go to professional events, and figure out whose message and style qualify them as your personal work hero or heroine. Then find out as much as you can about this person. He or she can be your inspirational mentor from afar or up close, but their message and vision should give clarity to your own pursuits. Leeza Gibbons, executive producer and TV and radio personality, recalled her process of identifying and eventually meeting her inspirational mentors:

> I recall being so inspired when Barbara Walters made news by being the first woman (I believe) to get a million-dollar contract. I told my friends at school that I wanted to be like that. She had redefined what was possible. Barbara Walters still leads the way for many and is a powerful example of what hard work, big dreams, talent, and heart will get you. After I became established in the business I wrote her a heartfelt fan letter. I just needed her to know that I was profoundly affected by her work and example. She replied and encouraged me. A warm handwritten note. A small thing? Not on your life. It was tangible evidence that good things happen to good people and it validated my "hero-worship" of her. Same thing for Oprah. I was at the Oscars one year when Oprah and I found ourselves outside one of the after-parties. At that time I was executive producing and hosting my own talk show. The afternoon television schedule then was crowded with talk shows, but much of it was exploitive and tawdry. Oprah approached me and said, "Keep doing what you're doing. You and I are doing it the way it should be done." It was so generous of her to put me in her company, and I heard her voice whisper in my ear many times before I would go out on the stage to tackle a show. A few other times she has sent me notes of congratulations and support. From these two outrageously successful women I learned that generosity of spirit is key. I rarely

miss an opportunity to make a call, write a note, or take the effort to support and encourage those whose path I share or those who are coming up next.

A number of the individuals interviewed in our study could name many people they admired. They took the time to read about these people through biographies or other means. They paid particular attention to the ways the inspirational mentor handled his or her own career, how they dealt with adversity, and how they related to others. Studying the inspirational mentor's life was a useful way to learn from wildly successful individuals with whom they might never come into contact.

In summary, then, there are many different ways and places in which a protégé can seek out a power mentor. Finding a power mentor differs from finding a traditional mentor, because power mentoring may not involve a typical one-on-one relationship. Power mentoring offers a broad array of choices, so you should be ready to take advantage of the diverse opportunities that arise.

CONCLUSION

In this chapter, we have given you a number of suggestions on how to get and keep a power mentor. We have discussed the importance of building a foundation of trust, setting goals, and managing impressions, and we have also provided a number of overall suggestions. Here we distill the important ideas down to three key questions:

1. *Are you willing to ask for help and take the advice and feedback offered?* One thing we heard again and again from our mentors that really fried them was that sometimes their protégés completely disregarded their advice or got defensive during a feedback session. Obviously, we are not suggesting that you become a "Stepford protégé" who blindly does whatever your mentor suggests. But we are suggesting that you keep an open mind, try to take the mentor's suggestions seriously, and then communicate with your mentor about any concerns you may have.

2. *Can you demonstrate your initiative in managing your own career?* One study showed that individuals who engaged in general career self-management had more positive and worthwhile mentoring relationships than others did.[18] In the interviews we conducted for

this project, the protégés had given a lot of thought to the character of the relationships they had with their mentors. They had thought specifically about their own strengths and weaknesses, what they wanted to improve on, and how their mentor could help their career. In other words, they had fairly clear career goals. In our interviews we found that as one advanced in his or her career, it was especially important to take the next step by having a plan and setting career-advancement goals.

3. *What can you do right now to make yourself as attractive as possible to a potential mentor?* You may want to go back to the previous chapter and consult the list of what makes a protégé attractive (intelligence, ambition, desire and ability to accept power and risk, initiative, energy, trustworthiness, integrity, high emotional intelligence, optimism, and complementary skills). We suggest that you determine not only how much of each characteristic you have, but to what extent you must signal to a potential mentor that you possess these characteristics. If you feel you are lacking in one or more areas, we suggest you look to other people you admire for these characteristics, then work on ways to emulate their values and behavior. Find situations in which you can demonstrate or practice these characteristics. Think about how you can be seen as trustworthy, and what you can do to "impression manage" in a way that feels positive and natural for you.

In the next chapter, we focus on bringing the mentor and protégé together and on ways they can deepen their relationship. We borrow ideas from those who have written about other types of interpersonal relationships (such as marriage) to suggest new strategies that both the mentor and protégé can use to develop a deeply productive and satisfying relationship.

CHAPTER SIX

UNLOCKING THE SECRETS OF GREAT POWER MENTORING RELATIONSHIPS

*I think mentors are important and I don't think anybody
makes it in the world without some form of mentorship.
Nobody makes it alone. Nobody has made it alone. And we
are all mentors to people even when we don't know it.*
—OPRAH WINFREY

Oprah Winfrey is an amazing person. She has built a career that not only has made her one of the richest people in the world, but according to *Time* magazine in 1998, in the opinion of many people, one of the most influential people of the 20th century.[1] Why do others consider her so influential? One might speculate that her ability to influence others comes from the respect people have for her actions. She is seen as strong, generous, kind, and caring. According to another poll, Oprah was the person most often mentioned when individuals were asked whom they would like to sit next to on an airplane flight.[2] One of Oprah's secrets to success is the ability to connect with people, all different types of people. People who are around her love to be near her. She also takes time to mentor others and realizes what the important ingredients in these relationships are. Someone such as Dr. Phil McGraw, the psychologist Oprah sponsored as a feature of her regular talk show, knows how important her mentoring was in making it possible for him to land his own daytime talk show.

Think of the many relationships you have in your life. You are in relationships with your immediate family, your extended family, your significant other and/or friends, your bosses, your coworkers, and possibly even with your work organization's customers and suppliers. You may also be a member of a club or community group, and perhaps you are involved in virtual relationships via e-mail or through your own personal blog (an electronic journal posted to the Internet for all to read). Now think about the quality of these relationships. Some of the relationships are so good that in fact sometimes you feel as though the other person can read your mind. In other words, they "get you" and know what you are all about. They comfort you and defend you even when you reveal the not-so-good side of yourself to the world. Some of the relationships you have may be less deep or maybe just not as important to you, but nevertheless you must maintain them. The mark of great relationships lies in giving each person in the relationship an opportunity to grow and expand in his or her own right.

Some people find themselves consistently in great-quality relationships; other people, however, find that some relationships are harder to maintain than others. Why it is that some relationships just don't work? It may be a lack of personal chemistry, or one person may not be comfortable in the relationship. Perhaps something in the history of the relationship has caused difficulties; alternatively, differing expectations about the roles in the relationships may have led to a decision to move apart. Whatever the cause, ensuring that relationships do not take a turn for the worse is important.

Mentoring relationships have much in common with the other types of relationships people experience. Mentoring relationships consist of many of the same ingredients, go through similar developmental phases, and present many of the same challenges. Power mentoring relationships present additional complexities. For example, in a power mentoring relationship, a protégé may have to manage more than one relationship, or a network of relationships. Often the stakes are higher for both parties in power mentoring relationships than in other mentoring relationships. Power mentors have a lot to lose if the relationship does not go well. They run the risk of being seen as a poor judge of talent if their protégés do not live up to their high expectations. Backing someone in an organization who turns out to be a less than stellar performer is risky. For the protégé, an inadequate mentor can cause many problems. Bad advice, career opportunities, or interpersonal problems such as abusiveness or sabotage could result from a rocky relationship.

In this chapter we dissect the nature of mentoring relationships to give mentors and protégés some specific ideas for enhancing their relationships with one another. In the following pages,

- We provide answers to the question, How does one bring a power mentoring relationship to its full potential from the perspective of both the mentor and the protégé?
- We give you an overview of the building blocks of other effective relationships (for example, high-quality marriages and friendships) and suggest parallels to power mentoring.
- You will learn about the role of defining moments in power mentoring relationships. A defining moment can be the point at which the protégés in successful relationships understand that the relationship has in fact taken off and is now characterized by a high level of trust and reciprocal benefits. A defining moment can also be a situation or challenge that emerges that causes the nature of the relationship to substantially change.
- We also provide many examples of how one deepens reciprocity in relationships. We spend time reviewing effective communication practices that incorporate the tools of emotional intelligence in the relationships.
- Because power mentoring often includes multiple mentors, we also spend time discussing how to manage these multiple relationships and how to know when to bring other people into your mentoring network.

BUILDING BLOCKS OF EFFECTIVE RELATIONSHIPS

What is a relationship? Or, in other words, what does it mean when someone says they have a relationship with another person? The very nature of interpersonal relationships has been of interest to philosophers and psychologists for many years. As social animals, humans are involved in many relationships, and one might say that these relationships form the basis of all human interaction, making up the fabric of society itself. Relationship researchers have been interested in how one person forms a bond over time with another person in what they call *close relationships*. Researchers who study various types of close relationships have uncovered the many different factors that affect the quality of relationships, including intimacy or connectedness, passion, and commitment.[3]

Even though you may not consider the relationship with your postal carrier as being very intimate, it is a relationship nevertheless. One way to think of how relationships differ is in the degree of social closeness, or what researchers call *intimacy*. You are unlikely to be socially close to your postal carrier. You do, however, experience a higher level of closeness to your work group members, and a still higher level of closeness to a significant other.

This closeness or intimacy can vary in intensity, frequency, or both. For example, closeness is often related to the level of self-disclosure that occurs in the relationship, how much trust is involved (both how much you trust the other person and how much they trust you), and the emotional intensity of the topics you might discuss (that is, whether they include the everyday "How's the weather," versus "This is what I'm thinking about doing with my career"). Self-disclosure often intensifies a relationship because of the mutual level of risk. If one person discloses something personal, it signals that she has a level of comfort with the person in whom she has confided. If the other person reciprocates by revealing something personal, then the first person feels they have both risked something. Closeness may also be dictated by the frequency with which you interact with one another. Typically, people consider themselves closer to those with whom they speak more often. However, in some cases, the level of closeness may be independent to some extent of the frequency of contact, and people may feel very close despite having little contact. This may be the result of a deep bond that has developed over time. As one of our friends puts it, "No matter how long it's been since I last spoke with you, I know when we talk again, we'll pick up where we left off." The intensity of the relationship at this point is independent of frequency of contact.

Through our interviews, we found that intimacy and commitment—and to some extent passion—were important components of mentoring relationships, though there were major differences depending on the profession. By intimacy or connectedness we mean the level of self-disclosure, the level of trust, and the interdependence of the relationship. We talk about self-disclosure as we discuss defining moments and communication practices in relationships, and we follow up on the issue of trust that we discussed in the previous chapter.

What leads to intimacy, passion, and commitment in mentoring relationships? Initial connection, frequent interaction, efforts to increase closeness, and defining moments are the building blocks that lead to effective mentoring relationships. Before we give examples of three building blocks of successful mentoring relationships, take a moment to answer the questions in Exhibit 6.1 about a mentoring relationship you currently have. The statements in the exhibit come from mentors and protégés in our study, who talked about both the good and the not-so-good relationships they may have had with their mentoring partners in the past.

EXHIBIT 6.1   RELATIONSHIP QUESTIONS

Positive Initial Contact and Connection

1. I met my friend doing an activity that we both enjoy.   Yes/No
2. I saw something similar to myself when I began talking to my friend.   Yes/No
3. We bonded over something similar in our backgrounds.   Yes/No

Frequent Interaction

4. Our relationship became closer as we did more things together.   Yes/No
5. We spent time outside of our regular jobs doing things we enjoyed.   Yes/No

Growing Closeness and Connectedness

6. I really felt this person understood me.   Yes/No
7. I shared some of my fears with this person.   Yes/No
8. This person disclosed some personal events to me.   Yes/No
9. I felt supported by this person when I talked about a problem I was having.   Yes/No

Defining Moments

10. There was a specific event that brought us closer.   Yes/No
11. There was a specific occurrence that cemented my trust in this person.   Yes/No

Positive Initial Contact and Connection

In Chapters Four and Five, we discussed the types of factors that attract mentors and protégés to one another. Here we take this concept further and uncover the process that increases the quality of the initial contact and growing bond between protégés and mentors. We found that in fostering an effective relationship, people are initially looking for things they have in common with one another. Growing up in the same type of neighborhood, enjoying the same sorts of television shows, playing the same sports, being interested in the same music, or having the same circle of friends—these are some of the commonalities people might have that make initial conversations easy.

The other personal factor that made for an initial quality interaction was the relationship partners' social skills. Of course, we all know that social skills are important for initiating and maintaining relationships. Take a look in any bookstore, mortar or online, and you will see a slew of books talking about how to strike up a conversation with strangers or how to win people over within just a few moments of meeting them. The social skills that allow us to put other people at ease are quite coveted. There is a story of a painfully shy famous scientist who forced himself to spend a set amount of time every day in a local park striking up a conversation with young women he did not know for the sole purpose (ostensibly) of improving his social skills. Initially his conversations were quite awkward, and the young women walked away; eventually, however, he became good at striking up a conversation, making small talk, and putting people at ease.

In the previous chapter, we related many stories of how our protégés and mentors met one another. Sometimes it was during very simple exchanges, at least from the perspective of one member of the pair. For example, as we mentioned, Dixie Garr and Anthony Hayter's first meeting was over a tray of doughnuts after Dixie gave a talk at a professional gathering that Anthony attended. From her perspective it was a simple conversation about doughnuts. As Anthony remembered:

> Dixie was there, doing what she does best. She was invited to speak by an organization called NSBE, National Society of Black Engineers, during the career fair at my alma mater, Georgia Tech. She'd

spent a little time at the Cisco booth and then gave her motivational talk to the group of students.

And for me, we just happened to be in that little break area at the same time. So we struck up a conversation over a doughnut. I told her I was working as a recruiter for TI [Texas Instruments]. She went, "Ah, I used to work for TI." We both had some history there. And then I told her that my plans were to go work in Dallas and then transfer within the year to San Jose to work for the TI office out there, which happened to be where her Cisco offices were.

According to Anthony, it was more than just a conversation over doughnuts. From there, the two bonded over their similar work experiences at TI and his interest in moving out to San Jose. During our interviews with them, they both spoke fondly of the mutual admiration they have for each other now and of the career advice they share—all after meeting over doughnuts.

What if their initial interaction had unfolded differently? Imagine that instead of continuing the conversation, Anthony had ignored Dixie's offer to make small talk and did nothing with it. One well-known psychologist's work on successful and not-so-successful marriages shows that not recognizing bids for closeness results in major problems in relationships.[4] Those who find their bids for closeness ignored become very hesitant to make bids in the future, and begin to withdraw even in established relationships. Eventually, the overall closeness of their relationships suffers. With respect to mentoring, what does a bid for a relationship look like? Sometimes a mentor will extend a helping hand to a would-be protégé in an effort to see whether the protégé might be interested in being mentored. How that potential protégé responds is very important.

As professors, we both have the opportunity to mentor many students; however, sometimes we are surprised by students who do not respond when we make an overture to mentor them. Of course, it may be that they are truly not interested in our advice, but we believe that some students simply fail to recognize the significance of our mentoring attempt. For example, one of us knew an impressive graduate student who was interested in becoming an executive coach. We e-mailed the student, asking if he would be interested in working for a few hours in a high school leadership program to give one-on-one leadership feedback to students and help them interpret performance feedback, a process that is also involved in executive coaching. Although the group did not include executives, the experience would have given the student hands-on coaching experience, which could have improved his skills and built his résumé. After a week had passed, the student finally e-mailed back, giving a very weak excuse as to why he would be unable to participate. He did not apologize or thank us for considering him for the position. Our bid for closeness within a mentoring relationship was ignored. In fairness, the student may genuinely not have been interested in our mentoring; on the other hand, we had many benefits to offer: access to research opportunities as well as training, consulting, and coaching opportunities. We have had other similar experiences involving students who are very skilled and with whom we have wanted to connect in order to get them involved, but they have not seen our bid for connection. It would be nice if mentors would be clearer and more direct in their mentoring overtures, but often these subtle invitations are part of the initial tests and challenges we mentioned in Chapter Five. The mentor is attempting to discover whether the protégé is a keen observer of subtle invitations.

In making initial contact with Bob Wright, Pamela Thomas-Graham was introduced to him through another common mentor, Jack Welch. Pamela followed Jack's advice and set up the meeting with Bob. She did not necessarily have high expectations for the meeting, because as she said, people often tell you that you must get in touch with so-and-so and you will definitely hit it off, and Pamela recognized that that scenario did not always come to pass. However, as a testament to the high level of social skills that both Pamela and Bob bring to a meeting, in fact their first meeting was characterized by great initial rapport:

> I met him on the 52nd floor of 30 Rock, which is where the NBC executive offices are, and immediately found him very warm and friendly and approachable and very, very smart. I had read about him and knew he was a lawyer. And because he had been running NBC for about 14 years when I met him, he was certainly very well known.
>
> And what was great was just how gracious he was and how approachable he was and how genuinely interested he seemed to be in understanding what I was about. When somebody says you

should meet this person, it's never clear how those conversations are going to go. But I think really right from the start we had a very good rapport and found that we had a lot of things in common, which was very helpful.

I do remember when I first met him how good he made me feel about myself, which is interesting, because in the first interview you generally don't expect this. But I remember one of the first things he said to me was, "It's just really great that there's a person like you out in the business world." And I was really struck by his candor and frankly his willingness to make me feel that good about myself in a job interview. Generally that's not the way that works.

When Bob was asked what he thought when he first met Pamela, he mentioned that what struck him was her poise, confidence, and eagerness to get things going. Had the two of them not had the interpersonal savvy to put each other at ease and to engage in a discussion to further explore the potential mentoring relationship, their first meeting might have gone nowhere. Fortunately, they each brought to the table a portfolio of benefits the other was eager to learn more about, and they presented these benefits in a congenial interpersonal style.

It appears that social savvy and follow-up on bids for mentoring interaction can carry a potential mentoring relationship forward. These skills add to other important relationship starters such as perceived similarity, a complementary skill or perspective, a compelling characteristic or skill, or demonstrated potential or performance, which we discussed in some detail in Chapter Four. However, it is then the responsibility of protégés and mentors to continue to connect, in order to move the relationship forward. Protégés and mentors must recognize bids for closeness and follow-up. Letting a valuable mentoring possibility pass by could be potential career suicide in an organization. Protégés should watch for the offer of mentoring from potential sources and take time to explore the possible fit with that mentor.

FREQUENT INTERACTION

Usually when we're getting to know someone, the time we spend with them allows us to learn more about the person and serves to deepen the relationship. In mentoring relationships, the frequency of interactions has been shown to be related to satisfaction with the relationship, especially in the early stages.[5] This makes a lot of sense. You need to spend time with one another to establish the relationship before anything really can be accomplished.

One way to ensure that relationships are satisfying to the people involved is to make sure that the frequency and intimacy of communication are appropriate. Linda Sanford provided a number of examples of the ways she communicates with her protégés in the organization, realizing of course that IBM is an international corporation. As she noted:

> I mentor a lot more through e-mail clearly, especially if we're geographically dispersed. If you look at officially whose mentor am I, there's probably close to 20. And then informally I have a lot more that both of us understand that it won't be necessarily as regular, but what I say to them is, "Feel free to give me a call, send me a note. If you're wrestling with something in particular, a job change or something personal you're dealing with."
>
> One of my mentees is in Japan right now. So when she comes here, I go there, we try to get connected. But usually when she's here I'm out of town. In her case I'll say, "Here's my home number. Call me at home," because of time zone difference and everything else.
>
> I prefer to connect by phone, but sometimes with my travel schedule I don't want that to be the inhibitor. So if I'm just literally on the road, I tell protégés, "Send me a note, and I'll get to you. And if I still need to talk with you person to person, we'll get something scheduled."

Linda Sanford also talked about how the type of communication depends on different factors in the relationship. For example, with people she has known for a while, she needs to put in a little less effort in their communication. As she put it when talking about her protégé Charles Lickel:

> I think it stems back from the fact that our basic fundamental leadership styles are similar in so many ways that I can start a sentence and he can finish it or vice versa. I don't have to do sometimes the extensive dialogue.
>
> With somebody who I know has a very different approach, well, I have to make sure I'm being clear about what I want, what I need,

or what my expectations are. I can have a two-second conversation with Charles because he knows exactly where I'm going.

As we talked to a number of our mentors and protégés, we found that there needed to be something in the relationship for both of them that would cause them to interact in the early stages. As the relationship developed, they may have contacted one another less often, but the intimacy and closeness that they had built early on helped sustain them so that when they spoke again, they often had fond memories of their previous interactions. For example, Diane Robina spoke about some of her first impressions of her relationship with Anne Sweeney, remembering Anne's lessons about the business:

> It was also a business when we kind of first came into it, it was just really changing over from being an all-male bastion. Women started to come into the marketplace of the television business. And there was a lot of partying and drinking. Especially if you're meeting people internationally, such as doing business with people from France for dinner, you can't not drink. But Anne would mention, "These are not your friends. These are people you're doing business with." And I still remember when we go to markets and I'm taking someone new, reminding myself again, this is business; these are not your friends. Always be conscious of that when you're at a dinner table or having a conversation at lunch.

It was those lessons that propelled their relationship. Anne was candid and gave Diane good advice that guided her throughout her career.

Unfortunately, in many of the mentoring relationships we studied, it was difficult for the mentor and protégé to have frequent meetings because of the high-intensity nature of their jobs. We initially had a question in our interview protocol asking the mentors and protégés to reflect on what they did for fun. Only a handful could answer that question, because most of their time spent together was work related. However, usually in the context of describing their defining moments with each other, some did talk about the importance of moving a relationship to more intimate territory (for example, dinner at each other's houses, a long business trip, and so on). It appears that for power mentoring relationships, the quality and not the quantity of interactions is most important for building a close relationship. Quality interactions appeared to be more goal directed and quite candid in their content. We turn to more examples of quality interactions in the next section.

GROWING CLOSENESS AND CONNECTEDNESS

Intimacy has been defined as a sharing of innermost feelings and thoughts in an atmosphere of caring, trust, and acceptance.[6] Intimacy in mentoring relationships must be both with oneself and with the other in the relationship. To have an effective relationship, the protégé must be aware of his or her own inner feelings and needs, or must experience self-awareness, and then a sharing of these feelings and needs through self-disclosure must take place.

SELF-DISCLOSURE

The following story of Ron Kirk and Ann Richards illustrates the level of closeness and intimacy that develops in a mentoring relationship. One of Ron Kirk's biggest fans early in his career was the former governor of Texas, Ann Richards. When he was an undergraduate at the University of Texas at Austin, he took a break, against his father's better judgment, and spent time in Austin working for the legislature, where he became acquainted with Ms. Richards. It was there that he found his passion for politics. Throughout his career she has appeared in his life to ask him to take the next step—whether it be to serve as her Secretary of State, as the mayor of Dallas, or eventually to challenge the Republican candidate for the vacant seat of Senator Phil Gramm. As their relationship progressed, they shared very personal stories. For example, she shared with him many of her struggles related to her very public divorce and bout with alcoholism. This level of self-disclosure made their relationship much closer.

INTIMACY OVER TIME

Intimacy is not immediate; it takes time to develop. Anthony Hayter, a protégé of Dixie Garr while he was at Texas Instruments [Dixie was already at Cisco], talked about how their relationship increased in closeness. He actually could pinpoint the time at which he felt they became more than mentor and protégé: "It was the time Dixie had me over to her house. We had maybe a couple of lunches prior to that, where I'd tell her about my wife and about the times I'm having, good or bad, with work. And she says, 'Anthony, we should have you guys over.' And the first time we were over at Dixie's we had a great time. And that was really the point where our relationship matured into a wonderful friendship."

Anthony and Dixie's relationship had come a long way, beginning with their conversation over doughnuts when she came to give a speech at his college, and moving ahead when he worked at Texas Instruments, to where she now works with him on projects from her job at Cisco. Many relationships show this natural progression over time. The question one might ask, though, is whether the individuals in the relationship can "hurry the relationship along," so to speak. In other words, what techniques would help the relationship progress to higher levels of intimacy more quickly? The old song, "You Can't Hurry Love"—sung by Diana Ross and the Supremes—might hold some truth in this situation. The song goes on to say that you have to wait, because love is a game of give-and-take. This sentiment probably makes sense for mentoring relationships (except for the love part!). Mentoring relationships that progress too quickly might leave the mentor or protégé feeling uncomfortable, if there has not been enough effort spent getting to know one another and self-disclosing information.

SHARING ONE'S INTERESTS

But what does intimacy and closeness look like once it is achieved? It is really about the sharing of interests. For example, when Barbara Corday talked about her relationship with Barbara Avedon, she emphasized the important bonds they formed:

> The mentorship that Barbara gave me then was twofold and could not have been more important to me in either case. Because on the one hand, she gave me life lessons in political activism, which I knew nothing about and had never done any of before. And we went to Washington, and we lobbied. And I was doing things that I never had thought about doing before.
>
> And then we began a nine-year writing partnership. A nine-year partnership in anything is pretty unusual, including marriage. And second, being partners with somebody whom you have become so close to and become even closer with over the years I think is an incredibly special thing. We knew every morning when we woke up we were going to see each other that day, we were going to spend

the day together, we were going to be talking about life and our kids and our husbands and our world and our mothers or whatever. I think all that came out in our writing.

So it was an enormously important relationship for me, because not only did I have an older woman who was my best friend and my confidant, but she really taught me how to write for television. She taught me everything.

Some people say that men bond in different ways, not so much through talk, but in the process of doing things together.[7] General Lee Butler shared the following story of a project he and his protégé Donald Pettit collaborated on, and of how they got acquainted through all the travel they did together:

Don's one of the most skilled people I've ever known. He helped me build a deck on our townhouse in Alexandria, Virginia. We spent a very happy two or three months one summer. But those kinds of things we did very naturally together.

Of course we were in each other's company all the time. It was his job to make all the travel arrangements. We were in airplanes, staff cars, and hotels. And so, we were constant companions. And it was always pleasurable. We had our little things. When we would get to our frequent destination at Bolling Air Force Base in Washington, D.C., we'd go straight to the Burger King and get our hamburger and fries, our little rituals and things.

Don and Lee's closeness came from interactions that were normal, everyday kinds of things they did as they traveled together. They built closeness from mundane sorts of interactions rather than from a more goal-directed mentoring relationship. What's important to note from these different stories of intimacy and closeness is that people in the mentoring relationships did what they felt was right for them in achieving closeness. In other words, there is no one right way to build closeness.

DIFFERENT DEGREES OF COMFORT WITH CLOSENESS

Unfortunately, people do not go into relationships with the same desire for closeness. Many psychologists have attempted to explain differences in how much closeness people want in relationships through a number of theories. One of the more interesting theories, called *attachment theory*, claims that individuals form a pattern of attachment very early in their lives through their attachment to their mothers or primary caregivers; this pattern is played out throughout their lives.[8] In keeping with these early attachment styles, some people later avoid close attachments altogether, while others may take longer to develop close attachments, and still others may jump into relationships rapidly, with a high level of trust of others. We could see different propensities for closeness in our study, but for the most part, given that these individuals were known for their successful mentoring relationships, few were hesitant to form close bonds with others. Our advice, however, to would-be protégés and mentors is to think about the level of comfort you have with close relationships. Making that clear to yourself will help you in forming the types of mentoring relationships in which you can feel comfortable with others. You might also think about the lessons we discussed in Chapter Four on how protégés can show potential mentors that they are in fact trustworthy.

LEVEL OF RELATIONSHIP INTERDEPENDENCE

A final consideration in the development of intimacy and connectedness in a relationship has to do with the structure of the relationship with respect to interdependence. In some relationships the outcomes of one person are strongly affected by the behavior of the other. This idea refers to the interdependence in the close relationship. Researchers find that there are three ways in which people partner in relationships. The first is as equals, the second is where one dominates, and the third is where people take turns dominating depending on the context.[9] In other words, a division of labor emerges in the relationship in order to achieve common goals.

For example, Lee Butler, retired U.S. Air Force General, described the relationship he had with Donald Pettit as being very egalitarian, even though they differed in rank: "The relationship that Don and I developed, at some levels like that of General Brown and myself, [was] that I always treated Don completely as an equal."

The relationships we surveyed in our study varied in terms of the kind of interdependence exhibited between the pair. These forms map somewhat back onto the mental models of mentoring we introduced in Chapter Four. For example, the mentor with a master-mentor mentality may be very interdependent with his or her protégés. Those who have a more pragmatic view of mentoring relationships may show less interdependence; instead the mentor may dominate. The level of interdependence in the dyad is also important to consider as the mentoring relationship progresses. Each mentor will have a different idea about the nature of the relationship that will affect how closeness and goals are achieved. You might also expect that a relationship may go through phases, in which it begins as more asymmetrical and moves into a more equal status; moreover, one party or the other may be dominant, depending on the context. It's important to be aware of these differences and to discuss them as the relationship progresses, so that there are no misunderstandings.

Intimacy is an important component of close relationships. It can be built from a positive initial connection, followed by getting together frequently enough to self-disclose about one's career hopes and aspirations. Self-disclosure also plays a pivotal role in the defining moments of many of our relationships—the subject of the next section of the chapter.

DEFINING MOMENTS

Intimacy can be hastened, sometimes serendipitously, by a defining moment. The concept of a defining moment is an important part of the leadership and career development literature. In their book *Geeks and Geezers,* Warren Bennis and Robert Thomas discuss defining moments as crucible moments that occur during the life of a leader.[10] A *defining moment* is typically an intense transformational experience that can and often does change one's life, for better or worse. In fact, connecting with a mentor was defined as one of the four types of crucible moments for the leaders in this book, along with a period of enforced reflection, insertion into a foreign territory, or disruption or loss. Another collection of interviews with leaders revealed the following defining moments: criminal indictments; serious, high-profile product failure; a 50 percent stock price drop in a 24-hour period; or an embarrassing or stupid event.[11] "I did not have sex with that woman" encapsulated a defining moment for former President Bill Clinton, who up until the Lewinsky scandal had enjoyed a robust approval rating. Like Clinton, most managers encounter defining moments in their careers and in their mentoring relationships. Defining moments can be caused directly by one's own behavior, or they can force people to respond to situations that are completely out of their control.

Defining moments among our power mentors and protégés were associated with a high degree of trust and intimacy, and the successful resolution of a problem or support during a defining moment brought the mentor and protégé closer together. However it happens, a defining moment can be a true test of an individual's character and of the strength of a relationship. We found that defining moments in mentoring centered around six types of experiences: (1) setting an expectation, (2) helping with work-family balance, (3) responding positively to a personal revelation (self-disclosure), (4) providing advice given during a critical juncture, (5) delivering critical feedback, and (6) giving unconditional support during a crisis. In the following section we provide examples of each of these experiences in the hope that when defining moments arise in your mentoring relationships, you will be prepared. You may want to bear in mind the following questions as you consider the defining moments described here.

- Would your mentor or protégé be an ally during a defining moment, or would they disappoint you?
- If you have already had a defining moment, how was it similar to and different from those mentioned here?
- And most important to consider, what did you learn from your defining moment with your mentor or protégé, and how did it affect your relationship and career?

Typically, defining moments occur in the context of more established relationships; however, they can also be a catalyst for getting a relationship off the ground. In this case, a mentor sets expectations for a protégé. We heard several examples of this in our interviews. This idea of setting expectations works much like the positive Pygmalion effect—or a self-fulfilling prophecy—in the sense that if someone else believes in you, you are more likely to believe in yourself.[12] This effect has been well documented in the social-psychological literature in populations ranging from schoolchildren to adults. Have you ever had the feeling when confronted with a new task that "I can't do that; I'm not ready; I'm not worthy"? But if you have someone like a mentor who tells you, "Yes you can; you are ready; you are worthy," it gives you confidence and can completely change your mindset. For several of our interviewees, this sense of readiness and worthiness was instilled by setting an expectation of greatness for one's protégé. Ron Dellums, former congressman, shared the following experience: "Dr. Lewis Watts, my mentor, called me in his office when I was working in San Francisco, and said, 'I want you to read this book,' *The Shoes of the Fisherman*. He said, 'Prepare yourself to lead because I see you as a leader.' He told me this is a story about the loneliness of leadership, and you need to prepare yourself on the one hand for the loneliness, and you need to understand how to fight against isolation in the role of leadership."

One of the most challenging aspects of work life today is the critical balancing act between work and family. In the past decade alone, U.S. workers have added 58 hours per year to their work schedules.[13] A survey by TrueCareers reports that 70 percent of workers feel they have no balance between their work life and home life.[14] While 70 percent of mothers with children under 18 are in the labor force, and whereas only about 13 percent of married couples with children consisted of families in which only the husband worked outside the home, 31 percent were dual-income families with children.[15] Moreover, those without children also have a number of family relationships and important extracurricular relationships that must be balanced with work. A recent research study suggests that employees involved in mentoring relationships had reduced work-family conflict.[16] Some evidence suggests that many women are leaving the confines of corporate America because of a lack of support for work-family balance, representing a significant loss of resources for corporate America. High-profile cases like those of Brenda Barnes and Karen Hughes exemplify this trend. Brenda Barnes currently is president and COO of the Sara Lee Corporation. She took a five-year leave of absence from corporate America to spend time raising her children. Karen Hughes, former press secretary for George W. Bush, has worked on and off for the administration, citing the need to spend time with her family as the reason for her breaks. However, she retains her relationship with President Bush as she recently played an active role as an advisor during his 2004 election and in March 2005 took a position in the State Department as Undersecretary of State for Public Diplomacy.

The birth of a child is often a defining moment not only personally, but also professionally. A mentor can help one balance this competing demand with a bit more grace and dexterity. Diane Robina recollected her defining moment with her mentor Anne Sweeney, and how it not only alleviated some of her work-family balance issues but also brought the two women much closer. As Diane related:

> The defining moment for me, which is what made me become loyal to Anne, is when I went on maternity leave with my first kid. We were launching a new network and it was probably the world's worst baby timing. We were running two networks and I went on maternity leave. And Anne called me, and I told her, "I can't find anyone to take care of the kids." She called me back the next day. And she said, "I just talked to my old nanny who had worked for me for four or five years. She's going to quit her job in Connecticut. She's coming to work for you. And she makes *X* amount of dollars, and I'm giving you a raise for that amount."

While work-family balance is definitely a challenge, it is an issue that can be openly addressed, because the experience of having children is socially acceptable and even socially desirable. However, what about personal situations that are less common or perhaps less socially acceptable in the mainstream? Like being gay or lesbian in corporate America? This was the case for Linda Sanford and her protégé, Charles Lickel, at IBM. It is estimated that gays and lesbians represent approximately 10 percent of the population, yet in many cases this group is still a hidden minority. Federally, gays and lesbians have few rights and little recourse against discrimination. Although some corporations—and states—have provided protection, by and large discrimination against gays goes unchecked. The stress of staying in the closet can decrease productivity and be a detriment to positive work relationships. It is no wonder that Charles Lickel stayed in the closet for the first 16 years he was at IBM. He was afraid that IBM was not ready for his openness and that any disclosure would harm his career. When Charles did decide to come out, he first came out to his mentor, Linda Sanford. Both described this as a compelling, defining moment in their relationship. In Linda's words, "With Charles, the defining moment was when he told me that he is gay. It was very, very difficult for him

to do this. And this was back in the 390 world [previous IBM main-
frame] when we were there. And we had built a very strong team.
And I've always respected him, but I think I even respected him
more at that point. Because not only did he tell me; he proceeded
to tell the team in his own way. And then he became a leader in
our diversity group around gays and lesbians."

Charles became a cochair of the gay and lesbian task force and
has been recognized as a top gay and lesbian leader in America.
His efforts brought positive recognition to IBM and helped them
to be seen as a leader on diversity issues.

Linda was able to give Charles important backing and advice
to pursue a leadership position on the diversity task force. Simi-
larly, Ron Dellums described a time when he was able to provide
advice during a critical career juncture and decision point for his
protégé, U.S. Representative Barbara Lee (D-CA), who had served
as Dellums's chief of staff from 1975 to 1987. Lee faced a decision—whether to go with the crowd or follow her heart and
head.[17] The issue was whether to give President George W. Bush
the unilateral authority to declare war after the 9/11 attacks on the
World Trade Center. She was the only one among the 421 members of the House of Representatives who voted no. She received
an outpouring of protest against her decision. Before making that
decision, Dellums gave her the following advice:

> I have never told her how to vote because I didn't think that was
> my role, but we talked every day. What I did say to her was, "How-
> ever you vote, be comfortable with your vote because people will
> sense your comfort or your discomfort and whether you're confi-
> dent in your stance or whether you are not. So be comfortable,
> whether you vote for this or whether you vote against it." Second,
> I told her, whenever I've confronted significant votes in my public
> life, I've always asked myself the following question: "What is in
> the best interest of the children?" And I asked myself that ques-
> tion, Barbara, one, because the children cannot be there to articu-
> late for themselves. And number two, to ask the question, "What
> is in the best interest of the future?" And then we talked analyti-
> cally. What do you think about the issue? I am meticulous in not
> saying, "This is what I think you ought to do." She is my represen-
> tative and my friend. So I approach it in those terms. This is her
> turf now.

In addition to giving advice during a critical juncture, one of the most important services that a mentor can perform for a protégé is to offer critical feedback. Judith Gwathmey recalled a situation when she had to confront a protégé for bad behavior during a conference and how it was a defining moment in their relationship:

> This occurred with a student of mine at a national meeting. I'm walking around during the meeting, and he has his poster. He did the work. He understands it very well. Very smart guy. And then one of my colleagues came up to me and said, "Judy, what is wrong with that student of yours?" I said, "What are you talking about?" "He's rude—he's not going to be invited and have another thing accepted here. He's a maniac." So I went there, and he was being nasty. So I took him aside. I said, "I'll tell you one thing about people who come from our lab. You represent me. And you represent everybody in that lab. And if you are smart, you don't need to shout it from the rooftop." I said, "So either you reflect what I've tried to teach you, or we can go home right now. You can take the poster down and we'll leave this minute."
>
> And I'll never forget what he said to me. He said, "I'm sorry. I thought that's what you wanted me to do." And I said, "Why did you think that?" He said, "Because that's the way they always did it at Johns Hopkins. If someone got up, you're supposed to aggressively shoot them down and fight with them. That's what we were taught." So he was mimicking his mentor. And that's why you must realize that when you get a whole bunch of mentees, in an environment who had that kind of mentor, you can understand why we have these problems at MIT for women and these problems at Harvard and bigger schools.

Defining moments played an integral role in the development of intimacy in our power mentoring relationships. These moments seemed to take many forms, but after they had occurred, usually both the mentor and the protégé felt as though the relationship had entered a new phase. Our purpose in sharing a sampling of defining moments from our interviews is to give you some hints on how you can take your own relationships to a new level. But unfortunately, as you can tell from many of the stories we cite, the defining moments cannot be forced. They happen, and as we mentioned earlier, you must be prepared to react accordingly. As we asked before, would your mentor or protégé be an ally during a defining moment, or would they disappoint you? Also, what have you learned from your defining moments with your mentor or protégé, and how did those insights affect your relationship and career? Knowing how to best leverage your defining moments takes skill.

Deepening the Mentoring Relationship

Now that we have introduced you to the building blocks of effective relationships, we would like to give you some specific tips for maintaining a relationship once you have established a good level of closeness. This is because mentoring relationships are similar to other important relationships in your life: they must be tended to reach the full potential for both parties. We have adapted tips for deepening the mentoring relationship from what is known about effective relationships.[18] They include

1. Develop a deep understanding of each other's work environment and issues.
2. Develop a mutual admiration society.
3. Treat each other as confidants instead of as competitors.
4. Be open to your partner's influence and ideas.
5. Help each other to focus on solvable problems.
6. Develop a relationship that is meaningful for both parties.
7. Consider the important role of gender, race, or generational differences in the relationship.
8. Know when to bring others into the mentoring network.

Take tip 1, for example. In any relationship—friendship or otherwise—we are very happy when someone knows what we are all about. This implies that each person in a mentoring relationship should take time to find out more about the person they are mentoring to gain that understanding. These might range from small things like their favorite foods to big things such as their hopes and dreams for themselves, their families, or their organizations. Listening plays a key role in many of these initial interactions. (We bring up more about listening later in the chapter.) An open discussion of other personal traits, such as how the two individuals handle emotions, can also make a difference for the relationship.

As our interviews made clear, an honest sharing of important information of this nature can help build intimacy.

For example, Bob Wright said that he wanted to see people in different contexts to get a sense of what they were really like outside of the office:

> Most of my work always had a lot of travel in it. And so sometimes, we travel places and are with people late at night or early in the morning, and you get to know a person better than you would in a traditional office environment. And I think one of the difficulties of knowing people and making judgments about people is when you only see them [in the office], you only see certain aspects of their personality and performance.
>
> Finding a way to try to get to know somebody when you don't have an opportunity to spend time with them socially or outside of the office or in less formal environments is important. I always try to find or look up people in social environments if I can. Because you do see other sides of people. Or maybe you don't see another side, you see the same person. But some people are different. And sometimes it's tension, and sometimes it's just you get more of a chance to see their personality and their interests.

Not only did Bob understand the importance of context for judging talent, he also realized it was important for getting to know the challenges a person might be facing in their work environment and how they might be helped.

In Chapter Five, on the protégé's perspective on mentoring relationships, we touched on the important topic of impression management—that is, the ability to make the best possible impression on others. The crux of impression management is emotional intelligence.[19] All of us can think of individuals who seem extremely attuned to the emotions of others or who move effortlessly between different types of social situations. These individuals often have high levels of emotional and social intelligence, which they use not only to manage the impressions people have of them but also to manage other important aspects of relationships. The concept of emotional intelligence includes the ability to handle one's own emotions, to recognize and understand the emotions of others, and to delay gratification. In other words, it is about people who are smart about the nature and consequences of their own emotions and the emotions of others. People who have high levels of emotional intelligence are said to do well in many inter-personal situations and are found at the highest levels of organizations for their ability to motivate others through their caring personalities.

As one writer puts it, nice people are not always represented in the highest ranks of professions. The person who makes it to the top is often the executive who is never satisfied with the status quo and is concerned with logic and rationality rather than with the feelings of others.[20] However, in our mentoring study we found countless examples of mentors and protégés who were well aware of the requirements of emotional intelligence in their relationships. For example, General Lee Butler showed a keen understanding that his job involved more than just technical know-how, as he indicated in this passage:

> At levels of responsibility that entailed missions involving combat, missions involving high risk, nuclear weapons, for example, or in bureaucratic circumstances where I was making judgments about national strategies or the career paths of more than a hundred thousand people; in the day-to-day myriad judgments that come with choosing amongst alternative approaches to a problem, or dealing with a large staff, how you sort out the egos and the relationships and get a strong grasp of day-to-day life of your business and how it's proceeding and where you intervene, when it needs to be tweaked, who needs to be taken out of it, much of that revolves around a keen sense of people and dealing with them in a very straight-up, honest way.

Emotional intelligence includes a number of perceptions and skills a person can develop through training, experience, and a conscious effort to make a change through self-awareness and goal setting. Improving emotional intelligence is an important goal for anyone who cares about the quality of their interpersonal relationships, mentoring or otherwise. Currently many assessments exist for determining your general level of emotional intelligence. Understanding where you might have strengths or opportunities for improvement will start you on the path to improvement. Chapter Seven contains a source for online assessments to get you started.

At the heart of all relationships are listening skills. Effective listening is not limited to the act of hearing and repeating what someone is saying, but instead involves understanding what they are really saying. A person can exclaim, "Whew, what a week!" One listener may just hear a mundane comment about a workweek, whereas another may hear that the person is at their wit's end struggling to hold themselves together. Books abound that provide practice with active listening skills. Active listening means not just nodding and saying, "Yes, yes," but actually reflecting back to the person in a way that they feel confident that you have heard them. This "reflection" takes the form of a paraphrase of "What I hear you saying is . . ." or other, less obvious responses that convey the same information. The part of reflection that people often forget to give involves reflection for emotions. In other words, trying to reflect back the emotion the person is conveying helps ensure that you are truly listening to their meaning, not just their words.

Within the context of mentoring relationships, listening skills are taken to another level. Most mentors, especially those at higher levels in the organization, are very busy. If they offer a protégé career advice, the protégé needs to listen, because they may never get this advice again. Dixie Garr (from Cisco) described what she likes in protégés (mentees), and especially in her relationship with Anthony Hayter:

> You know what I love about mentees? It's when they really listen. Don't ask me, if you aren't going to listen to the advice that I give you or the insight. And I don't mean you have to do what . . . but listen to it, and . . . Otherwise if you are going to do what you were going to do anyway, why did you come? And Anthony has a track record of really taking it to the next level. Not only listening but applying it in other situations. Like when we were talking about his career and his job, he—the things that I talked about, he did. He followed up. He followed through, and I liked that. I felt like I wasn't wasting my time.

The participants in our study provided many other examples of excellent listening skills. In fact, in the course of conducting our interviews, we couldn't help but notice the way the interviewees gave us their full attention as we explained the process and asked them the interview questions. Their attentiveness made us feel like we were important to them during the time we were there.

This first tip for deepening the relationship is really the way to get the relationship off on the right foot. Making a good first impression, and getting to know one another through good emotional intelligence and listening skills, are all-important keys to great relationships. Even though most of us have heard these suggestions many times, often we do not take the time to consciously practice them. We urge you to use these skills deliberately when first connecting with your would-be protégé or would-be mentor. If you are not utilizing your best skills, you may be missing an amazing opportunity for a fantastic relationship.

Tip 2 on our list of tips for deepening your mentoring relationships—nurturing fondness and admiration—can also be crucial to the success of these relationships. In his research, John Gottman found that many marriages do not do well because the bad times chip away at the initial admiration the partners have for each other.[21] In mentoring relationships, there can be periods when the two individuals are not sure they are still getting the things from the relationship that they used to get. Spending time focusing on the pride you have for one another in the mentoring relationship can be very helpful for future interactions. Here is how Ron Meyer expressed his admiration for one of his protégés, Richard Lovett, president of Creative Artists Agency: "What I get back from him is a feeling of a friend—someone I trust and admire. I'm very proud of him. I think he's accomplished a lot. He and his partners held that company together when all the founders left. They have done an amazing job not only in holding it together but by building a better company."

Tips 3 and 4 are especially important in reverse mentoring relationships. In Chapter Five we spent some time talking about the many organizations that have begun to use reverse mentoring to learn from younger workers. Being open to what your mentor has to say is important. Sometimes it is difficult for older employees to admit that they don't know something in front of a younger employee. The relationship must be developed so that the comfort level is there. On the other hand, listening to what a protégé needs is just as important in maintaining a mutually beneficial relationship.

Peer mentors may find it difficult to control their competitive streak when working with others. Both members of the dyad are usually bright and want to get ahead, so sometimes they may find they are in competition with one another. Some of us just have difficulty listening to feedback that is counter to the perfect image we want of ourselves. Seeking a mentoring relationship means we have accepted the inevitability that we will sometimes receive negative feedback.

Tip 5 points to the importance of working on solvable problems together. Problem solving is a process that mentors and protégés work on naturally. It may become dysfunctional if mentors try to solve all of their protégés' problems rather than having the protégés learn the techniques for navigating potential workplace issues. Mentors need to be careful that they do not operate from a hero complex where they swoop in to solve all problems. This tip also underscores another problem that could occur in mentoring relationships: the relationship may turn into an opportunity to hold gripe sessions. Although once in a while, trashing your coworkers might feel good, it is not advisable. As one moves up in an organization, remaining professional in the face of adversity is very important. Mentors can encourage protégés to see organizational issues in a more favorable light by giving them insights into the decision-making processes of others in the organization.

Tip 6 refers to building a mentoring relationship where the two parties understand that the relationship should benefit both of them. What is important here is that both the mentor and the protégé should have realistic expectations and goals; failing to arrive at shared meaning in the relationship can lead to problems. For example, in one pair a mentor and protégé may disconnect on the objectives of the relationship. In another pair the mentor may not feel the same level of trust for the protégé that the protégé feels for the mentor. Shared meaning in a mentoring relationship occurs when both people agree on these various factors and the relationship is equally fulfilling to each party.

Tip 7 calls attention to the key role that race, gender, or even generational differences may play in a mentoring relationship. Should we expect that same-sex mentoring relationships will function the same way as different-sex relationships? Yes and no. Gender differences do exist in relationships, especially friendships; however, in the workplace, the work culture usually determines many aspects of relationships. In the general population of working women and women who do not work outside the home, women usually talk more to increase the intimacy of a relationship. Women also tend to use more self-disclosure to gain intimacy. Men tend to be more activity based in their friendships, which produces the same level of intimacy.[22] This doesn't always hold true for all men. When we asked Ron Kirk what conversational topics come up between him and one of his peer mentors, Rodney Ellis (a Texas state senator since 1990), Ron said:

> Everything. We talk about family. We talk about careers. We talk about practicing law. We talked about our love of politics. I mean he and I and Royce West, who has come to be kind of what I'd call a peer mentor—but I've known Rodney longer. But Rodney and Royce are the two African American state senators. We're all lawyers. Rodney and I went to law school together. I met Royce literally when we were taking the bar. But I mean we all talked about the Senate race. We talked about timing. We talked about we've all got young families. I mean, Rodney was in my wedding. I was in his wedding. I mean my wife worked—I mean there's not anything I can't talk to him about.

Hilda Solis, also from the world of politics, talked about male and female mentor differences she has seen:

> They're very different. I think obviously because there are fewer women in higher office, I think men tend to be a little bit more guarded in how they conduct themselves with women, especially if your mentee is a younger female. So of course that's different.
>
> If the guys get together and they go play golf or whatever it is, then the women go and they have coffee and do their thing. And it's very different.

Hilda spoke more specifically about a peer/step-ahead mentor, Gloria Molina, on the Los Angeles County Board of Supervisors:

> She's the kind of person that says, "Come on in, Hilda. Sit down. Let's talk." We'll spend maybe an hour or so talking about issues or political concerns in the community in her office. And meanwhile she's catching the phone because her daughter's calling and she's got to go somewhere and finish work-related items. So she's in my opinion a real person. While maybe if it was a male elected official, all the calls are held over. So it's that informality that exists between women that would go on. If I was a male [mentor], there would be different nuances that go on.

Jacqueline Woods, executive director of the American Association of University Women, and an African American woman, shared her opinions on the role of gender and ethnicity in mentoring relationships. When asked about women mentors in her life, this is what she had to say:

> I can think of women who are still in my network, who were among the first women to embrace me and encourage me when I arrived in Washington. Many of them taught me how to interact within the higher ed community and then successfully outside of it. And we're still all friends.
>
> In profiling success characteristics in both men and women, we still view honesty, directness, and hard work as difficult traits if found in a woman. I'm considered safe, and I'm considered hard-working. I'm a tough, intimidating woman. And it hurts sometimes. It hurts a lot. I am all of those things. The lay public still want women to exhibit different, often more nurturing traits.
>
> And for any of us to think that even though we have made many, many strides, that we have come over that hump, it is not true, because we're far, far from coming over the hump. And I can make a really better set of comparisons now, having come to a women's organization.
>
> Women's networks were smaller and more homogenous in years past. I see more and more young women of all ethnic groups, all cultures, seeking to broaden their exchange and be a part of a network, and I like that. I really do.

A few women were quite conscious of how their gender was important in their industry. For example, this is the story Martha Coolidge told:

> I knew from college there were no women filmmakers out there doing speaking engagements. So from the time I did my first documentary I did speaking tours. So I've been speaking and sharing what I know with women's groups and other organizations since 1972.
>
> It's important to see the possibility of you doing a job you aspire to. There were some people I was able to look at, men directors, and say, "Oh, I can do that." But not everybody can do that. I know so many women say, "How did you do it?" For whatever

reason with my upbringing, I didn't look at those men and look at me and say, "I'm not like them. I can't do it."

I noticed very young that most artists were men. And the women were the wives of the artists. And having been raised in an art family, I said, "Jeez, how can I be a woman and be an artist? I have to figure that out." So I addressed it at a very young age. I'm saying I was aware of this at about six.

When I got older, it was presumed I would be an artist, and also my father died young. I didn't grow up thinking, "Oh, I'll just get married," and I didn't have those expectations laid on me. So I just followed my bliss, as Joseph Campbell would say, and went after filmmaking.

And everybody thought I was crazy. But because I didn't come from that traditional gender role perspective, I didn't see the problem. I'd look at Francis Coppola or Martin Scorsese and identify with them. The only people I got to meet were male filmmakers, so I'd look at them and say, "I can do that." And then I just talked about filmmaking.

So I have offered myself as an example even when I was just a documentary filmmaker to show people that yes, you're a woman and you can do this. Here's how I did it up to this point. I did this. So you can too.

When Linda Sanford was asked about the role gender might play in mentoring relationships, she focused on many of the individual differences she saw in mentoring:

I think individuals mentor differently. I really do. I always, when I talk with my team about diversity, I always talk to them about diversity in many dimensions. Yes, there is the gender and the ethnic diver-sity, but there's also diversity in thought and diversity in experience.

Not all men are the same either. And so, I mean, I see differences in different generations of men. I see differences in men who have come through one career path versus another. Because you might have thought—and this is where some of the generations come in. Sometimes you would think women would have more of the "How do I put balance in my life?" kind of issues. This next generation of men, same thing. They have the same issues. They worry about it. They worry about it. I've even met a customer who was what I would call a next-generation guy. We're having dinner, and he's getting text messages from his daughter. "Oh, I got to go. We have a little bit of swim together tonight." I mean, when would you ever see that in an older generation.

So I don't think it is as much a gender difference as it really is an individual difference. And so when you pick mentors, you pick individuals that have a certain either style or sort of experiences that you need right now in order to help you through some point in your business or your career here.

Acknowledging the possibility of gender differences in relationships is a good place to start when thinking about your interactions with someone of a different gender, but the exceptions to the rule also point to the need for finding your mentor's or protégé's own style of interaction. Generational differences may also play a role. As we have mentioned previously, Bennis and Thomas's book *Geeks and Geezers* underscores the impact of generational differences in the workplace.[23] Mentoring across ethnic lines may have an impact on relationship closeness because of potential cultural differences. For example, cultural differences could affect the use of self-disclosure, how individual explain or attribute the causes of their behavior, and attitudes toward hierarchical versus egalitarian relationships. Of course, how acculturated the group member is will determine whether ethnic differences in relationships become meaningful. Some research has shown that African Americans do not dive into relationships quickly with those of a different ethnicity. Some ethnicities, such as Asian Americans and Latinos, engage in more hierarchical relationships; they may be looking for more power distance in a relationship.[24] The way different ethnic groups explain or attribute the causes of their behavior may also differ. Asian Americans may tend to attribute their own good performance more to the efforts of their work group than to their own efforts. There is a caveat in looking at differences. Although these findings illustrate how groups of people may differ from one another, people are individuals, and the commonalities among group members will usually transcend their differences.

We asked our interviewees how race and ethnicity played out in their mentoring relationships and in the general work environment. As Dixie Garr put it:

Being a person is hard. Careers are hard, no matter if you are a white male, but . . . being a woman is harder, harder, harder, and being black, multiply that by a significant amount. Even now, the isolation . . . is amazingly underappreciated.

And because there is such unconsciousness around it. When I came to Cisco, I interviewed with every senior vice president here at Cisco, and I asked them all, "So what about diversity?" And they said, "Oh, you will love it here. We are just . . . Oh, we're so . . . And we're just . . . it's like utopia. You will come here." What not one of them had realized or said to me or even thought to say to me was, "Dixie, now you're going to be our only black vice president, and our only woman black vice president. Not even another male, but it's okay, we're going to . . ." It never even occurred to them.

Protégés of color specifically acknowledge the importance of having mentors of their own ethnicity. Araceli Gonzalez noted the following when talking about Rosario Marin:

What I was most impressed by with her was that for the first time I noticed a Hispanic leader speaking Spanish on television who was very articulate in Spanish. And she was very articulate in English. I knew this is the type of representation we needed in our government. Our Hispanic community is saying that we need more representation and we need to hear the important messages in English but reinforced in Spanish, I said, "She's it. She's it. Look at her."

What happened is that Rosario and I started to develop a relationship. And we developed that relationship because as we worked in our city council we found that we had a lot in common. We were the only Republican women elected in that area. We were both Hispanic.

And we both had, it seemed like, the same values. I had my family and she had her family, meaning my parents and her with her children and her husband. And there was a lot that we could talk about besides just the city council. We had other things in common. Our family structures, our language, and then being women, just the other things that we could just talk about as women.

If you are a protégé or would-be protégé, it is not imperative that you find a mentor of your own ethnicity, but as you look at your network of mentors, there may be something that a mentor who has a similar background to your own might contribute to your career. The same goes for mentors looking for protégés. You may have something specific to contribute to a protégé of the same gender or ethnicity that they may be missing in the career advice they have received thus far.

The last tip on our list, tip 8, mentions knowing when to bring others into your mentoring network. One of the great features of power mentoring is that a protégé is not just stuck with one mentor over time. Power mentoring involves utilizing various mentors at different times from different sources. Both mentor and protégé should be involved in determining when the relationship is not meeting their mutual goals. There are functional reasons for leaving a mentoring relationship, including a move to another part of the country or world. Other functional reasons come from the fact that protégés have outgrown their mentors. Revisiting career goals from time to time and assessing how well your current mentoring relationships are helping in achieving these goals is an important process. In Chapter Seven, we give you some assessment exercises for evaluating the adequacy of current mentoring relationships.

Sometimes, continuing a mentoring relationship may not be feasible if it has become dysfunctional. As many researchers have pointed out, all relationships can go through negative periods. In our interviews we asked participants to talk about any mentoring relationships that had difficulties or that did not work out. As one would expect, the interviewees indicated that they would rather not talk about those relationships. A few could think of relationships that did not end up going anywhere, often because there was a poor mentor-protégé connection, but none talked about finding themselves in a negative relationship. Research suggests that protégés report negative mentoring experiences when the mentor is not skilled, or when they do not share similar values, attitudes, and beliefs with the mentors.[25] Other negative experiences include mentors who, according to one source, can be critical, demanding, and authoritarian.[26] One can imagine mentors who use their powerful position to haze a protégé as part of the mentoring process. This may include dressing down the protégé for a mistake, either in private or in front of others. One could also imagine mentors who used the mentoring relationship for their own political gain within an organization. Although these negative behaviors sound quite serious, many protégés will find that they occur once in a while, but that the benefits of the relationship outweigh the occasional negative events.

A protégé and a mentor both need to become very concerned in a mentoring relationship when it shows signs of becoming consistently dysfunctional. Some relationships will end in anger and frustration, according to researchers.[27] One study noted that the dysfunctional reasons for termination could stem from (1) highly destructive relationships characterized by jealousy and the mentor stifling the protégé's advancement, (2) dependency and suffocation within the relationship, and (3) lack of support and the mentor's unrealistic expectations.[28] Unfortunately, some dysfunctional relationships will persist. It is incumbent on both the protégé and the mentor to realistically assess the relationship and watch for serious problems. Mentors should steer clear of protégés who are exploitative, egocentric, or deceptive; who engage in sabotage or harassment; who are too submissive; who perform below expectations; or who are unwilling to learn.[29] Protégés should avoid (or break off) relationships with mentors who engage in sabotage, ask the protégé to make impossible choices, steal ideas, bully, seek revenge, are exploitative, or engage in other negative actions.[30]

Mentoring relationships are not to be entered into lightly. They require a commitment of time and energy on the part of both mentor and protégé to produce worthwhile results. They also require prudence, so that dysfunctional situations can be avoided. With the proper levels of commitment and caution, power mentoring can immeasurably enrich your career—and your life.

CONCLUSION

Throughout this book, we have emphasized the importance of mentoring as a relationship. In this chapter we focused on the nuts and bolts of effective power mentoring relationships, including initial connection, frequency and quality of interaction, ways to increase intimacy, and the role that defining moments play in determining relationship quality. The tips we have offered in this chapter are not all inclusive; there are as many variants on mentoring relationships as there are individuals engaged in these relationships. In reading through the experiences of our successful mentors and protégés, focus on those ideas that suit your current situation best, or that with a bit of a stretch could be a goal for you to achieve as your relationship with your mentor or protégé deepens. In the next chapter, we give you tools for mapping out successful mentoring relationships by developing your own personal Relationship Development Plan.

CHAPTER SEVEN

POWER MENTORING AND YOU

Congratulations! Today is your day. You're off to great places! You're off and away! So be sure when you step, step with great care and tact, and remember that Life's a Great Balancing Act. And will you succeed? Yes! You will indeed! (98 ¾ percent guaranteed).
—DR. SEUSS, *OH, THE PLACES YOU'LL GO*

As a well-known writer of children's books, Theodor Seuss Geisel, otherwise known as Dr. Seuss, provided life lessons to both young and old throughout his career. His books, written in a lively rhyming style, have made reading fun for thousands of children over the years. In his book *Oh, the Places You'll Go,* which remains a best-seller, he emphasizes the importance of the drive to succeed, the choices you make, and the role of setting goals and self-determination in getting where you want to go in life.

Throughout our book, we have provided rich details from the work lives of individuals who have sought out the advice, guidance, and support of a network of powerful mentoring relationships rather than leaving their career development to chance. We have traced the stories of these mentors and protégés from their initial acquaintance, to their developing closeness and intimacy, and finally to the great rewards that the relationships have brought to each party. We have shared their stories to inspire you to take advantage of your own power mentoring relationships. Therefore, it is time to think about how to plan your next steps in pursuing the mentoring relationship of your dreams. You are off on a path that will require motivation, goals, and self-determination. Oh, the places you will go!

THE RELATIONSHIP DEVELOPMENT PLAN

In this chapter, we provide a number of interactive exercises that will assist you in working toward more positive and rewarding mentoring relationships. In the spirit of best-selling career development books like Richard Bolles's *What Color Is Your Parachute?* and Julia Jenson's *I Don't Know What I Want, But I Know It's Not This: A Step-by-Step Guide to Finding Gratifying Work,* our interactive exercises can lead to an action plan to be used in establishing productive mentoring relationships.[1] To capitalize on the many ideas we have shared in this book, we ask you to work through the following exercises to create a road map to successful mentoring relationships. We feel it is important to actively build a plan for entering into fulfilling mentoring experiences; we call it the *Relationship Development Plan* (RDP).

Most career development activities ask individuals to answer questions about their own career preferences and the goals they would like to accomplish. As we mentioned previously, books such as *What Color Is Your Parachute?* have been popular for years and have provided many people with valuable insight into their interests and goals as an important step in career planning. These books are important, because leadership development experts suggest that effective career development begins with a good level of self-awareness.[2] Also helpful are self-awareness scales that reveal individuals' preferred problem-solving styles, such as the Myers-Briggs Typology, as well as tests that reveal preferred learning styles, like Kolb's Learning Style Inventory.[3] Other types of assessments focus on determining whether individuals have appropriate skills. They may take the form of self-assessments of a person's skill level in particular areas, or assessments that come from others who have the opportunity to observe a person's skills. Many organizations use 360-degree assessments for their managers and leaders to help in the career development process. These assessments gather opinions of a person's effectiveness from his or her subordinates, bosses, peers, or customers, as well as incorporating self-ratings of effectiveness. These ratings are then used to provide an overview of the person's particular strengths and areas for improvement. If used properly, 360-degree assessments can be a very useful tool. If you have not already done so, you may wish to consider using some of these assessments as a precursor to the work we suggest here.

We combine some different types of activities to give both mentors and protégés insight into their preferences and skill sets surrounding effective mentoring relationships, as well as their own assessments of their current mentoring relationships. Some of these activities tap into a person's mentoring preferences, while others ask the mentor or protégé to gather feedback from others to gain an even higher level of insight. Many of these exercises have been road-tested by us during our work in designing mentoring programs. You can use them just as they are, or modify them as you see fit. Our intention is to provide exercises for *both* the mentor and the protégé here, so if one exercise does not work for you, keep reading, because you have a lot of options to choose from. We split the RDP into three phases:

1. *Getting started: Know what you want.* These activities include visualizing the perfect relationship, assessing the mentoring philosophy that works for you, and identifying the types of specific mentoring relationships you would like to pursue. The result will be a comprehensive profile of the types of mentors or protégés that will work most effectively with you.

2. *Getting involved: Know how to get what you need.* Getting involved requires that you identify methods for attracting the mentor/ protégé, approaching the mentor/protégé, establishing rapport, and making your pitch. Before beginning this process, however, we ask you to do a number of self-assessments to identify the types of benefits you may offer in the relationship, how you stack up as a potential protégé, and how your talents and skills match up with the potential mentor or protégé you have chosen. We also ask that you assess skills that will become necessary in developing the relationship such as your level of emotional intelligence and whether you will be ready for the tests and challenges posed to you in your first meetings. The result of these exercises will be a step-by-step plan for making initial contact with an identified mentor or protégé.

3. *Getting close: Know how to build and deepen the relationship.* In the final phase, we give you tools to further build the relationship.

There are also activities assessing current relationships and determining how they might be improved, activities for determining whether now might be a good time to bring others into the mentoring network to accomplish career goals, and activities for deciding whether to dissolve existing mentoring relationships.

Now that we have identified an overview of the general process, let's begin.

GETTING STARTED: KNOW WHAT YOU WANT

We will get started by offering exercises to help you identify the type of mentor or protégé that will best suit your current career needs.

VISUALIZE THE IDEAL RELATIONSHIP

Many self-improvement books recommend that if you want to accomplish something, visualizing it will help you achieve your goal. Visualization has been found to be an effective tool for improving performance in many arenas, including sports, public speaking, and other types of competitions. It is equally applicable in other areas of life—even in mentoring relationships. Read over the following questions one by one, thinking about them carefully and visualizing your optimal situation:

- Where does your ideal mentor work? What type of industry or organization?
- How do you feel when you connect with your mentor?
- How does your mentor help you?
- What might a typical conversation look like?
- How do you communicate with your mentor (that is, phone, e-mail, in person)? How often?
- At the end of the relationship, what will you have accomplished? What new skills will you have learned?
- Do any specific people come to mind?

Jot down whatever comes to mind with respect to your ideal mentoring relationship in the box in Exhibit 7.1.

In visualizing the ideal mentor or protégé, you may have tapped into your most important beliefs regarding the mentor philosophies that we introduced in Chapter Four. A mentor

EXHIBIT 7.1 MY IDEAL MENTORING RELATIONSHIP

philosophy includes assumptions about the role the mentor plays and the benefits he or she offers. You may have developed your mental models of mentoring from your previous mentoring relationships, or from mentoring relationships you have been aware of and have admired.

If you are a protégé, take the quiz in Exhibit 7.2 to see what characteristics you are looking for in your mentoring relationships.

Here are a few tips on interpreting your results:

- If you have relatively equal scores in each of the four categories, that means that you most likely do not have a preference for a specific type of mentor. You are more interested in finding a mentor who may provide you with all the benefits you want, but you do not have a preference for their style; you will adapt.
- A score of a 7 to 8 for one or more of the categories shows that you have a *strong* preference for certain types of mentoring philosophies.
- A score of a 5 to 6 for one or more of the categories shows a *slight* preference for those mentoring philosophies.
- A score of 2 to 4 for a particular mentoring philosophy indicates that you are really not interested in that type of mentor, and should look for mentors in higher-scoring categories.
- Calculating an overall score will also help you uncover the type of mentoring relationship you might be interested in. For example, if you have a score of 24 or higher, this indicates that you are interested in a wide array of benefits. This insight will help you realize that one mentor may not satisfy all of your needs. On the other hand, if you had a low score overall—18 or below—you may be looking for other things in mentoring relationships that are not captured by these philosophies.

When you complete this first section of the RDP, please fill in some of your expectations for your mentors. You may find because you are interested in peer mentors, or reverse mentors, the mentoring philosophies we list do not really fit your needs at the present time. The next section is for mentors to complete; please skip over it if you are a protégé.

If you are a mentor, complete the scale in Exhibit 7.3, thinking about your own conception of ideal mentoring relationships from your perspective as a mentor.

EXHIBIT 7.2   PROTÉGÉ PREFERENCES FOR MENTORING

	Strongly Agree	Agree	Disagree	Strongly Disagree
1. I want to be well connected within my organization because I plan to work there for most of my career.	4	3	2	1
2. I believe a protégé should have responsibility equal to the mentor's for making sure a mentoring relationship succeeds.	4	3	2	1
3. I think a mentor who can give me technical skills within my industry will be most beneficial.	4	3	2	1
4. I want specific career advice for promotions from my mentor in exchange for the hard work I will do for him or her.	4	3	2	1
5. I need a mentor who will take me under his or her wing to show me the ins and outs of my profession.	4	3	2	1
6. I want a mentor who has experience with many different protégés.	4	3	2	1
7. My mentor needs to be a well-respected expert in my field.	4	3	2	1
8. My mentor should be recognized by others for his or her mentoring skills.	4	3	2	1

Scoring for Mentoring Preferences Scale: Protégé Results

Total scores for questions 1, 3   _____ Corporate-citizen mentor

Total scores for questions 2, 4   _____ Pragmatic mentor

Total scores for questions 5, 7   _____ Global-citizen mentor

Total scores for questions 6, 8   _____ Master mentor

EXHIBIT 7.3 MENTOR PREFERENCES FOR MENTORING

	Strongly Agree	Agree	Disagree	Strongly Disagree
1. I am well connected within my organization, which will benefit a protégé.	4	3	2	1
2. I believe a protégé should have responsibility equal to the mentor's for making sure a mentoring relationship succeeds.	4	3	2	1
3. I think mentoring is an important part of our corporate culture.	4	3	2	1
4. I want a protégé who recognizes what I give to him or her, and gives me back benefits of equal importance.	4	3	2	1
5. I really think I would like to take someone under my wing to show them the ins and outs of our profession.	4	3	2	1
6. I value mentoring many different protégés.	4	3	2	1
7. It is very important that I am a well-respected expert in my field.	4	3	2	1
8. I am recognized by others for my effective mentoring skills.	4	3	2	1

Scoring for Mentoring Preferences Scale: Mentor Results

Total scores for questions 1, 3 _____ Corporate-citizen mentor

Total scores for questions 2, 4 _____ Pragmatic mentor

Total scores for questions 5, 7 _____ Global-citizen mentor

Total scores for questions 6, 8 _____ Master mentor

A few comments may help you interpret your results:

- If you have relatively equal scores in each of the four categories, that means that you most likely do not have a specific mentoring style. You are more interested in doing whatever a protégé may need in terms of mentoring, and what will provide you, as a mentor, with desirable benefits. You will adapt.
- A score of a 7 to 8 for one or more of the categories shows that you have a *strong* preference for certain types of mentoring philosophies.
- A score of a 5 to 6 for one ore more of the categories shows a *slight* preference for those mentoring philosophies.
- A score of 2 to 4 for a particular mentoring philosophy indicates that you are really not interested in that type of mentoring and should not mentor protégés who are looking for those types of mentors.
- Calculating an overall score will also help you uncover the type of mentoring relationship you might be interested in. For example, if you have a score of 24 or higher, this indicates that you are interested in a wide array of mentoring philosophies. This insight will help you realize that you may be able to satisfy the mentoring needs of protégés with different interests.

Exhibit 7.4 provides more detail on the mentoring philosophies explored in the previous exercise. Looking at the definitions in the exhibit, what philosophy of mentoring is most appealing to you, either as a mentor or as a protégé? As we mentioned in Chapter Four, our treatment is not exhaustive. People may mentor for other reasons; these were merely some of the more salient philosophies we uncovered in our interviews.

One last exercise we have mentors and protégés do when thinking about mentoring is contained in the worksheet in Exhibit 7.5. In training sessions, we often ask mentors and protégés to think about the perfect metaphorical image for what a mentor represents to them. Our participants come from diverse backgrounds—sometimes they mentor other managers, or sometimes they mentor students in youth programs—so we get very different answers. But they all show special insight into the various forms the ideal mentor can take. For example, one student mentioned that

EXHIBIT 7.4 MENTORING PHILOSOPHIES

Mentoring Philosophy	Definition	Advantages	Disadvantages
Corporate-citizen mentor	This mentoring relationship is rooted in an organizational culture that believes mentoring is important for employee development and succession. This philosophy may imply a relationship that is business based; in other words, the mentor and protégé are mentoring for the good of the corporation.	Through this type of mentoring, the protégé learns specifics of career advancement within a specific corporation.	This model gives the protégé only one perspective for career advancement. The protégé may end up in the mentor's shadow in smaller organizations.
Pragmatic mentor	This mentoring relationship is largely characterized by an equal exchange of effort and benefits on the part of the mentor.	The relationship may be very goal focused.	This type of relationship may offer slightly less in the way of psychosocial support (the softer side of mentoring).
Global-citizen mentor	This mentoring relationship may exist outside of a specific organization. The mentor seems to be interested in mentoring in the service of his or her profession.	This approach is good for comprehensive mentoring within one's profession.	It may be difficult for protégés to remove themselves from the mentor's influence.

Mentoring Philosophy	Definition	Advantages	Disadvantages
Master mentor	These mentors have vast experience mentoring others and pride themselves on the large number of protégés they have helped throughout their careers.	The mentor's experience helps identify ways to assist different protégés.	The mentor may be too busy to always give the type of support needed by all types of protégés.

EXHIBIT 7.5   METAPHOR FOR MENTORING

A mentor is like a _____

Extend the metaphor, explaining how a mentor serves as that object.

mentors are like pace cars in professional car racing. They come out to get the race started, but once it is going, the pace car goes back to the pits. If there is an accident or other danger on the track, the pace car will return to guide the rest of the field of cars again. To this person, mentoring was somewhat hands-off unless the person needed it; when trouble arose the mentor would spring into action to do what was necessary to solve the problem. Although not a very proactive model of mentoring, this metaphor revealed some of the ideas that this person held around mentoring.

Completing the worksheet in Exhibit 7.5 will give you further practice in identifying the types of mentors or protégés you feel would be most useful in your career. These results will be used in the next section, on targeting mentors who will meet your expectations of the ideal mentor or protégé.

Target Potential Relationships

We introduced you to the range of potential single mentors or possible networks of mentors you might utilize in Chapter Two, and we included suggestions on places to find these different types of mentors in Chapter Five. Exhibit 7.6 provides a review of types of mentoring. It also outlines the possible benefits these offer for both mentor and protégé as well as the challenges that might occur in working with these different types of mentors.

Inventory Your Network

Here we ask you to actively inventory your network for possible mentoring relationships. We provide a worksheet in Exhibit 7.7 to get you started. You do not have to fill in something for every single type of mentoring relationship. Just pick the types of mentoring relationships that interest you. For each type you are interested in, list possible benefits they could provide, as well as possible drawbacks. Assessing your possible network for these different types of mentoring relationships is a powerful way to identify potential mentors or protégés. Although this exercise can be time consuming, once you are clear about the types of individuals you would like to target, the next steps in the RDP become very straightforward.

EXHIBIT 7.6 INNOVATIVE FORMS OF POWER MENTORING

Type of Mentoring	Description	Benefits	Challenges
Barrier busting	Mentoring relationships that occur across traditional boundaries such as competitive organizations or political parties	—Fresh perspective —Nontraditional alliances	—In-group or social censor —Risk to reputation
Boss	Boss provides both emotional and career support to subordinate-protégé, both within formal boundaries of relationships and informally	—Provides opportunity to groom for successor —Daily opportunity to learn and develop, thus generally high performance and job satisfaction	—Transitioning away from boss mentor can be challenging —Reputations and work credit inextricably linked
E-mentoring	Mentoring relationships that use primarily computer-mediated communication (that is, e-mail, instant messaging, chat rooms, and so on)	—Greater access —Equalization of status —No boundaries of time and space	—Increased propensity for miscommunication —Telecommunication difficulties

Type of Mentoring	Description	Benefits	Challenges
Family member	An immediate or extended family member who provides instrumental, psychosocial, and role-modeling support, usually from a very young age; often a person of considerable influence and accomplishment within his or her own family circle or community	—The ultimate mentoring relationship in terms of trust —Early and ongoing development of protégé self-esteem and self-efficacy	—Dysfunctional family dynamics can erode quality of mentoring —Perceived nepotism by others
For hire	A mentor who primarily provides job- or career-specific advice or help in exchange for tangible (usually financial) remuneration	—Clearly defined relationship boundaries and expectations —Efficient and task specific	—Relationship can be perceived as cold or mechanistic —Lack of loyalty or trust prohibits deep knowledge or learning
Group	A senior-level mentor provides ongoing coaching to small groups of junior-level protégés	—Maximizes access to senior executive and efficiently uses his or her time —Provides opportunities to develop peer mentors among others in their mentoring group	—May breed competition among protégés —Can be difficult to obtain feedback on confidential or personal issues

(Continued)

EXHIBIT 7.6 INNOVATIVE FORMS OF POWER MENTORING *(Continued)*

Type of Mentoring	Description	Benefits	Challenges
Inspirational	A role model who is one's ideal mentor and an important person to learn from and emulate; usually protégé has no direct contact with this person	—Provides the protégé with vision, identity, and a sense of purpose	—Difficult or impossible to obtain tangible career or emotional support
Moment	A situational, intense relationship that has lasting, sometimes life-changing, impact by virtue of the advice given, by the role modeling, or simply by the affiliation	—Often happens just when it is needed the most —Short relationship but lasting lessons	—Usually short-lived and temporary —Seems to be a function of serendipity rather than planning or strategy
Peer and step-ahead	A mentor who is at the same level or just one step ahead of the protégé but has a different set of skills or experience that complements the other	—Can empathize with work and life situation —Can provide even and immediate exchange of benefits	—Does not have the power or connections that a more senior mentor provides —Can be a source of competition

Type of Mentoring	Description	Benefits	Challenges
Reverse	A younger/less experienced person mentors an older/more experienced person	—Often context specific, such as teaching new forms of technology —Provides an exchange: enhances younger generation retention, and older generation gets fresh ideas	—Benefit and purpose can be hard to distinguish —Loss of face and potential for embarrassment on both sides
Traditional	An older, more experienced person mentors a younger, less experienced person in a one-on-one relationship, usually within an organization	—Can sponsor, coach, motivate the younger individual —Often is what individuals are looking for when thinking about the ideal mentor	—May not be readily available —May limit protégé's potential if relying on only one person

EXHIBIT 7.7 INVENTORY YOUR POSSIBLE NETWORKS FOR MENTORS

Type of Mentor	Possible Candidates	Benefits They Might Provide	Possible Drawbacks to Having This Person as a Mentor
Barrier busting	1. 2. 3.	1. 2. 3.	1. 2. 3.
Boss	1. 2. 3.	1. 2. 3.	1. 2. 3.
Electronic	1. 2. 3..	1. 2. 3.	1. 2. 3.
Family member	1. 2. 3.	1. 2. 3.	1. 2. 3.
For-hire	1. 2. 3.	1. 2. 3.	1. 2. 3.
Group	1. 2. 3.	1. 2. 3.	1. 2. 3.
Inspirational	1. 2. 3.	1. 2. 3.	1. 2. 3.
Moment	1. 2. 3.	1. 2. 3.	1. 2. 3.
Peer and step-ahead	1. 2. 3.	1. 2. 3.	1. 2. 3.
Reverse	1. 2. 3.	1. 2. 3.	1. 2. 3.
Traditional	1. 2. 3.	1. 2. 3.	1. 2. 3.

PULL IT ALL TOGETHER TO FORM A PROFILE OF
YOUR IDEAL MENTOR OR PROTÉGÉ

As a first step in developing a road map to great power mentoring, we have suggested you do several things:

1. Visualize the perfect mentor or protégé.
2. Determine the types of mentoring philosophies that suit your needs.
3. Identify the types of people and types of mentoring that might assist in your career.

Exhibit 7.8 contains a blank worksheet on which to record the characteristics of your perfect mentor or protégé for that perfect mentoring relationship. Make copies if you are targeting more than one person. So pick a person, and complete the form for him or her. If you do not have a specific person in mind, complete the form for the type of person you would like to target.

GETTING INVOLVED:
KNOW HOW TO GET WHAT YOU NEED

Once you have identified what characteristics you are looking for in a mentor or protégé and have located a possible candidate, your next step is determining exactly how you can start a mentoring relationship with that person. Sounds simple, doesn't it? Actually, as you can imagine, it is not so straightforward. Successful individuals, whether potential mentors or protégés, often receive the attention of others, therefore, in approaching them do not waste their time. Have a plan. Bring your "A Game." For example, as we found in our interviews, successful mentors were regularly approached by would-be protégés asking for career advice. Many mentors found it difficult to determine immediately whether a potential protégé might be worth mentoring.

The skilled protégé makes it apparent that he or she offers some very tangible benefits to the mentor. As mentioned in Chapter Four, protégés with particular characteristics and skills are attractive to mentors. Protégés are looking for mentors who can provide a wide range of benefits that enhance their careers. As a mentor, it is important to realize the types of opportunities you

EXHIBIT 7.8 DESIRED MENTORING RELATIONSHIP

These are the most important benefits I want in my mentoring relationships:

1.

2.

3.

I expect my mentor (or protégé) to:

1.

2.

3.

The following types of mentoring relationships (for example, boss, reverse, barrier busting, and so on) would meet my expectations:

1.

2.

3.

The following people (or types of people) are potential mentors (or protégés) whom I plan to target:

1.

2.

3.

could provide for protégés that would make you attractive to them in guiding their careers.

In this section, we focus on methods to assist you in attracting a potential mentor or protégé first by focusing on the particular benefits you would bring to the relationship. We specifically ask protégés to examine how they stack up as a potential protégé. Then we ask you to examine how the benefits you provide match up with the potential mentors or protégés you targeted in the last section. We give mentors advice on how they should manage these initial meetings with protégés to set the tone for the relationship. We ask protégés and mentors to make a plan and use their best skills for making initial contact with their potential partners and facing initial tests and challenges.

ATTRACT POTENTIAL MENTORS OR PROTÉGÉS

To attract a potential mentor or protégé, it is first important to understand what you may have to offer. We take you through some exercises that will help you examine the many benefits you can provide a mentor or protégé in a mentoring relationship. First we have you interview a close work acquaintance about some of your strengths. Next you evaluate your possible benefits against the list of benefits we cited in Chapter Three. Finally, we have protégé and mentors assess how their skills and characteristics stack up against the ideal protégé and mentor characteristics.

IDENTIFY POSSIBLE BENEFITS YOU OFFER

In Exhibit 7.9 we ask you to take an inventory of the many things you have to offer in a mentoring relationship. To get you started, informally interview three of your work contacts, colleagues, or work friends, and ask them the questions in the benefit interview. You might start the conversation by talking about your interest in pursuing mentoring relationships to enhance your career, either as a protégé or as a mentor. As we described in Chapters Three and Four, the benefits to the mentors in mentoring relationships are substantial, but whether you are a mentor or a protégé, it is important to identify what you bring to the mentoring relationship.

Now that you have gathered the perspectives from these different people, it is your responsibility to sort out what is true, and

EXHIBIT 7.9   BENEFIT INTERVIEW

Acquaintance 1

What strengths do you think
I bring to my work?

How might a mentor [or protégé]
help my career?

What benefits might I offer a
mentor or protégé in exchange
for his or her help?

Acquaintance 2

What strengths do you think I
bring to my work?

How might a mentor [or protégé]
help my career?

What benefits might I offer a
mentor or protégé in exchange
for his or her help?

Acquaintance 3

What strengths do you think
I bring to my work?

How might a mentor [or protégé]
help my career?

What benefits might I offer a
mentor or protégé in exchange
for his or her help?

---

maybe what you feel is less true. As we mentioned when we introduced the RDP, many techniques exist for getting insight into your preferences and expectations. You may want to refer to other resources for more activities of these types. Here are a few other techniques you can use to accurately assess what you have to offer a mentor or protégé:

- Scrutinize the results of your recent performance appraisals. What are your strengths and weaknesses?
- Ask your boss during your next performance appraisal interview to identify places you can improve.
- Utilize your work group peers, if you feel comfortable doing so, to seek feedback about some of your strengths and opportunities for improvement.

In Chapter Three we provided an extensive list of the benefits that both protégés and mentors can provide in the mentoring relationship. We have recreated them in Exhibits 7.10 and 7.11, so that you may determine what you have to offer. These exhibits include only benefits that you as a protégé or you as a mentor might provide. You personally may have additional unique benefits to offer in a potential relationship. We left space at the bottom of each exhibit for you to add other benefits you might provide. Place a check mark next to those you feel very comfortable offering, as either a mentor or a protégé. Be honest with yourself as to which benefits you became aware of in listening to your colleagues.

You will need to use both exhibits in completing this exercise. *Mentors:* If you are completing this exercise from the perspective of a mentor, you will fill out Exhibit 7.10 by checking off the types of benefits you think you could provide to a protégé. In Exhibit 7.11, you will check those benefits that you would like to receive in mentoring a protégé. *Protégés:* You should complete the exercise in Exhibit 7.10 by thinking specifically about the types of benefits you would want to receive from potential mentors. You should use the list in Exhibit 7.11 to identify the types of benefits you think you could provide to a mentor in a relationship.

How Do You Stack Up as a Potential Protégé?

In Chapter Four, we discussed 10 attributes that mentors often find appealing in their protégés: intelligence, ambition, willingness to

EXHIBIT 7.10   PROTÉGÉ BENEFITS

Career Support	Check	Personal/Emotional Support	Check
Promotion opportunities	❑	Self-efficacy at work	❑
Job mobility	❑	Interpersonal growth	❑
Pay raises	❑	Sponsorship and protection	❑
Job involvement	❑	Advocacy	❑
Career and job success	❑	Friendship and social interactions	❑
Organizational commitment	❑	Counseling and listening	❑
Job- and career-related feedback	❑	Support and confirmation	❑
Challenging assignments	❑	Acceptance	❑
Access to resources/ information/people	❑		
Exposure and visibility	❑		
Other benefits_____		Other benefits_____	
_____		_____	
_____		_____	

take risks, initiative, energy, trustworthiness, integrity, high emotional intelligence, optimism, and complementary skills. Chances are good that you have many of these attributes, though you may need some help in becoming aware of them and then determining the best way to communicate these characteristics. We offer a few suggestions about the best way to do this.

Exercise 1: Analyze your résumé. First, take a look at your résumé. What does it say about you? In general, you want your résumé to reflect something like the words of the *Saturday Night Live* character, Stuart Smalley: "I am good enough, smart enough, and dog-gone-it, people like me!"

EXHIBIT 7.11 BENEFITS TO A MENTOR I CAN PROVIDE AS A PROTÉGÉ

Career Support	Check	Personal/Emotional Support	Check
Recognition as a developer of others	❏	Rejuvenation	❏
Recognition as a leader	❏	Personal satisfaction	❏
Reputation enhancement	❏	Increase in knowledge, empathy, and skills relating to diverse groups	❏
Increase in influence and power	❏	Greater collegiality	❏
Increased network	❏	Friendship	❏
Career satisfaction	❏	Sense of pride and personal satisfaction	❏
Career and job motivation	❏	Support and confirmation	❏
Improved management and leadership skills	❏	Respect and empowerment	❏
Improved job performance	❏	Greater confidence	❏
Job-related feedback	❏	Interpersonal skill development	❏
Assistance in doing job	❏	Satisfaction in role as mentor	❏
Insight into different role or area of the organization or profession	❏	Transmission of knowledge, skills, and values	❏
Challenge and stimulation	❏	Excitement and inspiration	❏
Visibility and exposure	❏	Greater consciousness of what you are doing by teaching another	❏
Other benefits_____		Other benefits_____	
_____		_____	
_____		_____	

How well does your résumé communicate your intelligence, ambition, willingness to take risks, and the other important protégé characteristics? It would be helpful to analyze this for yourself, as well as asking friends or colleagues to do the same. (Note: This would be a terrific exercise if you are designing a career workshop.) Consider the first attribute: intelligence. We would not recommend that you list your IQ score or your designation as mentally gifted in first grade; however there are other ways of communicating that message without being arrogant. Intelligence can be communicated by your grade point average, if you are a recent college graduate, educational pedigree, work experience, or even volunteer accomplishments.

What about ambition or willingness to take risks? If you do not feel that those qualities are reflected well in your work history, what else have you done that communicates those attributes? For the purposes of soliciting a mentor, you may want to personalize your résumé so that it reflects your extracurricular interests and accomplishments as well as your more traditional ones. Of course, everyone knows that personalizing your résumé is important for different jobs, but it makes sense to share with a potential mentor the side of yourself that is important for making a connection.

Exercise 2: Conduct an informational interview with a potential mentor. Approach a would-be mentor with a request to conduct a short, informational interview with them. Ideally, this should be done in person to build rapport. Informational interviews often start out as one-way queries and transition into dialogues. You can formulate questions around key attributes. For example, you might ask, How important is risk taking in this job, and can you give me an example of a risk you took that paid off for you? Then, if it seems appropriate, you can share your experiences in this area. This way you build on the similarity you have with your mentor and communicate that you have these important skills as well.

During the meeting with your mentor, be sure to communicate your high level of energy and an optimistic attitude. The best way to communicate energy is nonverbally through good eye contact, voice intonation, posture, and liveliness. The best way to evaluate how you come across in terms of energy is to videotape yourself making a presentation or having a conversation. We know this may be painful to execute, but it can be quite revealing. Studies have conclusively shown that job candidates who demonstrate high energy get considerably more job offers than their counterparts with the same academic degrees and experience.[4]

Optimism is an interesting concept and one that is highly valued these days. Research shows that optimists have lower levels of depression and other mental health problems.[5] Traditional views of optimism suggest that optimists are those who often expect things to work out for the best on the whole. More recent studies suggest that optimism relates to how people ascribe causes for their successes and failures. An optimistic person is likely to take personal credit for the good that happens and somewhat discounts his or her own role in negative events. Pessimists, on the other hand, do just the opposite. Moreover, people often want to be around optimists, and avoid the office pessimists. Think about how you can put an optimistic spin on challenges that you have overcome and about how you can communicate this to a mentor.

When the information interview is concluded, send a thank-you note promptly. Keep in touch with your potential mentor by sending him or her news articles of interest, or updates about your progress. If the chemistry feels right, approach her with an offer of a lunch or coffee get-together. This will go a long way toward showing your willingness to take initiative. Try to think of the skills you might have that are complementary to the mentor's, so that you can become a valuable member of his network.

Match Your Benefits and Skills with the Targeted Mentor or Protégé

Using the information you gleaned from your conversations and from completing the preceding checklists, combine that information with the potential mentors or protégés you listed in the first section of your RDP and answer the questions in Exhibit 7.12. If you haven't yet identified specific individuals, complete the exhibit for the type of person you have in mind as a mentor or protégé.

Mentors, you also need to think about what makes you appealing to a potential protégé. Research shows that more effective mentors are skilled in mentoring, provide career, emotional, and role-modeling functions, and are empathetic.[6] In our study, mentors who provided powerful connections, who devised worthwhile tests and challenges, and who worked to develop outcome-oriented relationships were very effective in the eyes of their protégés.

EXHIBIT 7.12   MATCHING BENEFITS WITH TARGETED MENTOR OR PROTÉGÉ

1. How are you similar to your targeted mentor/protégé? How can you communicate that similarity?

2. How are you different in a way that could be helpful to your mentor/protégé? (This gets at the idea of complementary skill or perspective.)

3. What characteristic or skill do you possess or could you develop that this mentor/protégé would find appealing?

4. What is your past performance or demonstrated potential? (This is a good chance to update your résumé.)

5. As a protégé, how can you communicate your willingness to learn?

MENTOR: ESTABLISH THE RELATIONSHIP THAT BENEFITS YOU AS WELL AS YOUR PROTÉGÉS

We hope that at this point we have convinced you that it is in your best interest to develop a posse of protégés. Fortunately, if you follow the five tips listed next, you will not have to do too much work to develop this cadre because the protégés will come to you!

1. *If you build it, they will come.*[7] In other words, develop a reputation for excellence. Become involved in your professional community and take advantage of opportunities for visibility. This might involve writing a column for a professional organization or by taking on a leadership role. Become media savvy by taking a class in how to perform well with the media or solicit personal coaching from a PR professional. Develop an area of expertise and then share it with others.

2. *Once they come, be approachable.* Once you are approached about being a mentor to someone, make sure you treat that person with respect even if their approach was not the smoothest. Most of the mentors we spoke with said they would usually talk to a potential protégé once, even if just on the phone. Then after that, they might refer them to someone else for mentoring.

3. *Set the ground rules.* Be approachable, but not too approachable, or else you will be deluged. Paula Madison humorously noted that whenever she went to a speaking engagement, her assistant shuddered, because Paula inevitably received a flood of requests, many from would-be protégés. Think ahead of time about what you can and cannot do in terms of time limitations. Provide alternatives to potential protégés. One of our mentors, a busy management consultant, said she refuses to have lunch because it takes too much out of her day. Instead, she designates Saturday mornings between 10:00 and 12:00 at a local Starbucks as her mentoring time, and her protégés come to her. One of our own early mentors used to tell us that our relationship was a blank check that we could cash anytime. In his view, he was here to help, but we were the ones who needed to go to the bank. We had to make "deposits" by initiating contact and following up on his suggestions.

4. *Touch base.* Many of our power mentors had developed a system of periodic follow-up with their protégés. This may be an electronic reminder to send their protégé an e-mail from time to time.

5. *Share the wealth.* Manage your growing network by referring protégés to other qualified mentors. Paula Madison likes to connect new protégés with past protégés. This is a terrific way to develop a loyal group of protégé supporters and provide both parties with opportunities to grow and develop.

APPROACH POTENTIAL MENTORS OR PROTÉGÉS

Once you have found the mentor or protégé of your dreams, how do you approach that person and begin this much sought-after relationship? There are a number of ways to do this, as we mentioned in Chapter Five, but the right strategy will depend on your current relationship with this person. If you have just identified the type of person you are looking for, you need to take some initial steps before making contact. On the other hand, if this is someone you have worked with over time, approaching them may be somewhat easier. You may begin with a lunch invitation, and make it clear to them that you are interested in talking about your career or theirs. As we mentioned before, many of the relationships in our study were simultaneously initiated, with both the mentor and protégé noticing something that the other had to offer. By now, in your RDP, you have a good idea as to what you have to offer a potential mentor or protégé, so now is the time to decide how you will approach the mentors or protégés you have targeted. Using the following outline, come up with your approach plan.

1. Find the type of mentor or protégé you identified in the previous section.
   a. Utilize the resources of professional associations, either those that meet in person or online.
   b. Seek mentors or protégés in your workplace.
   c. Connect through one of your friends or acquaintances.

2. Research the person's background as thoroughly as you can.

3. Come up with a plan.
   a. Mode of first meeting: Decide among a lunch meeting, office meeting, e-mail introduction, or phone call.
   b. Script for discussion: What will you say? What is the purpose? What do you hope to accomplish? How formal do you want the relationship to be? How might they react?
   c. Role play of discussion: Pick a work friend and tell them

about your plan and what you want to say. Get their reactions.

d. Goal for accomplishing the plan:

- By such and such a date, I will have called X number of potential mentors or protégés.
- By such and such a date, I will have set up meetings with X number of potential mentors or protégés.
- By such and such a date, I will have had initial conversations with the following individuals—1. _____; 2. _____; 3. _____—and talked about the relationship.

USING EMOTIONAL INTELLIGENCE IN ATTRACTING MENTORS AND PROTÉGÉS

We have repeatedly mentioned the importance of emotional intelligence (EQ) in mentoring relationships for both the protégé and the mentor. Although it comes into play throughout the mentoring relationship, EQ is very important during the initial stages when you decide to approach a potential protégé or mentor. Although very popular these days, the idea of emotional intelligence actually has a long history. It includes a number of important elements, such as the ability to handle one's own emotions, understanding as well as recognizing the emotions of others, and the ability to delay gratification.

One instrument we have used in assessing some of the facets of emotional intelligence is called the Social Skills Inventory.[8] This gets at a person's level of emotional and social intelligence. Social intelligence goes further than the concept of emotional intelligence by incorporating how well people interact with others in social situations. Exhibit 7.13 includes a shortened version of that scale.[9]

Here are a few tips that may help you interpret your scores:

- A score of 6 to 8 on each dimension means you are relatively skilled in this area.
- A score of 4 to 5 indicates a moderate skill level, with some room for improvement.
- A score of 3 or below indicates a lower skill level.

EXHIBIT 7.13 SOCIAL SKILLS INVENTORY

	A Little Like Me	Like Me	Very Much Like Me	Exactly Like Me
1. People tell me I have an expressive face.	1	2	3	4
2. I always seem to know what other peoples' true feelings are no matter how hard they try to conceal them.	1	2	3	4
3. I am very good at maintaining a calm exterior even if I am upset.	1	2	3	4
4. It is very important that other people like me.	1	2	3	4
5. I usually take the initiative to introduce myself to strangers.	1	2	3	4
6. I often show my feelings or emotions.	1	2	3	4
7. I enjoy going to parties and meeting new people.	1	2	3	4
8. It is very easy for me to control my emotions.	1	2	3	4
9. I can instantly spot a "phony" the minute I meet him or her.	1	2	3	4
10. I can easily adjust to being in just about any social situation.	1	2	3	4
11. There are certain situations in which I find myself worrying about whether I am doing or saying the right things.	1	2	3	4
12. When in a group of people, I rarely have trouble thinking of the right things to talk about.	1	2	3	4

Scoring

In each blank below, insert your score from above and add the figures to come up with a score on each dimension.

Emotional Expressivity: This score reflects your report of how expressive you are in communicating your emotions to other. Managers need to use emotions well to show their enthusiasm or other feelings that may be important to communicate.

1. ____ People tell me I have an expressive face.

6. ____ I often show my feelings or emotions.

Score Emotional Expressivity _____

EXHIBIT 7.13 SOCIAL SKILLS INVENTORY *(continued)*

Emotional Sensitivity: This score shows how well you can tell what emotions other people are feeling. This is an important skill in that it helps understand what motivates others, and it can help you make sure you get your ideas across to others by reading their reactions to your ideas.

2. ____ I always seem to know what other peoples' true feelings are no matter how hard they try to conceal them.

9. ____ I can instantly spot a "phony" the minute I meet him or her.

Score Emotional Sensitivity _____

Emotional Control: This score reflects both how much you are able to control your emotions, and how much you choose to control the emotions you show to others.

1. ____ I am very good at maintaining a calm exterior even if I am upset.

8. ____ It is very easy for me to control my emotions.

Score Emotional Control _____

Social Expressivity: This score reflects your report of how verbally expressive you are in communicating with other people. Effective managers and leaders need a good level of expressiveness to motivate others and get them to work together.

5. ____ I usually take the initiative to introduce myself to strangers.

7. ____ I enjoy going to parties and meeting new people.

Score Social Expressivity _____

Social Sensitivity: This score shows how well you can read the cues in social situations. If you score high on this dimension, it means that you can easily tell what is going on in any social situation. This is an important leadership skill, because it helps you figure out the rules for any given group of people very quickly.

4. ____ It is very important that other people like me.

11. ____ There are certain situations in which I find myself worrying about whether I am doing or saying the right things.

Score Social Sensitivity _____

Social Control: This score reflects how you can change your social behavior to fit any situation. You know how to become a social actor in new situations. Good leaders know how to make others feel at ease in social situations by fitting in well with any crowd.

10. ____ I can easily adjust to being in just about any social situation.

12. ____ When in a group of people, I rarely have trouble thinking of the right things to talk about.

Score Social Control _____

In thinking about your scores on the Skills Inventory, it is important to look at the three emotional dimensions and the three social dimensions together. These different dimensions have been found to be important in many areas of workplace effectiveness. For example, leaders and managers with high levels of emotional expressivity are seen as more effective. In the same vein, though, individuals also need to have a corresponding level of emotional control. If a person has high control and low expressivity, many people find it difficult to work with them because they may feel as though they never know what the person is thinking. On the social side, a similar result is seen. Social expressivity is an important attribute in today's work world, but it also requires a good level of social control to make sure that behavior is appropriate for a given situation. Moreover, the ability to read social situations to know what is appropriate behavior is an extremely important skill. Many of us know people who can come into a social situation, read it, and act accordingly to make everyone comfortable. Regardless of your political affiliation, you'll probably agree that both former Presidents Bill Clinton and Ronald Reagan were very skilled in this arena.[10]

How can you improve your scores? Sometimes it just takes awareness of the importance of the different dimensions. For example, many of us are good at reading the emotions of others who do not communicate much. However, we do less well when interpreting the emotions of others who are talking all the time. Taking time to determine if a person's facial expressions match their words is an important step in becoming more skilled. If people find it difficult to read your emotions, you may want to work on sharing those emotions more often. On the other hand, if you show your emotions constantly, people will start disregarding your input. In social settings, there are many ways to increase your skills. For example, many people enroll in public speaking courses, which not only help with public speaking, but also are a way to develop networking skills.

Lengthier scales exist that will help you assess many aspects of emotional intelligence. For example, the Hay Group has developed a scale in conjunction with Daniel Goleman to assess many facets of emotional intelligence. This scale is available on their Web site.[11] Emotional intelligence also plays a large role in doing well when given specific tests and challenges in the initial stages of a mentoring relationship.

PREPARE YOURSELF FOR INITIAL TESTS AND CHALLENGES

Both mentors and protégés need to be aware of the role that tests and challenges play in the early stages of the relationship. The first step is recognizing when the challenge is offered. For example, we shared how Pamela Thomas-Graham and Bob Wright's positive first impressions of one another led to Pamela taking over at CNBC and leading the organization through a massive period of dot-com staffing ups and downs.

Recall the following four initial tests we described in Chapter Four. We suggest that you use these in the following way. For mentors—take a look at the four initial tests and feel free to customize them for yourself. What would you add to or delete from this list? You may find it helpful to use these as a way to set expectations with your protégé in your initial meeting. Also, you can use them as a tool to evaluate a potential protégé after your first meeting with them. For protégés, we suggest that you may find it helpful to assess what type of message you were trying to convey after your first meeting with a mentor. How well do you think you performed on these first four tests?

1. Does the protégé have a goal?
   - What are the protégé's goals, and are they aligned with what the mentor is willing and able to provide?
   - What ideas does the protégé have in terms of where they want to be at the peak of their career?

2. Can this be a win-win relationship?
   - What will the mentor gain from the relationship?
   - What are the specific ways the mentor can be of assistance to the protégé?

3. What is the mentor's first impression of the protégé?
   - How does the protégé's nonverbal communication style (for example, eye contact, body language, and energy) check out?
   - Does the protégé have—or do they have the potential to develop—that "special something" or executive presence?

4. Is this protégé a winner or a whiner?
- Does the protégé describe problems and challenges in their career and job constructively (that is, without whining or slamming other people)?

GETTING CLOSE: KNOW HOW TO BUILD AND DEEPEN THE RELATIONSHIP

In this section we give you worksheets and checklists that help you focus on the adequacy of the mentoring relationships you are currently involved in and to identify ways to improve or deepen these relationships. We draw on the findings we described in Chapter Six, as well as in other chapters, to help you make sure your relationship is productive.

ASSESS YOUR CURRENT RELATIONSHIPS

Research shows that mentors provide three broad categories of assistance: career, emotional, and role modeling. Research has also shown that the more of these that are offered to the protégé, the more satisfied the protégé is with the relationship.[12] The statements in Exhibit 7.14 are taken from an assessment of mentoring functions that you can use as either a mentor or a protégé to determine to what extent your relationship is providing all of the support necessary.[13]

In looking of the list of behaviors in Exhibit 7.14, think specifically about which ones are present or absent in your current relationship and what you can do to improve the support you receive. For example, as a protégé, you might talk to your mentor about other types of support you might need in the relationship. As a mentor, you might talk with your protégé about what other kinds of support you might provide him or her to improve the relationship. You may decide that for your specific mentoring relationship there are other types of behaviors you would add to the list. Regardless, using this list as a touchstone from time to time to determine whether you are in an appropriately rewarding relationship will be helpful.

ASSESS THE LEVEL OF TRUST IN YOUR CURRENT RELATIONSHIP

In a number of chapters in this book, we have discussed trust as a powerful ingredient in successful mentoring relationships.

EXHIBIT 7.14 MENTORING FUNCTIONS IN YOUR RELATIONSHIP

Career

1. My mentor takes a personal interest in my career.

2. My mentor places me in important assignments.

3. My mentor gives me special coaching on the job.

4. My mentor advises me about promotional opportunities.

5. My mentor devotes special time and consideration to my career.

6. My mentor shares valuable information with me.

7. My mentor helps me make contact with other people who might be helpful to me at work.

8. My mentor helps me to prepare for advancement.

Emotional

1. I consider my mentor to be a friend.

2. I share personal problems with my mentor.

3. I socialize with my mentor after work.

4. I exchange confidences with my mentor.

5. I often share a meal (for example, go to lunch) with a mentor.

Role Modeling

1. I imitate the work behavior of my mentor.

2. I admire my mentor's ability to motivate others.

3. I respect my mentor's knowledge of his or her field.

4. I respect my mentor's ability to teach others.

Researchers have identified a number of elements that play into feelings of trust, or "the idea of one party's willingness to be vulnerable to another party based on the belief that the latter party is (a) competent, (b) open, (c) concerned, and (d) reliable."[14] The exercise in Exhibit 7.15 asks you to rate your current mentoring relationship with respect to trust.

Add up your scores and divide by 10 to determine the average level of trust in your current relationship. Average scores at 3 or 4 indicate a very good level of trust. Scores less than 3 but more than 2 indicate that there is room for improvement. A score less than 2 indicates a low level of trust in the relationship.

EXHIBIT 7.15 TRUST SCALE

	Not At All True	Not True	Somewhat True	Very True
1. I consider this person competent in his or her job.	1	2	3	4
2. This person is a competent mentor/protégé.	1	2	3	4
3. I know where I stand with this person.	1	2	3	4
4. This person reveals appropriate personal stories about him- or herself.	1	2	3	4
5. This person communicates honestly.	1	2	3	4
6. I feel as though this person is concerned about my career.	1	2	3	4
7. This person shows concerns for others in his or her job.	1	2	3	4
8. I think this person is concerned about me as a person.	1	2	3	4
9. I can count on this person to do what she or he says will be done.	1	2	3	4
10. This person's actions match his or her words.	1	2	3	4

This scale can also be used to assess your own level of trust-worthiness. In other words, if you are a trustworthy person in your current mentoring relationship, you would be able to rate yourself highly on all the dimensions of trust. In Chapter Five, we gave numerous examples of relationships where trust was built from simple incidents. As an individual, you will have to decide what kinds of things prove another's trustworthiness for you. Research does show that while trust takes a while to develop in relationships, it can be lost quickly if one is not careful.

ASSESS TESTS AND CHALLENGES IN THE DEEPENING RELATIONSHIP

In Chapter Four, we looked at how the tests and challenges a mentor may pose to a protégé change as the relationship moves forward. For example, in Gale Anne Hurd's words, "Everything with [mentor] Roger Corman was a test!" because he was constantly presenting her with new challenges. The tests and challenges at this stage affect both the protégé and the mentor. For the protégé, it is important to handle the different types of tests deftly and to learn from them. For the mentor, we identified six categories of tests, and now we expand the discussion and provide specific ideas about how to use tests in your own relationship with a protégé. Often the nature of the first test varied considerably depending on the industry, relationship, and professional level of the mentor and protégé. However, we provide a list of generic examples that you might consider adapting.

1. "Can the protégé 'put their money where their mouth is'?" was often the first significant test. In other words, when the mentor gave the protégé his or her first assignment, did the protégé complete it and if so, how well? Typically, failing at the first assignment hurts only the protégé—the only loss to the mentor is the time spent giving the advice or suggestion. Here are some types of assignments a mentor may give:

- Give the protégé something important to read or review. This may be a report you have written or simply a book that is pivotal to your thinking. For example, Ron Dellums shared that one of his first mentors tasked him with reading *Shoes of the Fisherman* as a means of eliciting his philosophy of leadership. Discuss the protégé's thoughts and ideas at the next meeting.
- Ask the protégé to do some research. This might be something simple, such as determining when the next professional meeting of the American Society of Training and Development will be held, or it might be much more complex.
- Suggest that the protégé contact a colleague or friend for additional information about your industry or something else of interest. This will be a great way to determine how well they follow up, and what kind of impression they make on others.

- Give the protégé a simple but important task that can form the basis for your next discussion or meeting. This task can be something simple, such as updating their résumé and creating a list of career goals.
- Give the protégé a job-specific test. For example, Congresswoman Hilda Solis tasked Sharon Martinez with raising her first $10,000 for her campaign.
- What other ideas for appropriate and meaningful first tests do you have?

2. The second test relates to the question of whether a relationship with this protégé will hurt the mentor or help the mentor. Ultimately, the protégé's performance on this test will be telling in terms of whether this relationship is likely to be beneficial for the mentor. How well did the protégé handle the first challenge that had direct work implications or repercussions for the mentor's career? Typically, the second challenge is more serious, because failure can have serious work or reputation repercussions for the mentor. This challenge is often job related and really ties the protégé to the mentor's reputation. This is very context specific, but typical examples include such things as asking the protégé to deliver a professional presentation, allowing the protégé to speak or act on the mentor's behalf in a professional capacity, or tasking and trusting the protégé with a key piece of research.

- What do you think is an appropriate "benefit test" to give your protégé?

3. The third set of challenges is based on the idea that to err is human, to forgive divine . . . that is, if you learned something. This test comes into play when the protégé fails. This type of test cannot be manufactured and usually happens at the most inconvenient time possible. However, foreseeing what might go wrong and anticipating appropriate responses might be one way to avoid a relationship blowout. The following questions can be useful tools to assess your past and present mentoring relationships:

- How have you failed in the past? Think about relationships where you did poorly. What was the fatal flaw that caused it to end, or how did you salvage it?

- Think about your past relationships with mentors or protégés. What is an unforgivable act from your standpoint? What is the worst they could do?
- What would make you angry? If your protégé apologized in the right way, what could you forgive?
- Imagine a situation where your protégé failed. Is he or she likely to be defensive, receptive to your criticism, swift to make amends?
- What is a "deal-breaker" failure for you?
- How could you recover if your reputation was damaged or tainted by the actions of your protégé?
- What did the protégé really learn? What about you? Was the lesson worth the cost?
- Is the relationship worth salvaging?

4. Can I trust this protégé to tell me the truth and really hear me? In other words, how well does the protégé provide useful opinions, advice, and/or feedback to the mentor?

- List three areas in which you would appreciate candid feedback from your protégé.

5. As the relationship continues to evolve, there is a set of tests around the issue of whether the protégé is doing the work and whether he or she appreciates the mentor. Carefully examine the following diagnostic questions and assess how well your protégé is meeting your expectations:

- Is the protégé continuing to act on your suggestions?
- Is the protégé communicating to you how they acted on your suggestions, corrections, or advice?
- Is the protégé communicating appreciation of you, the mentor?
- Be honest: How do you want to be appreciated? For example, we appreciate thank-you notes and small tokens of appreciation, and we like to hear that our protégés are saying good things about us to others. How do you like to be appreciated?

6. The final test is about determining what the protégé is *really* like, as a whole person. Consider the following questions:

- How does your protégé behave in social settings, and how comfortable are you with each other outside of work?
- How does your protégé respond under pressure, and how does that help the mentor?
- Is the protégé fun to be with?
- Consider assessing your protégé in situations outside of the office, such as at lunch or at a sporting event. How does their behavior in a social setting relate to their behavior on the job, and how they might represent you and your organization?

IMPROVE YOUR CURRENT RELATIONSHIPS

In Chapter Six we provided eight tips for deepening your current mentor relationships and offered some examples. Exhibit 7.16 presents these tips, as well as space for you to record the steps you should take to achieve whatever the tip involves. So for example, you might find that in some ways the mutual admiration society is lacking. Why is that? Is it either person's fault? What can be done about it? What is your responsibility? What is your partner's responsibility?

In completing this exercise, you may decide you need to take some action to move your relationship to the deeper relationship it can be. Alternatively, you may decide that your current relationship is not meeting all of your career needs, nor is it meeting your relational needs. If you feel it is impossible to deepen your current relationship, it may be time to move on.

How do you know if your relationship is dysfunctional or no longer useful? Individuals involved in mentoring relationships often go through ups and downs in the relationship. A relationship may feel as though it has stalled. We covered some of the negative experiences mentors may have in a relationship in Chapter Six. We revisit these ideas here and ask you to take a close look at your own relationship. To what extent is your current protégé

- Exploitative
- Egocentric
- Deceptive
- Engaging in sabotage
- Overly submissive
- Performing below expectations
- Unwilling to learn[15]

EXHIBIT 7.16 DEEPENING YOUR CURRENT RELATIONSHIP: STEPS YOU WILL TAKE

1. Develop a deep understanding of each other's work environment and issues.

2. Develop a mutual admiration society.

3. Treat each other as confidants instead of as competitors.

4. Be open to your partner's influence and ideas.

5. Help each other to focus on solvable problems.

6. Develop a relationship that is meaningful for both parties.

7. Consider the important role of gender, race, or generational differences in the relationship.

8. Know when to bring others into the mentoring network.

To what extent does your mentor

- Sabotage your work
- Ask you to make impossible choices
- Steal your ideas
- Bully you
- Seek revenge
- Exploit you
- Engage in other negative actions[16]

As you complete this section, both on attempting to deepen your current relationship and on assessing whether it has become too negative, we also want you to think about whether the relationships you currently have are giving you the level of benefits you need in your career. We have described seriously negative mentoring experiences that characterize dysfunctional relationships. If the downside of the relationship outweighs the good, it may be time to start the relationship development process over again to modify your current mentoring network.

SAYING GOOD-BYE

You may find that the mentor you have is not fulfilling the many functions and expectations we have described throughout this book. We all know that breaking up is hard, and breaking up gracefully is even harder. Unfortunately, none of our power mentors and protégés had a magic potion for smooth endings, but we can share with you some of the ideas they offered that worked most of the time:

1. *Start with a positive action.* If possible, begin the transitional process by showering the mentor or protégé with appreciation for all they have done for you in the past. Be sincere. If the relationship has recently soured, reflect on what they provided for you initially and why you worked so well together. You may even want to put your thoughts into writing or present the mentor or protégé with a token of your appreciation. Next, depending on the situation, you may want to have a formal conversation or simply begin to lessen your contact with your mentor or protégé. If the parting of the ways seems mutual and amicable, this may be the easiest approach. However, if this relationship is characterized by confusion or rancor, then a more formal conversation may be necessary.

2. *Be direct and tactful.* You must be as truthful as you possibly can about why the relationship is ending. It is always better if they hear the information directly from you rather than from someone else. Just as you may have practiced "break up boyfriend" speeches with your friends in high school, you can do the same here. Talk to a trusted advisor (if not a work colleague, then a spouse, parent, or therapist). Rehearse exactly what you are going to say to your mentor or protégé and how you are going to say it. Be ready to give specific examples of behavior rather than inferences or impressions.

3. *Choose your time and place carefully.* Think carefully about meeting in a neutral location and giving enough time to this meeting. Prepare yourself for high emotions. Communicate your caring, yet be assertive about your need to move on.

4. *Tie up loose ends.* Mentors and protégés often become enmeshed in each other's work lives. Be graceful and generous, and do not leave annoying details undone. If possible, provide alternatives or even other referrals.

5. *Keep it confidential.* Remember the axiom, "If you don't have anything nice to say, say nothing at all"? This applies to ending mentoring relationships as well. Resist the urge to publicly debrief—if you must vent, do it in private with someone you trust very much and who is ideally outside of your work circle.

CONCLUSION

Developing a mentoring relationship that is truly satisfying with respect to your career is a crucial goal. Throughout this chapter, we have provided activities that focus your efforts on finding mentoring relationships to satisfy your specific career goals. Within the context of the *Relationship Development Plan,* you were asked to identify what you wanted out of the relationship. Once you decided what you were looking for, there were a number of tips for ensuring that you got what you needed, and there were methods for approaching a potential mentor or protégé. Finally, we gave methods for continuing to build and improve on the relationship you developed. As we mentioned in the beginning of this chapter, all of these activities engage the reader in careful planning and self-examination. By understanding yourself more fully, you are in a unique position to begin the journey of finding the most satisfying mentoring relationship out there—in other words, the mentoring relationship of your dreams.

The information we have presented in this chapter can be used to enhance either the relationships you seek out on your own, or those relationships that are part of a formal mentoring program. Tools to strengthen the ties formed in formal mentoring programs are very important. Unfortunately, some individuals find the mentoring programs offered by their organizations to be frustrating, either because they had little say regarding the mentor or protégé with whom they were paired, or because the training that accompanied the program was minimal. In the next chapter we discuss many of the lessons we have learned about how formal mentoring programs can be improved. Combining the activities in this chapter with the lessons learned from some of the formal programs will help you determine if you are truly making the most of the opportunities formal mentoring programs present.

CHAPTER EIGHT

CONCLUSION

What We Have Learned About Mentoring in Today's Work Environment

> *Work is love made visible. And if you cannot work with love but only with distaste it is better that you should leave your work and sit at the gate of the temple and take alms of those who work with joy.*
> —KAHLIL GIBRAN, *THE PROPHET*

We began this book by asking you some difficult and important questions around the subject of your career and your attitudes toward work. We hope that by now we have convinced you that power mentoring can increase the joy and success your work brings you. Throughout this book, we have shared with you stories of successful mentoring relationships in the hope that these important lessons would inspire your own mentoring relationships. In this last chapter, we briefly summarize what we have learned about today's mentoring landscape from our own study and from the research of others. We also point out aspects of mentoring that could still benefit from additional discovery.

In our summary in the following pages, we move from applying what we learned on an individual basis to applying what we know to organizations. To do this, we review what is known generally about setting up great programs, and then we describe some of the mentoring program practices from a selection of companies in which our study participants worked. Our recommendations will not only help organizational professionals design successful mentoring programs (or improve existing programs), but will help individual mentors and protégés take full advantage of their own companies' formal mentoring programs.

TURNING EVERYDAY MENTORING INTO POWER MENTORING

Power mentoring represents a new way of viewing traditional mentoring for today's organizations. With the changes that have occurred in the way we work in the 21st century, and the need to take charge of our own careers, a new view of mentoring is important in order to move ahead in both the corporate world and the world of not-for-profit organizations. In Chapter Two, we shared compelling examples from our participants that described how power mentoring differs from traditional mentoring in *what it does, how it looks,* and *where it lives.* We explained how power mentoring can include many aspects of traditional mentoring but expands, and in some cases radically departs from, what we consider to be traditional mentoring. To reiterate, *power mentoring* is defined as a network approach to mentoring that provides those involved with mutually beneficial outcomes related to career growth and development.

In the next section, we review our findings and those of others who have spent many years studying mentoring.

WHAT WE KNOW ABOUT EFFECTIVE MENTORING RELATIONSHIPS

As we mentioned previously, research on mentoring has demonstrated that great benefits accrue to protégés in both formal and informal relationships. Studies have shown that those who are mentored earn higher salaries, receive more promotions, and have greater career and job satisfaction than those who are not mentored.[1] Research has also demonstrated that mentoring quality makes a difference; in other words, not all mentoring relationships are created equal. Effective mentors provide career and emotional support, as well as serving as positive role models for their protégés. Research shows that gender and ethnic pairing also has implications for the initial attraction and later success of pairs.[2] We know that mentoring relationships, like other relationships, go through phases and may require different skills on the part of the mentor and the protégé to allow the relationship to reach its full potential.[3]

More recent mentoring research has begun to look at some of the complexities of mentoring. These researchers acknowledge that there is even more to effective mentoring relationships than initially anticipated. Different forms of mentoring can exist, and more reciprocal benefits can be reaped.[4] We also know that many people are finding mentoring in nontraditional sources, such as in step-ahead situations or peer groups, as well as using networks of individuals to assist in their career development.[5]

We recommend that you take the following steps in pursuing your future mentoring relationships as well as assessing your current ones:

1. *Recognize the drivers of change for today's mentoring relationships.* As we mentioned in Chapter One, the work landscape has continued to evolve dramatically in today's competitive global economy. For many, the nature of work itself has changed, as a more knowledge-based workforce has emerged. This new workforce finds itself in organizations for which there are no clear-cut corporate ladders to climb. Instead, information for career advancement must be gleaned from many different sources. Finding mentors who can help you move ahead in your profession, wherever these mentors may exist, will benefit you immensely.

2. *Broaden your definition of mentoring.* In our own research we found that it was important to broaden our definition of mentoring—in other words, to think outside the box that contained traditional ideas of mentoring. The idea that "everyone who makes it has a mentor" was uncovered in one study sponsored by Heinrick & Struggles, the executive recruiting firm.[6] Another article, by Harvard Business School's Linda Hill, argues that the perfect mentor does not exist, recommending instead that individuals look for a network of people to provide developmental support throughout their careers.[7] We agree. Effective and powerful mentoring should be utilized wherever possible. Thinking only of traditional mentoring relationships is too limiting.

3. *Expand your assumptions about mentor and protégé benefits.* Through our interviews we uncovered additional examples of the many types of benefits that both protégés and mentors receive from a mentoring relationship. Although we have often thought more in terms of the benefits accruing to the protégé, recent research and our own mentors' stories revealed many additional areas of benefits.[8]

4. *Get plugged into successful mentoring lineages if possible.* In large organizations it may be important that your mentor is tapped into the core set of powerful individuals in the organization. Of course, seeking powerful individuals as mentors has many obvious advantages, the most important being that these people have access to resources and insights about the inner workings of the organization that others might not have. Moreover, these relationships can get you recognized early in your career. But pursuing these types of "plugged-in" relationships has the disadvantage that many others in the organization are attempting the same strategy. Once you make the commitment to pursue these high-powered relationships, you have to back up your efforts with hard work, through loyalty, and by being someone others can trust. This is a high-risk strategy, but it comes with the possibility of a large payoff.

5. *Recognize the importance of different mentoring philosophies.* Individuals begin mentoring relationships with different ideas about what makes the ideal relationship. These ideas come from previous mentoring relationships they may have experienced, or from popular fictionalized mentoring relationships they have admired. Whatever the source, these ideas play a large role in the expectations individuals have for how a mentoring relationship will play out. We introduced four main types of mentoring philosophies in Chapter Four, but also noted that there are most likely a few more. The ones we identified included corporate-citizen mentor, pragmatic mentor, global-citizen mentor, and master mentor. In Chapter Seven we asked you to identify your own philosophy, and as you discovered, that philosophy plays a large role in determining your expectations and the types of mentoring relationships you plan to pursue.

6. *As a protégé, play a much bigger role in determining the type of mentoring relationship that works for you.* Another exciting feature of power mentoring that we uncovered through our research was the important influence a protégé can have over his or her mentoring relationships. Often, in the traditional view of mentoring, it

appeared that protégés waited for the mentor to choose them and then decide how they would be mentored. In other words, the mentor largely controlled the relationship. What we saw in our interviewees were protégés who did whatever they could to shape their mentoring relationships. As we mentioned, many were goal directed in their relationships and identified the type of mentoring that would most benefit their careers.

7. *Utilize goal setting or self-awareness to maximize mentoring relationships.* In Chapters Five and Seven we showed how protégés could utilize goal setting and self-management techniques to determine the outcomes of a mentoring relationship. Goal-directed protégés are very attractive to mentors; however, goal setting alone is not useful unless it is paired with a number of effective self-management strategies. Monitoring one's own performance, seeking feedback from others, rewarding oneself when achieving goals, and setting up cues to ensure that goals can be attained are just a few of the ways you can ensure that goal setting works.

8. *Be prepared for the tests and challenges that might occur in your relationships.* Both mentors and protégés need to be aware of the role that tests and challenges play, at the beginning as well as in the later stages of the mentoring relationship. These tests and challenges seem critical to ensuring that the relationship progresses. As a mentor, it is important to be clear on the purpose of the tests you might pose to a protégé. As a protégé, it is important to recognize that you are being tested or challenged, and that your performance may determine whether the relationship continues. Stepping up to the tests and challenges and overcoming them is the next important step for a protégé. Learning from the challenges and incorporating them into your future work efforts will ensure that your mentor's efforts—as well as your own—were not wasted.

9. *Develop great relationship skills.* The people we interviewed were skilled communicators—not just good at relaying facts, but people with emotional intelligence, with great listening skills, and with important insight into what makes people who they are. Understanding the use of self-disclosure and how to respond to bids for closeness are also very important relationship skills that make the difference between a weak connection with another and a mentoring relationship that satisfies both parties.

10. *Recognize defining moments.* Defining moments cannot be scheduled in advance; they can happen unexpectedly, serendipitously,

and often at busy or inconvenient times. The axiom "Expect the unexpected" applies here. The key is to realize that these moments represent an opportunity for a turning point in the relationship. When you see a defining moment arise, recognize it as an opportunity and make it a priority. What you can do ahead of time is to think about effective ways to respond; you can also try to cultivate those responses in other unexpected situations.

WHAT WE ARE STILL LEARNING ABOUT MENTORING RELATIONSHIPS

Many facets of mentoring relationships are still not well understood. Why not? First, it is difficult to study all aspects of these relationships. Getting individuals to reflect accurately on their actions in giving or receiving help is not easy. How people remember behaving with one another in general is colored by their own perceptual biases, which cause them to see themselves in a slightly more favorable light than the situation might warrant. Second, some things that take place in the mentoring relationship involve feelings that are difficult to measure carefully through rigorous scientific research. The good news is that we do know to a large extent where the gaps in our knowledge about mentoring relationships lie—that is, where more research is needed. We are left, then, with the following challenges and cautions in thinking about establishing and maintaining the right type of relationships:

1. *We need to learn more about how to make all mentoring relationships equally successful.* Although research has shown that mentors can be very helpful, not all mentoring relationships provide the same benefits. After all, mentors are not miracle workers who can solve all of a protégé's career problems. As we have outlined, protégés have to take initiative. At the same time, however, showing too much initiative could be a turnoff for some potential mentors. We do not have research that shows the proper balance of initiative with appropriate deference that makes for good initial impressions in mentoring relationships. Also, how protégés use their own career management strategies to find the type of mentoring relationships they desire requires some further investigation. In addition, although the quality of a mentoring relationship is not guaranteed, quality is very important in ensuring important out-

comes. Past research showed that mentors who were marginal in effectiveness (that is, neither on the highly effective nor highly ineffective end of the continuum) did not provide as many benefits as those who were seen as highly effective by their protégés.[9]

2. *We need more information about what it takes to maintain successful mentoring relationships.* Just as we find it difficult to keep our many life relationships running smoothly, one can expect a mentoring relationship to also take some effort to ensure that each relationship is productive for each participant. Researchers and consultants do not have all the answers about how to keep a mentoring relationship running smoothly through trying times. More research should address the problems inherent in the relationships. We have a good start when looking at some of the things that protégés or mentors have done to affect their relationships negatively. These were discussed more fully near the end of Chapter Six.

3. *Mentors and protégés need to be explicit about benefits they expect.* We have mentioned that recently mentor benefits have been studied more extensively than ever before in mentoring research.[10] With the increasing awareness of these benefits comes more responsibility on the mentor's part for identifying what he or she wants from the relationship up front. We do not know, however, exactly how that process might work. In a formal program, training mentors to identify their expectations for the relationship is one way to accomplish this. But mentors in informal relationships may not have taken the time to make sure that they understand the specific benefits.

4. *We need to understand more about the negative side of mentoring.* Although mentoring provides many advantages, it can also have a dark side, as we mentioned in Chapter Six.[11] The following example reveals one such issue. A 2004 *Wall Street Journal* article profiled a successful individual who had worked very closely with a person who mentored her.[12] A drawback the article highlighted was how working with a powerful mentor over time might make it difficult for the protégé to escape the mentor's shadow. Understanding more about how to transition away from a mentor would be an important skill to learn, especially when engaging multiple mentors. Several of our protégés shared stories of making conscious efforts to break away from their previous mentors for just those reasons.

5. *We need to uncover additional effects of mentoring on the bottom line.* Mentoring has been shown to positively affect retention,

organizational commitment, turnover, and organizational-citizen-ship behaviors. However, increasing our understanding of how mentoring helps an organization in other ways that affect the bottom line will help underscore the importance of mentoring as an organizational intervention.

Recapping what we know and what we still need to know about mentoring illustrates the complexity of mentoring relationships for mentors and protégés alike. It also illustrates many of the important concepts to both understand and put into practice as you begin to embark on new mentoring relationships, or think of ways to improve your existing relationship. In the previous chapter, we provided you with a step-by-step process to develop or improve on mentoring relationships. Now we use a wider lens to determine how what we learned can be applied to formal mentoring programs in organizations.

THE LESSONS OF POWER MENTORING FOR FORMAL MENTORING PROGRAMS

Various companies have taken advantage of the benefits of mentoring relationships in their organizations, with 60 percent of *Fortune*'s 100 best companies having formal mentoring programs.[13] They have developed comprehensive mentoring programs to fulfill a number of business needs within their organization or even to address issues in their industry. Many of these companies are very effective in developing these programs and making sure that they contribute to the bottom line.

Some of the companies initially started formal mentoring programs as a way for women and minorities to get connected into the powerful networks in organizations. Companies realized that, in fact, people tend to mentor those most like themselves, so women and minorities were being left out. Once these programs were established, many were so popular that the organizations implemented them on a larger scale, recognizing the many benefits they brought to the entire organization. In fact, whether or not a company has a formal mentoring program has become a criterion on which the "Best Companies to Work For" are judged.[14]

Although we have talked mostly about mentoring programs in structured organizations, mentoring resources also exist for those interested in owning their own businesses. A 2003 study by the National Women's Business Council examined existing, formal mentoring programs for women and men business owners.[15] They found that it was very useful for people in different stages of business ownership to have different types of mentors. For instance, for those just starting out in business, looking for someone who has been successful is a good way to get help. As examples, different Silicon Valley business incubators and the Women's Technology Cluster focused on providing assistance to new businesses. As the organizations grew, the entrepreneurs needed other types of mentoring that could be satisfied through peer-to-peer contact.

All in all, a large body of research exists that can help make formal mentoring programs very successful in the workplace. Through our interviews, however, we found some added lessons for transforming typical formal mentoring programs into power mentoring relationships. In our recommendations following, we incorporate an overview of some of the best practices from a select group of organizations whose employees participated in our study. Throughout our interview process, we were fortunate to gain access to the best and brightest individuals in some of the top U.S. companies. In our multiple interviews with employees in such companies as IBM, Cisco, Disney/ABC, and NBC/Universal, we found mentoring entrenched in the various organizations. The fact that these organizations, like many others, are required to remain at the cutting edge of technology, prepare for executive succession, build strong organizational cultures, create shareholder wealth, and attract and retain top talent underscores the importance of mentoring for their continued success.

Throughout our interviews, we found many other examples of individuals who worked in companies where mentoring was quite important. They each brought unique insights into how other organizations might improve their formal mentoring programs. These insights led to the following recommendations:

1. *Experiment with different forms of mentoring.* This includes group mentoring, reverse mentoring, multiple mentoring, e-mentoring, and other forms. We encourage organizations to think outside the

box of traditional mentoring. Determine the major goals of the mentoring program, and then decide if alternative forms might work better than traditional mentoring.

2. *Encourage mentoring and coaching as part of the organization's culture.* In the organizations we profiled and in countless others, corporate leaders realize the importance of mentoring and coaching, so much so that they include these activities as part of their official management performance appraisal system. At IBM, for example, as we've mentioned earlier, mentoring has always been used as an important tool in the development of new talent.[16] We had the good fortune of talking with a number of individuals at IBM who were closely connected to various facets of their mentoring programs. One was Joan Buzzallino, from IBM's Human Resources Department, who talked about the extent to which mentoring is part of the organization:

> For the WMC [World Wide Management Committee], which is the top 55 or so executives in the corporation, reverse mentoring is in their PBCs [personal business commitments]. So they must be able to answer the question, "Who is your reverse mentor?"
>
> We have online in our management development database lots of materials. For some people, the quick guides work for them. Some of the guides have forms where they sign mentoring agreements. This appeals to the real techies, who love everything in black and white. Other people are just as comfortable with, "Hey, you want me to be your mentor?" They work it differently, but it works fine for the different kinds of folks there are.
>
> For some of our client executives or consultants, it's in their job description that once you reach this level, you will mentor. It's viewed and observed and evaluated. It's part of the content of your job. For the rest of the employees it may be in their performance plans. So it's at different levels of the business.

What is also interesting about the mentoring programs at IBM is that they often start outside the company and involve graduate, undergraduate, and high school students interested in careers in science, especially women and minorities. If just a small percentage of those individuals join IBM, they are already acquainted with the culture of mentoring at IBM, having been mentored before they arrived at the company.

Since the idea behind power mentoring is to utilize a network, we strongly recommend that organizations build participation in mentoring into their rewards systems. Simply put, make mentoring part of your employees' performance appraisals. If employees feel rewarded and recognized for mentoring, they are more likely to participate.

3. *Utilize both formal and informal mentoring in organizations.* Formal and spontaneously developed mentoring relationships do not have to be mutually exclusive events. Both types of mentoring can coexist and even complement each other, as they do at IBM.

4. *Regard mentoring as an important way to develop executive talent.* In 2000, Linkage Incorporated (a consulting group that gathers trends on organizational practices) asked a number of companies to list the top leadership development challenges they expect to face in the years ahead.[17] Following are some of the issues they identified:

- Globalization
- Improving productivity
- Competitive pressures
- Customer focus
- Rapid growth
- Focus on corporate vision
- Entrance into new markets
- Postmerger integration
- Strategic partnerships

All of the reasons organizations feel pressure to develop leadership potential can be addressed through the use of formal mentoring programs. For example, although the effects of globalization may differ for each company, this process may still affect the type of leadership you need. Companies that have already done what they can to globalize need leaders and managers who have an appropriate worldview and can work to integrate operations around the world. Their mentoring of young up-and-comers in the organization can help these employees adopt the kind of global, cooperative perspective that will help the organization succeed. Companies just beginning to take steps toward the globalization of their operations will likewise need managers to mentor new employees as the organization works to keep up with economic developments already taking place. In this case, leaders and managers must be continually looking for changes in their competitive markets. Mentors who are able to impress on protégés the importance of globalization for the company will make an important contribution.

One company that Linkage profiled, Dow Chemical, was acutely aware of the importance of both mentoring and coaching within their leadership development program. They used these techniques to ensure that their new managers and leaders were acquainted with the leadership requirements of the culture.[18] Other companies have implemented similar programs. In our conversations with Anne Sweeney and Kathleen Von der Ahe from Disney, we learned a great deal about the program Disney had put in place to make sure that individuals were advancing appropriately in the organization. We also learned that Disney recognized the importance of cross-organizational mentoring in such a large corporation. Another part of the organization also emphasizes the importance of mentoring. For example, the ABC Corporate Mentoring Program pairs a senior executive with a protégé for one year. The program targets talented minority and women employees at the senior management level who have demonstrated ability and commitment to the company. The program gives protégés exposure to business strategies across the media networks, as well as networking opportunities with other executives from a cross-section of businesses. The organization also recognizes that the program gives both mentors and protégés an opportunity to enhance leadership skills.[19]

5. *Understand the importance of knowledge workers.* Organizations should realize that human capital is important and that the knowledge that workers bring to the organization is indeed a very valuable asset. Organizations should also realize that tapping into the knowledge that workers possess is not always easy. However, modeling an easy exchange and effective utilization of information could be an important role for mentors. According to some experts, mentoring in information technology (IT) companies such as Cisco or IBM is somewhat more difficult because of the more linear thinking that dominates the workforce. They go on to suggest that in IT companies, it is imperative that a program be set up competently, with specific goals to encourage participation.[20] High-tech companies such as Hewlett-Packard, Microsoft, Intel, and SBC Communications have used mentoring for many years. Cisco most likely finds that other techniques—such as helping protégés set specific development goals, as well as pinpointing learning objectives—

help guarantee the success of the organization's mentoring efforts. Consultants who work with high-tech companies say a variety of tools are important, including checklists and worksheets as well as online training guides. Even though these organizations are high tech, however, consultants find that encouraging more one-on-one time for a culture that prefers e-mail is very worthwhile. Finally, they note that giving praise in a mentoring relationship goes a long way, because people in these organizations are often not used to receiving overt praise when they are doing well.

6. *Develop a formal mentoring program philosophy.* The formal mentoring programs in the companies we studied seemed to make a special effort to develop a corporate philosophy of mentoring. In Chapter Four we talked about the importance of clarifying one's mentoring philosophy so that mentors and protégés have a complete understanding of the expectations of the relationship. With a formal program, developing a unifying philosophy helps those in the program manage expectations and look to others as their guides for the type of mentoring that is in keeping with the company culture.

7. *Emphasize complementary skills approach.* The individuals we interviewed ended up with their protégés or mentors not necessarily because of what they had in common but more because of the complementary skills they brought to the table. In other words, some of the most successful mentoring relationships were more like partnerships, with the members receiving mutual benefits. NBC's emphasis on mentoring seems less formalized, at least as far as we could tell from our interviews with NBC employees. Bob Wright, Pamela Thomas-Graham, and Paula Madison all worked together in the same manner as Bob Wright had done when he worked his way through GE under Jack Welch's guidance.

8. *Make development of trust a foundation of formal mentoring.* Because we found that trust played a large role in mentoring relationships, we thought that making this explicit in mentoring relationships or formal mentoring programs would go a long way in capitalizing on the benefits of trust. For example, mentoring relationship partners could develop confidentiality agreements, take a course on trust building and maintenance as part of their mentor training, and work toward developing a reputation and concern for trust. The idea of trust could be part of a larger training module on the ethics of mentoring.

Getting a Formal Mentoring Program Off the Ground

Fortunately for those creating formal mentoring programs, a large amount of advice on planning, implementing, and evaluating programs of this nature is available. In this section, we outline advice to program managers about how best to work through the process of implementation by sharing some of the specific lessons we have learned through our interviews and from other sources.

Top Management Support

Most consultants say that gaining top management support is a prerequisite to a successful formal mentoring program. We found this to be very true when we looked at the companies that had mentoring ingrained in their organizational culture. Mentoring was encouraged, supported, rewarded, and modeled by top management.

Voluntary Participation

It's important to reward people for participating instead of punishing those who do not participate in a mandatory type of program. Once individuals see the rewards they gain from the relationship, others will be eager to join the program.

Proper Prescreening

We suggest that you carefully prescreen potential mentors and protégés. Assess their motivation level. Also, do a thorough assessment of their skills, and use this information to match them with an individual who has similar values but complementary skills. In addition, tap into their expectations regarding the types of benefits they expect from the relationship.

Proper Pairing

Organizations today choose mentoring pairs in many different ways. Make it look and feel as much like a spontaneously developed relationship as possible. Give people a choice. Educate them about the vast array of power mentoring options. We suggest that you provide some initial direction in terms of matching mentors and protégés, and then allow them to make the final choice. The initial matching can be fairly simple or very sophisticated, depending on your organization. For a simple approach, you might have participants complete a one-page questionnaire that indicates their interests, skills, and preferences. For a very sophisticated and innovative approach, check out MentorNet, a formal online mentoring program.[21] MentorNet uses a computer-based algorithm program that matches mentors and protégés and that has been shown to be extremely successful.

ENHANCED TRAINING AND SUPPORT

We would argue that for every company serving as an exemplar of the best training and ongoing program support, there are many others that do not have the necessary time and resources. Chapter Seven contains many exercises that can be used individually or adapted for use in a training program. Individuals need the help of others who have been there before them in establishing a mentoring relationship to share their experience with mentoring. For example, Anne Sweeney from ABC/Disney described her own experiences in early mentoring relationships after overcoming her initial reservations:

> I remember being a little nervous about it [being part of a mentoring program] as I was new to the company. I was worried that I was expected to be perfect or know it all, and I think the best thing about a mentor-mentee relationship is accepting each other, warts and all. You really have to be able to let your hair down and say, "Let me tell you about my biggest mistake" or "the day I totally bungled this because I didn't listen to what the client was really saying or the direction their business was going." Just being able to share that kind of thing is invaluable.

Testimonials such as Anne's go a long way in demonstrating to a new mentor that some of the uncertainty that occurs in the early stages of the relationship is natural, but eventually goes away as the relationship develops.

MUTUAL BENEFITS

By now you should be convinced of the mutual benefits that are available to both mentors and protégés. Although formal mentoring programs emphasize the benefits for both, most programs seem to concentrate on the benefits for protégés. Alerting potential mentors to the various benefits when advertising formal programs will go a long way toward making sure that the mentors gain valuable experience from the program—experience that will enhance their own career development.

EXPANDED ROLE OF TESTS AND CHALLENGES

Educate mentors and protégés about how tests and challenges will likely affect their mentoring relationship, both in the initial stages and throughout. Provide coaches who can help mentors and protégés with some of the tests and challenges they will face.

PROPER FEEDBACK AND PROGRAM EVALUATIONS

Professionals managing formal mentoring programs are well aware that any organizational initiative must show results. Some tie their results to the bottom-line outcomes, while others track participant satisfaction and other program outcomes. We suggest that besides using typical indices, program administrators also assess process measures. For example, they might evaluate the pairing methodology as soon as it is completed. Were the initial matches satisfactory? Did individuals find common values and goals on which they could build a relationship? Evaluate the mentors' and protégés' readiness for the mentoring relationship in addition to their performance in the relationship. Moreover, if your organization is interested in specific workforce outcomes such as increased incidence of general coaching behavior, those could be additional behavioral measures included in a manager's annual performance review.

TIME LIMITS

Knowing the right time to end a mentoring relationship is an important feature of a formal mentoring program. Giving participants a time frame for determining how long the relationship should last will help them determine what goals can be realistically accomplished in the given time. Without an ending date, participants may find that the relationship has outlived its usefulness but still feel pressure to continue. If participants want to continue a formal mentoring relationship past the allotted time frame, it is most likely a successful relationship, so that the benefits for both mentor and protégé will continue.

CONCLUSION

In researching and writing this book, we learned more about effective mentoring than we thought possible. Our interviewees were not only successful but also incredibly insightful about their career journeys and about who helped them along the way. We are grateful for the time they took with us and for the examples of power mentoring they provided us with. We set out to write this book because we wanted to build bridges between bodies of knowledge, such as academic research and practitioner know-how. We also wanted to build bridges between you and your respective mentors and protégés. There is much to be learned from each other as we integrate our knowledge and experience.

The wisdom and stories shared by our interviewees resonate for us as we bring this work to a close. We recall the words of Araceli Gonzalez in describing how she initially felt about her mentor, Rosario Marin, before she approached her and they became close. Araceli said with great conviction, "She's way up there, and I am way down here." As Araceli got to know Rosario, she felt more confident about what she had to offer and less like she was beneath Rosario. Rosario also seemed more down to earth to her as well, as she got to know her as a whole person. If you have ever felt "way down here" or that someone you are interested in being a mentor for you is "way up there," we hope you remember that it is possible to connect with the mentors of your dreams by using some of the strategies we have outlined in this book. Remember, if you don't ask, you don't get. Ask for the assistance you need—you will be amazed that there are mentors just waiting to help you in your career journey.

On the other side, if you are a mentor, recall the benefits of being a mentor. Here the words of Rosario Marin, Araceli's mentor, resonate for us. We wish you could hear the passion and truthfulness in her voice when she said, "I get such a sense of tremendous joy in being a mentor." We know you are busy, and relationships with others do take time and energy. However, when you think about spending those 50-plus hours a week at work, we hope that you take away from this book the important idea that having a circle of protégés can bring great meaning to your work life right now and be a tremendous source of help for you. What you give, you get back. Start giving—you will be amazed at the rewards you receive.

Our most important decisions in life often require us to choose only one option, and then we have to live with the consequences for quite some time. Think about it: you have to choose one university and/or graduate school to attend. You have to choose one career or job to pursue at a time. We have to choose one spouse or partner. Often we are forced into positions of monogamy or at least serial monogamy with our schools, jobs, and life partners. However, as we move through life and through our careers, our needs are in constant flux.

Consider the people in your life who enable you to keep up with your rapidly shifting needs. Usually it is your circle of friends, which may change depending on your circumstances and interests. You can have work colleagues to write articles with, tennis pals, running buddies, or mommy friends for play dates. In their book on friendship, Ellen Goodman and Patricia O'Brien talk about the idea of friends of the road and friends of the heart.[22] *Friends of the road* are crucial during certain times in your life, but you often lose touch with them when you change jobs or move away. *Friends of the heart* are with you for the long haul. The idea is that you can have a circle or a community of friends who fulfill different needs for you. So it is with power mentoring.

Different mentors meet different needs for you at various times along your career journey. Some will form the nucleus of your community and be with you for the long haul. Others will be a part of your community only temporarily but will have a lasting impact on your thoughts and work behavior. Just as you can effectively nurture a community of different friendships, you can do the same for mentors. When it comes to mentoring, you don't have to choose just one—you really can have it all.

APPENDIX A

THE INTERVIEWEES

FRAN ALLEN has made outstanding contributions to the field of programming languages for almost 40 years, and her work has significantly influenced the wider computer science community. Ms. Allen is a pioneer in the field of optimizing compilers. Her achievements include seminal work in compilers, code optimization, and parallelization. In the early 1980s, she formed the Parallel TRANslation (PTRAN) group to study the issues involved in compiling for parallel machines. The group was considered one of the top research groups in the world working with parallelization issues. Her work on these projects culminated in algorithms and technologies that form the basis for the theory of program optimization and are widely used in today's commercial compilers throughout the industry.

Ms. Allen's influence on the IBM community was recognized with her appointment as an IBM fellow; she was the first woman to receive this recognition. She also was president of the IBM Academy of Technology. The Academy plays an important role in the corporation by providing technical leadership, advancing the understanding of key technical areas, and fostering.

Allen is a member of the National Academy of Engineering, the American Philosophical Society, and the American Academy of Arts and Sciences. She is a Fellow of the ACM, the IEEE, and the Computer History Museum and has two honorary doctorate degrees as well as several awards for her work for women in computing. She has been inducted into the WITI (Women in Technology International) Hall of Fame and last year she received the Augusta Ada Lovelace Award from the Association for Women in Computing. For her work on behalf of women in IBM, the company established the Frances E. Allen IBM Women in Technology Mentoring Award in 2000 and made Fran the first recipient.

PATTY ARCHIBECK currently manages Investor Relations for Cisco Systems in Europe, the Middle East, and Africa and is based out of London. She has spent over five years at Cisco Systems, primarily in the role of senior manager, executive communications for the chief financial officer and the Office of the President based in San Jose, California. Patty earned a B.S. degree in business administration–accounting from Santa Clara University in 1991 and her license as a Certified Public Accountant in 1993 while working at Coopers & Lybrand. Patty lives in London with her husband, David Charles, and their son, Archie Charles.

LILACH ASOFSKY is the senior vice president of marketing/research/creative services for CNBC, the global leader in business news, providing real-time financial market coverage and business information to more than 175 million homes worldwide. In this position, Lilach is responsible for the overall marketing and management of the CNBC brand, including advertising and sales marketing for the network. Based in Englewood Cliffs, New Jersey, she also oversees CNBC's research operations. Lilach joined CNBC in 1999 as vice president, product development and marketing for CNBC.com. In this position, she built and led a world-class team responsible for overall customer experience, including core financial tools and applications, site navigation, content expansion, and site product innovations as well as advertising, promotion, and research. Previously, Lilach was the vice president of Internet marketing and business strategy for e-Citi, a division of Citigroup. While there, she built an organization focused on online marketing, Web site construction, portal deal negotiation and execution, and relationship management of other business units. In that role, she also led a Global Internet Steering Committee to maximize successful transfer and communication between all of Citi's consumer businesses. As the vice president of access marketing, Lilach was responsible for the mass market launch of Direct Access, Citi's online banking service, in which she increased users by 650 percent over a one-year period through an integrated marketing campaign consisting of broadcast and print advertising, direct mail, promotions, and the creation of a trade show strategy. As a result of her successful programs, including an award-winning online campaign introducing "trial without purchase" within financial services, she has spoken frequently on the topic of "brand-action marketing" both at industry events and academic forums.

ANITA BORG (1949–2003) was the founder of the Institute for Women and Technology (IWT). On her passing, IWT was renamed in her honor as the Anita Borg Institute for Women and Technology. The Institute is supported by Xerox, Sun Microsystems, Hewlett-Packard, Compaq Microsoft Corporation, and individuals as it works to bring women's perspectives, needs, and brilliance to the development of future technologies for a better world. Dr. Borg has been featured in numerous national print, television, radio, and Web publications, including CBS's *60 Minutes*. In 1999 she was appointed by President Clinton to the Commission on the Advancement of Women and Minorities in Science, Engineering, and Technology (CAWMSET) and in 2002 she was recognized with the Heinz Award for Technology, the Economy and Employment. Throughout her career, Dr. Borg has worked to encourage women to pursue careers in computing. In 1987 she started *systers,* an electronic community for technical women in computing. Today, *systers* has 2,500 members in 38 countries and provides an international community of advice and support. Dr. Borg was born Anita Borg Naffz in 1949 in Chicago, Illinois. She grew up in Palatine, Illinois; Kaneohe, Hawaii; and Mukilteo, Washington. She moved to Palo Alto, California, in 1986, where she was an outdoorswoman, enjoying hiking, backpacking, mountain biking, scuba diving, gardening, and flying.

MARC BUCKLAND began his career as a production assistant at Steven Bochco Productions. After working his way up to associate producer, he wrote, produced, and directed *Dead Guy,* a 16-minute short film that received accolades on the festival circuit and caught the attention of industry professionals. He then produced and directed the critically acclaimed Bochco series *Murder One* for two seasons, followed by a stint as supervising producer and director of the drama *Brooklyn South.* Following that, Marc directed episodes of *The West Wing, NYPD Blue, Felicity, Sports Night, Buddy Faro, Maximum Bob, Popular,* and *Scrubs,* for which he received an Emmy nomination. He also directed the pilot episodes of *My Name Is Earl,*

Medical Investigation, Cracking Up, Partners, It's Not About Me, Couples, News from the Edge, and *Brutally Normal.* Marc executive produced and directed the series *Ed, It's Not About Me, Brutally Normal,* and *Medical Investigation.*

LEE BUTLER was in charge of the United States' strategic nuclear forces—encompassing the nation's long-range bomber and land- and sea-based intercontinental ballistic missiles, which are equipped to carry up to ten thousand nuclear warheads—from January 1991 to February 1994. In this position, he was also responsible for developing the nuclear war plan and was the principal advisor to the President on the execution of that plan. He is a 1961 graduate of the Air Force Academy and was an Olmsted Scholar at the University of Paris, where he earned a master's degree in international relations. General Butler has flown more than three thousand hours in 15 different types of aircraft. He flew the F-4 in combat in Vietnam. He has been a member of numerous civic organizations, including the Council on Foreign Relations and the Committee on International Security and Arms Control of the National Academy of Sciences. He served on the Boards of several service organizations while living in Omaha, Nebraska. He has received numerous awards and honors, both military and civic, including the Heinz Award for Public Policy. He is married to the former Dorene Nunley of Norwalk, California. He and his wife have two children, Brett and Lisa, and six grandchildren. General and Mrs. Butler make their home in Laguna Beach, California.

JOAN BUZZALLINO is vice president, human resources, technology, and manufacturing at IBM. She joined IBM 30 years ago as an educational services representative in New York City and has held positions covering all aspects of sales, including sales manager in Philadelphia and branch manager in Morristown, New Jersey. She was appointed to her first executive position in 1990 as director of human resources, operations, for the IBM United States Marketing and Services organization. In 1994 she was named director, executive programs, responsible for succession planning and executive compensation programs for IBM North America. Joan has served as vice president of HR for IBM Global Industries, responsible for human resource programs for the seventeen thousand employees across 127 countries worldwide. She has been the vice president, human resources, for two of IBM's global brand units—the personal systems group and the storage products group. She spent the last two years as vice president of HR for IBM's new strategy to become the premier e-business on demand focusing on the cultural impact of major transformation. She assumed her current role as HR leader for IBM's 195,000 technical resources in October 2004. Joan graduated from Cabrini College in Radnor, Pennsylvania, with a B.S. degree in education and she currently serves on the college's Board of Trustees.

LARRY R. CARTER is a senior vice president in Cisco's Office of the President and a member of the Cisco Board of Directors. Carter joined Cisco as chief financial officer (CFO) in 1995 and developed a world-class finance organization during his eight-year tenure. Under his leadership, the Cisco Finance Organization leveraged Internet technologies to pioneer daily financial reporting on crucial metrics for company executives and made the one-day worldwide "virtual close" a reality that cuts finance costs almost in half as a percentage of revenue.

   During his career as CFO at Cisco, his finance organization was spotlighted in major publications, such as *Fortune, Harvard Business Review,* and *Financial Executive.* His expertise has been recognized with awards such as the CFO Excellence Awards. Carter was appointed to the Cisco Board of Directors in July 2000. He has brought more than 25 years of experience to this role as well as a thorough understanding of the industry from a business and financial perspective. In May 2003, he stepped away from his day-to-day financial management role as CFO and was appointed senior vice president in Cisco's Office of the President. Carter also serves on the Board of Trustees at Loyola Marymount University and on the Board of Directors for QLogic Corporation.

JUDY CHU was elected to the California State Assembly in May 2001. She represents the 49th Assembly District, which includes Alhambra, El Monte, Monterey Park, Rosemead, San Gabriel, San Marino, and South El Monte in Southern California.

   She chairs the State Assembly Appropriations Committee, which oversees all legislation that has a fiscal impact on the state. As such, she serves as a member of Speaker Nunez's executive leadership team and plays a pivotal role in the development and passage of policy through the state legislature. As a member of the Budget Conference Committee, which is responsible for negotiating the final version of California's $99 billion annual budget, she has worked to maintain critical healthcare programs and social services for seniors, children, and the developmentally disabled. She chairs the Select Committee on Hate Crimes and the California Asian and Pacific Islander Legislative Caucus. She is also a member of the Assembly Revenue and Taxation, Labor and Employment, and Environmental Safety and Toxic Materials committees.

Dr. Chu has authored a landmark tax amnesty bill that is expected to produce over $300 million in revenue for the state budget without raising taxes. She fought to protect victims through her Sexual Assault Survivors' DNA Bill of Rights and through her bill protecting the assets of domestic violence survivors. She has authored measures to protect immigrants from victimization by fraudulent immigration consultants and from deceptive bait-and-switch practices in car dealerships. Her hate crimes bills provide for an automatic protective order for hate crimes victims, improve the prosecution of hate crimes, and allow courts to mandate anti-bias counseling for perpetrators. Her legislation enables aging schools greater access to state modernization funds. Her environmental bills ban toxic chemicals in packaging and establish an environmental justice small grant program. Her healthcare bills improve access to MediCal and the Healthy Families program by those using community clinics, increase training for acupuncturists, and improve accountability by requiring an audit of the state's contracts for prescription drugs.

Prior to serving in the State Assembly, Dr. Chu served on the Monterey Park City Council for 13 years, from 1988 to 2001, and served as Mayor three times. Dr. Chu has been dedicated to education for decades and was a community college professor in psychology for 20 years.

MARTHA COOLIDGE is one of the more prominent female directors working in Hollywood. She received extensive training at the Rhode Island School of Design, New York's School of Visual Arts, and the New York University Institute of Film and Television graduate school. During the period of her education, she made many prize-winning films and documentaries. Her first directorial job was a short film, *Not a Pretty Picture* (1975), which examined high school date rape. It won acclaim and attention, as did her feature-length *City Girl* (1983), which led to her subsequent job directing the modest commercial feature comedy *Valley Girl* (1983) with Nicolas Cage in his first starring role. This film's unexpectedly positive reviews won Coolidge major studio assignments. Coolidge also found satisfying work in television and made the hit movie, *Rambling Rose* (1991), the story of a free-spirited young woman in a small Southern town, which earned Oscar nominations for its stars Laura Dern and Diane Ladd. Recent credits include *The Prince and Me* (2004) starring Julia Stiles. Coolidge is currently in production on Hillary Duff's latest movie, *Material Girls*. Long active in the Directors Guild of America, she was elected its first female president in March 2002 and she held the position until 2003.

BARBARA CORDAY is recently retired as chair and professor of the Production Division of the world famous USC School of Cinema Television. Previously, Corday was president of Columbia Pictures Television; she was the first woman in Hollywood to hold that position at a major studio. She was also the first woman to head all primetime programming at a network, CBS. She was cocreator of the multiaward winning series *Cagney & Lacey,* cocreator of the Emmy nominated series *American Dream,* and writer or producer of many others. Corday lives in Los Angeles with her husband, Roger Lowenstein, and has a grown daughter.

RONALD V. DELLUMS is founder and senior partner of Dellums and Associates, L.L.C. He retired from Congress in 1998 after being first elected in 1970. During his tenure in the House of Representatives, Mr. Dellums occupied a number of top leadership positions, including the chairmanship of the House Armed Services Committee. As chairman of the Congressional Black Caucus, he was renowned for his visionary leadership in helping to end the U.S. support for the racist apartheid regime of South Africa. Upon retiring from the House of Representatives, Mr. Dellums accepted the position of president of Healthcare International Management Company. Mr. Dellums conceived the AIDS Marshall Plan for Africa, which evolved into today's Global Fund to Fight AIDS, Tuberculosis and Malaria. President Clinton appointed Mr. Dellums to chair the Presidential Advisory Council on HIV/AIDS in 1999. Mr. Dellums currently serves as chairman of the Board of

Directors for the Constituency for Africa. Mr. Dellums has received numerous honors and awards, including the eponymous naming of two buildings in Oakland, California. His contributions to higher education have earned wide recognition. Mr. Dellums has authored two books, including *Lying Down with the Lions: A Public Life from the Streets of Oakland to the Halls of Power* (2000). His family was the focus of a 2000 Disney movie, *The Color of Friendship,* which depicted their experience hosting a white South African exchange student in the 1970s.

Nick M. Donofrio is the senior vice president, technology and manufacturing for IBM. He is the leader of IBM's technology strategy and is a champion for innovation across IBM and its global ecosystem. His responsibilities include IBM Research, the Integrated Supply Chain and Integrated Product Development teams, Governmental Programs, Environmental Health and Product Safety, Quality, and IBM's enterprise on-demand transformation team.

Since joining IBM in 1967, Mr. Donofrio has held numerous technical management and executive positions throughout IBM's product divisions. He holds seven technology patents and is a member of numerous technical and science honor societies. He serves as a member of the Board of Directors for the Bank of New York and the Board of Trustees for Rensselaer Polytechnic Institute. Mr. Donofrio holds a B.S. degree in electrical engineering from Rensselaer Polytechnic Institute and an M.S. degree in the same discipline from Syracuse University. He also holds an honorary doctorate in engineering from Polytechnic University and an honorary doctorate in sciences from the University of Warwick in the United Kingdom. In addition to his strategic business mission, Mr. Donofrio leads the development and retention of IBM's technical population and strives to enrich that community with a diversity of culture and thought.

David Dreier was born in Kansas City, Missouri, where he remains active in his family's real estate investment firm. Dreier graduated cum laude from Claremont McKenna College in 1975 and earned a master's degree in American government from Claremont Graduate University the following year. From 1976 to 1978, Dreier served as director of corporate relations for Claremont McKenna

College. He also worked in marketing for a San Dimas industrial firm until his election to Congress in 1980. Congressman Dreier has established a record of leadership through honesty, integrity, and accountability. At the start of the 106th Congress in January 1999, Dreier joined the House Leadership when he took the helm of the powerful House Committee on Rules. One of the youngest as well as the first Californian Rules Chairman in history, David Dreier plays a pivotal role in fashioning key legislation. In May 2001 Dreier was unanimously selected by his California colleagues to chair the state's Republican Congressional delegation. As chairman, he leads the Congress's largest Republican delegation on matters of importance to California. In the fall of 2003, he was asked by California Governor Arnold Schwarzenegger to chair his transition team. As a member of the House Republican leadership, he encourages bipartisan solutions, while sticking to his core principles of working to promote individual liberty, economic opportunity, strong U.S. global leadership, and limited but effective government.

KIM FISHER is a director at Prologue International, which provides the expertise and technology required to effectively and efficiently build world-class centers of innovation that foster entrepreneurship. Through her role at Prologue, Ms. Fisher has started, run, turned around, and built sustainable revenue models for incubators, technology parks, and business centers.

Previously, Ms. Fisher was executive director of the Women's Technology Cluster (WTC), the world's leading incubator for women-led companies, where she helped over 50 companies raise over $350 million in venture capital. Prior to working at the WTC, Ms. Fisher was CEO and cofounder of AudioBasket, where she raised over $25 million and formed partnerships with leading companies, such as Microsoft, AOL, Time Warner, and Deutsche Telekom. (AudioBasket was acquired by EMotion.) Ms. Fisher also has worked for Motorola Ventures and was marketing director for a wireless operator in Lithuania, where she grew revenue from $0 to $200 million.

As a leading female CEO, she has been featured in four books, has appeared on the cover of *U.S. News & World Report,* and has been mentioned in numerous other media. She has also been awarded the Price Fellowship for Entrepreneurship and serves on the Advisory Boards of the Haas School of Business, the Lester Center for Entrepreneurship, and Nokia Innovent (an investment division of Nokia Corporation).

Ms. Fisher has a B.S. degree in economics from the Wharton School of Business and an MBA from the University of California at Berkeley, Haas School of Business.

DIXIE GARR has been vice president of customer success engineering at Cisco Systems, Inc.—the leader in Internet communication solutions—for the past six years. The scope of her direct teams has included specialized technical support, laboratories, and client-funded strategic cross-corporation initiatives. During Ms. Garr's tenure, the level of customer satisfaction improved from a 3.85 baseline to 4.78 of 5.0 maximum; a single cross-functional improvement program saved over one half billion dollars last year. Prior to joining Cisco, Ms. Garr held leadership positions in six large corporations. As director of software engineering at Texas Instruments, Ms. Garr led a team of more than nine hundred software engineers responsible for hundreds of development projects as well as office automation. Her industry recognitions include being named one of the 50 Most Important African-Americans in Technology (2004), NSBE Technology Woman of the Year (2002), IT Executive of the Year by Career Communication (2000), Black Engineer of the Year for Professional Achievement in Industry, and Corporate Most Influential African American in the Bay Area. She is an alumnus of Leadership America and Leadership Texas. She was cofounder and president of the Minority Leadership Initiative at TI. Ms. Garr is married to David Schultz. Her greatest in-progress masterpiece is her daughter, Alexandra Garr-Schultz, a high school senior.

LEEZA GIBBONS has been entering America's living rooms for over 20 years. In 2004, Leeza and Westwood One launched *Leeza at Night*. Gibbons currently hosts Lifetime's successful primetime magazine, *What Should You Do?* Gibbons left her daily post as managing editor and host of the newsmagazine *EXTRA* in order to form the Leeza Gibbons Memory Foundation. Gibbons has been a national anchor/reporter on *Entertainment Tonight* and has hosted and served as executive producer of her own daytime talk show, *Leeza*. Gibbons received nominations for both Outstanding Talk Show and Outstanding Talk Show Host every year she was eligible, and *Leeza* garnered 27 Daytime Emmy Nominations and won three Emmys. Gibbons was awarded with a star on the Hollywood Walk of Fame. Televised projects produced by or in association with LGE and Leeza include a CBS special with IWON.com, E!'s *Assignment E! with Leeza Gibbons,* the highest-rated non-news series in the channel's history, and the Emmy-winning *Teen Files.* Gibbons is the national spokesperson for Kids Peace, a celebrity ambassador for ChildHelp USA, and a Board member of Marc Klass's Beyond Missing. Gibbons has testified before Congress and is most proud to have received the Congressional Horizon Award for her crusade on children's issues. Gibbons is married to architect/actor Stephen Meadows. They have three children—a daughter, Lexi, and sons, Troy and Nathan.

LESLI LINKA GLATTER's first film, *Tales of Meeting and Parting,* received an Academy Award nomination. Glatter made her feature directorial debut with New Line's successful coming-of-age comedy, *Now and Then.* Previously, she directed HBO's highly acclaimed *State of Emergency,* which received a Cable ACE nomination for Best Picture as well as a nomination for the Humanitas award. Lesli is based at John Wells Production and is in development on numerous film and television projects. Currently she is directing the final two episodes of the upcoming NBC miniseries *Revelations* with Bill Pullman, by David O. Seltzer. She directed episodes of *The O.C., Jonny Zero,* and *Numbers.* Lesli has also directed multiple episodes of *The West Wing, ER*—including the 1998 season finale—and various episodes of *Third Watch, NYPD Blue, Brooklyn South, Murder One,* the highly acclaimed *Freaks and Geeks,* Stephen Spielberg's *Amazing Stories,* and *Twin Peaks* for David Lynch, for which she received a Director's Guild Nomination. She also directed the pilot *In My Life* for Francis Ford Coppola's American Zoetrope and the WB and *Newton* for Joel Silver and Warner Bros. Lesli presently serves on AFI's Education and Training Board, the Western Directors Council of the Director's Guild of America, and the Silver Circle of Women in Film and is a mentor for the Independent Feature Projects' Project Involve.

ARACELI GONZALEZ is an American of Mexican decent. Gonzalez's dedication to assisting working families and improving their quality of life led her to a career as a small business consultant in which role she helps aspiring entrepreneurs start and grow new businesses. She is the proud owner of AG Business Services, which provides small business consulting, document preparation services, and business plan preparation. In 1996 Gonzalez became the first and youngest Latina to be elected as city council member and Vice-Mayor of Cudahy, California. In 2000 Gonzalez was a regional co-chair and national Hispanic media spokesperson on the Bush for President campaign and was a delegate at the Republican Convention in Philadelphia. Later in 2000 Gonzalez announced her intentions to run for the State Senate when she became increasingly frustrated with political leaders in Sacramento. In 2002 President George W. Bush recognized her for outstanding Hispanic leadership. She is a 2003 nominee for the American Institute of Young Political Leaders and currently serves on the Republican Central Committee of Orange County for Senate District 34. In 2004 she served as a delegate for the convention in New York and was selected as platform chair for California. She is a founding member and former member of the Board of Directors/President for the National Latina Business Women Association of Orange County (NLBWA-OC) and a JAYCEES member.

JUDITH GWATHMEY is the founder and CEO of Gwathmey, Inc., a pre-clinical contract research laboratory that supports small to mid-sized biotechnology companies in getting safe drugs to the FDA for approval to enter clinical trial. She formerly was an associate professor of medicine at Harvard Medical School and she currently is professor of medicine and physiology at Boston University Medical Center and senior lecturer at Harvard Medical School in the Department of Medicine. She has received two of the highest awards from the Ohio State University—the William Oxley Thompson Distinguished Alumnus Award for Excellence in Science Before Age 35 and Distinguished Alumnus for Outstanding Accomplishments in Science and Mentoring from the School of Veterinary Medicine. Dr. Gwathmey is a highly respected and referenced thought leader in cardiovascular disease, who has received over $12 million in funding from the National Institutes of Health and the National Science Foundation. With these funds, she has published over 160 papers. Dr. Gwathmey wrote and edited a landmark book on cardiovascular disease entitled *Heart Failure: Basic Research and Clinical Aspects* and is the author of the most cited paper in heart failure research on the role of calcium in heart failure. She is an elected Fellow of the American Heart Association and the first nonphysician Fellow elected to the American College of Cardiology. In 2001 Dr. Gwathmey was awarded the Presidential Mentoring Award in Science, Mathematics, and Engineering. Since that time, Dr. Gwathmey has coauthored a major mentoring article published in the *Journal of Social Issues.* Judith lives in Virginia with her family.

ANTHONY HAYTER is the owner and operator of a Marble Slab Creamery ice cream shop. He is the CEO of VHA Creamery, Inc., the business entity behind the shop, and is currently in the process of opening his second Marble Slab. Mr. Hayter earned his bachelor's degree in electrical engineering at Prairie View A&M University in 1996 and completed his master's degree in electrical engineering at the Georgia Institute of Technology in 1998. He began his career in technical sales and marketing at Texas Instruments. After spending five years at the company, he worked for several high-tech startups and eventually traded in his world of chips and silicon for scoops and cones in 2003. Anthony enjoys giving back to an organization called BUILD, which helps at-risk youth groom their entrepreneurial skills while preparing them for college. He lives in San Jose with his wife Vickye Hayter.

GALE ANNE HURD is one of the most respected and accomplished movie producers in the entertainment industry and is the chairman of her own production entity, Valhalla Motion Pictures. She has more than two-dozen feature films to her credit, including the three blockbuster *Terminator* movies, *Aliens, The Abyss, The Hulk, Armageddon,* and the award-winning indie, *The Waterdance.* Her films have grossed over $2 billion at the box office and garnered numerous Oscars. A Phi Beta Kappa graduate of Stanford University with a degree in economics and communications, Hurd began her entertainment career as an executive assistant to legendary filmmaker Roger Corman. At New World Pictures, she became the head of marketing and later a producer. Hurd has received many honors and awards for her producing and charitable work, including the prestigious Crystal Award from Women in Film, which honors those "outstanding women who have helped enhance the role of women within the entertainment industry." In 2004 the National

Board of Review honored her with a Special Achievement in Producing Award and in March 2004 Hurd received the Millennium Award for Entertainment Industry Environmental Leadership from former Russian President Mikhail Gorbachev's Green Cross.

RONALD KIRK is a partner in the Dallas office of Vinson & Elkins L.L.P. Mr. Kirk earned his J.D. degree from the University of Texas School of Law in 1979. Kirk served as Mayor of the City of Dallas from 1995 until 2001, and in 1994, he served as the Texas Secretary of State. He has over 20 years of experience as legislative counsel for numerous public and private entities. He is a former Dallas Assistant District Attorney for Governmental Relations and has served as an aide to U.S. Senator Lloyd Bentsen. Currently, he serves on the Board of Directors for Brinker International, Dean Foods Company, and PetsMart, Inc., and he is a National Trustee for the March of Dimes. Mr. Kirk lives in Dallas with his wife, Matrice Ellis-Kirk, and their two daughters, Elizabeth Alexandra Kirk and Catherine Victoria Kirk.

KAY KOPLOVITZ is the founder of USA Network, Sci-Fi Channel, and USA Networks International, a company launched in 1977. Ms. Koplovitz served as chairperson and CEO until the company was sold for $4.5 billion in 1989. She is the principal of Koplovitz & Co., LLC. Ms. Koplovitz created Springboard Enterprises, which was launched in 2000 to raise venture capital for women entrepreneurs and has since then presented 275 companies with $2 billion in capital. In 2001 she cofounded Boldcap Ventures, a venture capital fund that invests in technology and life science, mid-stage companies. She is presently on the Boards of Liz Claiborne and Instinet and is chairman of Reality 24/7 Network and a partner in The Directors' Council. She is the author of *Bold Women, Big Ideas* (2002), which she wrote to inform and inspire women entrepreneurs to create wealth through equity.

MITCHELL KOSS has a bachelor's degree in political science from the University of Michigan and a master's degree from the Writing Seminars at Johns Hopkins University. He started in the television news and documentary business in the fall of 1983 at KCET, the Los Angeles PBS station. At KCET he worked the *Newshour* on PBS, as a writer, associate producer, and producer of documentaries for the

PBS system, and for the science series *Nova*. Some of his projects won awards, including a Peabody. He has also produced for National Geographic. He joined Channel One News in the fall of 1992, where he worked with Lisa Ling from 1994 to 1999. Through Channel One, he also produced segments or documentaries for ABC News, *Nightline*, the *Today Show*, CBS News, CNN, KCET, PBS, the WB Network, and HBO. With Serena Altschul, Laura Ling, and Pat Lope, he created the MTV investigative documentary series, *Breaking It Down with Serena*, which ran from 2000 to 2002. He has contributed to the *Detroit News, Advertising Age, National Review,* the *New York Times*, the NewsAmerica syndicate, the *Los Angeles Herald Examiner,* the *Los Angeles Weekly,* and the *Los Angeles Times.*

CHARLES LICKEL is vice president, systems software and storage development, Systems & Technology Group at the IBM Corporation. Mr. Lickel is responsible for development activity for IBM TotalStorage solutions, software development for the IBM eServer iSeries, pSeries, xSeries, and zSeries, and the Linux Technology Center. Mr. Lickel joined IBM in 1978 as a software engineer after graduating with a B.A. degree from the State University of New York at Albany. In the course of his IBM career, he has contributed significantly towards "reinventing" the S/390 and creating the OS/390 operating system, in addition to pioneering efforts to propel IBM's family of data management products to the leadership position in the industry. Mr. Lickel is a Senior Fellow of the American Leadership Forum in Silicon Valley, is on the Board of Directors for United Way of Southern Arizona, and serves as IBM's senior site executive for Arizona—IBM's principal link with Arizona's state and federal elected officials. Recognized as a leader of diversity within IBM, then-chairman Lou Gerstner appointed Mr. Lickel co-chair of the corporation's GLBT diversity task force in 1998. In 2001 he was honored as one of the "Gay Financial Network 25" for his effectiveness in shaping a diversity-friendly climate at work as well as for service as a role model in business leadership. Mr. Lickel currently lives in Tucson, Arizona, with his partner.

LISA LING has been working in television for 14 years and is currently with *National Geographic Explorer*. Most recently, she co-hosted *The View*, sitting alongside Barbara Walters, Meredith Vieira, Star Jones, and Joy Behar.

A Northern California native, at age 16, Ms. Ling auditioned for and was chosen to be one of four hosts of *Scratch,* a nationally syndicated teen magazine show out of Sacramento. By the time she was 18, Ms. Ling had moved on to become one of the youngest reporters for Channel One News, the network seen in middle schools and high schools across the country. Despite working more than 40 hours a week, she also attended the University of Southern California where she managed to make the Dean's list during her first year. In her years at Channel One, she reported from more than two dozen countries, including Afghanistan, Iraq, Colombia, Algeria, Cambodia, Vietnam, China, Japan, India, and Iran, and produced eight documentaries for PBS, several of which won awards.

Before the age of 25, Ms. Ling became Channel One's senior war correspondent. In October 2000 Ms. Ling began work as a contributing editor for *USA Weekend,* researching and writing exclusive stories on a range of topics. She hosted the television special *Teen People's 20 Teens Who Will Change the World* in February 2001.

PAULA MADISON is the president and general manager of NBC4 (KNBC), NBC's owned and operated station in Los Angeles. She is the first African American woman to become general manager at a network-owned station in a top five market. She was also named regional general manager for the NBC/Telemundo television stations in Los Angeles (KNBC, KVEA, and KWHY) when the NBC network purchased the Telemundo network in April 2002.

In addition to her duties as president and general manager, Madison served as vice president and senior vice president of diversity for NBC. Madison joined NBC4 from WNBC, NBC's station in New York, where she was the station's vice president and news director starting in March 1996. Madison has earned awards including the "Citizen of the Year Award" in 2004 from the City of Los Angeles Marathon, California National Organization of Women's 2003 Excellence in Media Award, the 2002 National Association of Minority Media Executives' Diversity Award, Los Angeles County Commission for Women 2002 Woman of the Year Award, Los Angeles NAACP President's Award (2001), the United Negro College Fund's Frederick C. Patterson Award (2001), the Asian-Pacific American Corporate Impact Award, and the Organization of Chinese Americans Greater Los Angeles Chapter Image Award for Corporate Achievement.

ROSARIO MARIN was sworn in as the 41st Treasurer of the United States in August 2001. She was the first immigrant ever to hold that honor and the highest-ranking Latina in President George W. Bush's first administration. A council member and Mayor of the City of Huntington Park, she was elected in 1994 and overwhelmingly reelected in 1999. Ms. Marin served in Governor Pete Wilson's administration for seven years. Her last position was Deputy Director of the Governor's Office of Community Relations. As a result of her first son, Eric, being born with Down syndrome, Ms. Marin became an advocate for people with disabilities. Her work in this field has earned her numerous awards, including the distinguished Rose Fitzgerald Kennedy Prize given to her at the United Nations in 1995. A graduate of the California State University, Los Angeles, with a bachelor's degree in business administration, she completed the Senior Executives of State and Local Government Program at John F. Kennedy School of Government at Harvard University. She received an Honoris Causa Doctorate of Laws Degree from her alma mater CSULA in 2002. She resides in Huntington Park with her husband of 23 years, Alvaro Alejandro Marin, and their three children—Eric, Carmen, and Alex.

SHARON MARTINEZ is founder and president of SMART Temporary Personnel Services, a woman- and minority-owned employment agency that specializes in clerical, bilingual, and promotional staffing founded in Monterey Park and now located in Alhambra, California. SMART Temporary Personnel Services was founded in June 1993 and now services the greater Los Angeles area, including the counties of Orange, Riverside, San Bernardino, and Ventura.

Sharon Martinez also enjoys the political arena. Before serving as Mayor for Monterey Park from 2003 to 2004, Sharon won a seat on the Monterey Park City Council in November 2001, beating her opponents by a 2 to 1 margin. Sharon was re-elected in March 2005 to again serve on the Monterey Park City Council.

Sharon is equally active in and devoted to community service. She is currently an appointed member of the Los Angeles County Commission on Local Government, Monterey Park/Rosemead Soroptimists, Monterey Park Rotary, San Gabriel Valley Council of Government (SGVCOG), League of California Cities Community Services Committee, the San Gabriel Valley Animal Control

Authority, West San Gabriel Valley Rebuilding Together (formerly Christmas in April), MTA San Gabriel Valley Sector Board, Boy Scouts of America Mission Amigos District Board, Monterey Park Chamber of Commerce, Monterey Park Library Foundation, and the Monterey Park Hospital. Sharon is a former Board member of the Latin Business Association, West San Gabriel Valley YMCA, former chairperson of Monterey Park Art and Culture Commission, Library Board, former elected national vice president of Young Adults of the League of United Latin American Citizens, former secretary of Hispanas Organized for Political Equality (HOPE) PAC, and former member of the United States Commission on Civil Rights—California Advisory Committee.

Sharon Martinez received her bachelor of science degree in public administration from the University of Southern California. She also received her master of science degree in public administration in management from the University of Southern California. During her college career, she had the opportunity to study abroad in Madrid, Spain, and also received a fellowship to study at the Lyndon B. Johnson School of Public Policy in Austin, Texas.

DEBRA MARTUCCI is the vice president of information technology (IT) at Synopsys. Debra has been with Synopsys for over 12 years and has contributed to the success of many mergers and acquisitions in her role as vice president of IT as well as through her responsibilities in managing the Release Engineering functions and driving the Porting and Licensing teams. Her IT group provides a strategic advantage for Synopsys. Prior to her time at Synopsys, Debra worked in the area of software simulation, which included positions within NASA in the Space Shuttle Training Division as well as managing teams responsible for developing code with object-oriented design methodologies for very large-scale real-time embedded microprocessor and database generation systems for advanced aircraft radar simulation. She earned her bachelor of science degree in physics from North Adams State College (Massachusetts) and completed a master's degree in physics from the University of Houston, publishing her thesis entitled "The Optical Degradation of Solar Absorbing Black Chrome Thin Films." She is originally from Boston and now lives in San Mateo, California, where she enjoys family time with her husband and two dogs.

LAURA J. MEDINA's life and show business career both began in New York City—although not at the same time. After receiving a bachelor of arts degree in political science from Antioch College in Yellow Springs, Ohio, Laura's film career began at New York University Graduate Institute of Film and Television, Tisch School of the Arts, where she earned a master's degree in fine arts in film directing. After graduation, her student film, the documentary short, *Leslie Tulips* (about a young exotic dancer/stripper and her mother), won Laura a Directing Fellowship from the Astoria Studios/New York State Council of the Arts. Within a few years, Laura's career took an unexpected detour into the production side of filmmaking. Based in New York and later Los Angeles, Laura worked as a production manager, then as a line producer, and eventually as a producer on over a dozen feature films and assorted other media projects, filming all over the United States, Mexico, Europe, and North Africa. With the coming of the millennium, Laura decided to return to her directing career by writing, directing, and producing a short comedy film, *Heart Attack,* which was an official selection at numerous film festivals. Since then, Laura has continued to pursue directing film and television, while also writing and developing her own feature film projects.

RON MEYER was appointed president and chief operating officer of Universal Studios on August 1, 1995. Prior to joining Universal Studios, Mr. Meyer was president of Creative Artists Agency, Inc., which he founded in 1975 with four fellow agents from the William Morris Agency. Over the years they built the company into the preeminent talent agency, representing many of the industry's most influential and talented people, and later expanded its range of services to include consulting with leading American and international corporations. Previously, Mr. Meyer was a television agent with the William Morris Agency from 1970 to 1975. Prior to that, he worked as a messenger at the Paul Kohner Agency in Los Angeles from 1964 to 1970. Before joining the Paul Kohner Agency, Mr. Meyer served in the United States Marine Corps. He lives in Malibu, California, with his wife, Kelly Chapman, and his three daughters and son.

MARTHA J. MORRIS is currently on leave of absence from IBM Corp. Prior to her leave, she served as vice president of global services procurement in Somers, New York. Martha earned her degree in engineering from the University of Tennessee, Knoxville, in 1980. She served in many executive positions during her career at IBM, including vice president of world wide server and storage manufacturing. She has served on the Global Women's Board and as a trustee of Marist College and has been recognized for her commitment to mentoring by the YWCA and other nonprofit organizations. Martha lives in Tennessee with her husband, John.

JUAN (JOHN) NOQUEZ was raised in the diverse community of Boyle Heights, a small suburb just three miles east of downtown Los Angeles. John later received his formal education at California State University, Los Angeles. His concentration was in real estate, which greatly assisted him in his more than 18-year career with the Los Angeles Assessor's Office. John's current assignment— to value the most architecturally significant properties in downtown Los Angeles—has allowed him to become a specialist in the Historic Core of downtown Los Angeles. In John's leisure time, he plays an active role in the community of Huntington Park. In September 2000, he was appointed City Clerk, and in March 2003, he received the greatest number of votes in the race for City Council. His peers on the Council immediately selected him as Vice-Mayor. In March 2004, John was selected to be Mayor of the City of Huntington Park. He is actively educating Huntington Park and the Southeast areas of Los Angeles in historic preservation. He is also very active in transportation issues, senior health care, and youth activities in his city.

DONALD P. PETTIT is a retired Air Force Brigadier General. He has 28 years of experience working in space and strategic force mission areas. During his time of service, he held numerous senior command and management positions. In his last USAF assignment, he served as the commander, 45th Space Wing, Patrick Air Force Base, Florida, with responsibility for all space launch operations (civil, commercial, and DoD) on the Eastern Range, the busiest spaceport in the world. Other key senior leadership positions he has held include director of plans and programs, Headquarters Air Force Space Command, chief, Nuclear Operations Division, and deputy director for operations, NMCC, Operations Directorate, the Joint Staff, commander, 341st Space Wing, Malmstrom Air Force Base, our nation's largest ICBM complex. Additionally, he has been a member of the Air Force Space Panel and the Air Force Scientific Advisory Board (SAB) and currently serves on several U.S. government commissioned senior level study/review groups. He is currently the executive director, operations and programs, for Aero Thermo Technology (AT2), Inc., a small business with highly experienced technical and managerial professionals specializing in engineering services, design and analysis, program management, and ballistic missile technology development.

General Pettit and his wife, Carol, live on Marco Island, Florida.

JIM ROBBINS founded Business Cluster Development in 1993. BCD has helped over twenty organizations with the formation of sector-focused incubators. The latest BCD projects are an open source software incubator in Beaverton, Oregon, and a homeland security incubator in Annapolis, Maryland. Jim is executive director of the Software Business Cluster, the first software incubator in California. The Software Business Cluster was named Incubator of the Year for 2000 by the National Business Incubation Association. Over $550 million in venture investment has been made in SBC companies over the last four years, and four SBC companies have gone public. Jim is also director of the Environmental Business Cluster in San Jose, California. The EBC was the first environmental incubator in the United States when it was formed in 1994. The EBC specializes in technology commercialization of clean and renewable energy technology. Jim developed the Panasonic Incubator in 1999. It incubates early stage companies in order to create technology partnerships for Panasonic. Jim is also on the Board of Directors of the National Business Incubation Association. He has worked for Digital Equipment Corporation and the U.S. Supreme Court and was a trial attorney.

DIANE L. ROBINA is a 17-year veteran of MTV Networks. Her latest assignment at Viacom is as executive vice president for acquisitions strategies for MTVN. Robina was executive vice president and general manager of TNN cable network. The New TNN—which was a country music/country lifestyle network for most of its 20 years—went national in appeal and enjoyed a 100 percent ratings increase in its target demo of 18–49. Formerly ranked 28th among basic cable networks, it jumped to top ten, becoming the fifth highest prime time. During the relaunch, Robina managed the successful transition of cable's high-rated program, *WWE RAW*. She also led the New TNN's efforts to acquire some of television's top franchises, including *Star Trek: The Next Generation, Star Trek: Voyager,* and the powerhouse *CSI: Crime Scene Investigation*. Previously, Robina was associated general manager and senior vice president of programming of TV Land starting in 1997 and played a key role in the programming strategy for both Nick at Nite and TV Land, while leading TV Land's distribution and advertising goals. Robina quickly rose through the ranks to become director of acquisitions and then vice president of acquisitions before moving to TV Land. Robina was named vice president of programming for Nick at Nite/TV Land and was charged with programming the launch of the new network. A year later, she was promoted to the top post at the network.

NIKKI ROCCO has resided as president of Universal Pictures Distribution organization since 1996 and has been with Universal Pictures since 1967. With Nikki heading the distribution strategy, the studio opened three movies in a row at $50-plus million domestic gross (*Bruce Almighty, 2 Fast 2 Furious,* and *The Hulk*) and had five $100-plus million domestic–grossing films in one summer.

Rocco has continued to see success in overseeing distribution for *Along Came Polly* and *Dawn of the Dead*. That success was furthered in the second half of 2004 with the studio's $150-plus million summer blockbuster, *The Bourne Supremacy,* Academy Award nominee *Ray,* which has remained in theaters for over 15 weeks, and *Meet the Fockers. Fockers* is now the second highest grossing live action comedy of all time. In 2000 her work on such films as *Dr. Seuss's How the Grinch Stole Christmas,* the most successful film of the year, the blockbuster comedy *Meet the Parents* as well as the Oscar-winning smash *Erin Brockovich,* and the hit sequel *Nutty Professor II: The Klumps* contributed to the studio's best overall year with more than $1 billion in domestic box-office revenues.

Rocco began her career at Universal in New York in the sales department. Throughout her tenure with Universal, she served as the assistant to the general sales manager, vice president of distribution, senior vice president of distribution, and marketing and executive vice president of distribution.

BETHANY ROONEY has directed over 100 hours of prime-time network series television and eight TV movies. Her series work includes *Joan of Arcadia, Crossing Jordan, One Tree Hill, Ally McBeal, Beverly Hills 90210,* and *St. Elsewhere,* among many others. She received a master's degree from Bowling Green State University in Ohio and currently teaches directing at UCLA Extensions and numerous acting workshops in the Los Angeles area. She is married and lives in Los Angeles with her family.

LINDA SANFORD, senior vice president, Enterprise On Demand Transformation and Information Technology, is leading IBM's internal transformation to the industry's premier on-demand business. In this role, Ms. Sanford is responsible for working across IBM to transform core business processes, create an IT infrastructure to support those processes, and help create a culture that recognizes the value that on-demand leadership can bring to IBM.

Previously, Ms. Sanford was senior vice president and group executive, IBM Storage Systems Group, where she helped take IBM from fifth to second place in storage market share in two years. Prior to assuming that position, Ms. Sanford headed IBM Global Industries, the organization that manages relationships with IBM's largest customers worldwide and is responsible for generating almost 70 percent of IBM's revenue. Before that, Sanford was General Manager of IBM's S/390 Division, which develops, manufactures, and markets large-enterprise systems.

During the early 1990s, she guided the S/390 Division through one of the most comprehensive product transformations the computer industry has ever seen, reinventing S/390 as an open, enterprise-level server.

One of the highest-ranking women at IBM, Ms. Sanford is a member of the Women in Technology International Hall of Fame and the National Association of Engineers. She has been named one of the 50 Most Influential Women in Business by *Fortune Magazine,* one of the Top Ten Innovators in the Technology Industry by *Information Week Magazine,* and one of the Ten Most Influential Women in Technology by *Working Woman Magazine.*

Ms. Sanford serves on the Board of Directors of ITT Industries, St. John's University, and Rensselaer Polytechnic Institute. She also serves on the Board of Directors of the Partnership for New York

City, the Business Council of New York State, Inc., and the Westchester Arts Council.

Sanford is a graduate of St. John's University and earned an M.S. degree in operations research from Rensselaer Polytechnic Institute.

HILDA L. SOLIS was first elected to Congress in 2000. Currently, Congresswoman Hilda L. Solis (CA-32) is serving her third term in the U.S. House of Representatives. She represents parts of the San Gabriel Valley and East Los Angeles. Solis serves on the powerful House Energy and Commerce Committee; she is the first Latina to serve on this committee. She is the Ranking Member of the Environment and Hazardous Materials Subcommittee. She is also chairwoman of the Congressional Hispanic Caucus's Task Force on Health and Democratic vice-chair of the Congressional Caucus on Women's Issues. Solis's hard work and passion to fight for environmental justice is nationally recognized. In August 2000 she was awarded the John F. Kennedy Profile in Courage Award for her pioneering work on environmental justice issues in California. She has proven her dedication to the pursuit of good environmental public policy. Her priorities are protecting the environment, improving the quality of healthcare, and fighting for the rights of working families.

ANNE SWEENEY is the cochairman, Media Networks, for the Walt Disney Company and president of Disney–ABC Television Group. Named the "Most Powerful Woman in Entertainment" by *The Hollywood Reporter,* one of the "50 Most Powerful Women in Business" by *Fortune,* and one of "The World's 100 Most Powerful Women" by *Forbes,* Anne Sweeney is responsible for all of Disney's nonsports, cable, satellite, and broadcast properties globally, including ABC Television Network, Touchstone Television, and the DISNEY ABC Cable Networks Group. She also oversees Walt Disney Television Animation and Buena Vista Domestic and International Television and manages Disney's equity interests in Lifetime Entertainment Services, A&E Television Networks, and E! Entertainment Networks.

From 2000 to 2004, Ms. Sweeney was president of ABC Cable Networks Group and Disney Channel Worldwide. She joined the Walt Disney Company in 1996 as president of Disney Channel and executive vice president of Disney/ABC Cable Networks. Starting in 1993 she was chairman and CEO of FX Networks, Inc., and before that she spent 12 years in various executive positions at Nickelodeon/Nick at Nite. Ms. Sweeney has received numerous awards, including the 2004 Muse Award from New York Women in Film and Television, the STAR Award from American Women in Radio and Television in 1995, induction into the American Advertising Federation's Advertising Hall of Achievement in 1996, Women in Film's Lucy Award in 2002, and the Cable Television Public Affairs Association's President's Award.

PAMELA THOMAS-GRAHAM is the chairman of CNBC, the global leader in business news. CNBC provides business news programming and financial market coverage to more than 201 million homes worldwide. Prior to her promotion to chairman, Thomas-Graham served as president and chief executive officer of CNBC. Under Thomas-Graham's leadership, the network has achieved record profitability, and CNBC's audience continues to be the wealthiest in all of cable television. Previously, Thomas-Graham served as president and chief executive officer of CNBC.com. Thomas-Graham is a Phi Beta Kappa graduate of Harvard College and a 1989 graduate of Harvard Business School and Harvard Law School, where she served as an editor of the *Harvard Law Review*. Before joining NBC in September 1999, Thomas-Graham was a partner at McKinsey & Company, the global management-consulting firm. She joined the firm in 1989 and six years later became its first black woman partner. She has received numerous awards, including being named "Woman of the Year" by *Glamour Magazine, Ms. Magazine,* and the Financial Woman's Association. *Fortune Magazine* named her one of the "50 Most Powerful Blacks in Business." In addition to her corporate work, Thomas-Graham is the best-selling author of the critically acclaimed "Ivy League Mystery Series," which includes three novels published by Simon & Schuster.

KATHLEEN VON DER AHE is a vice president in Affiliate Relations for the ABC Television Network. Kathleen earned her B.A. degree in communications and broadcasting from Slippery Rock University and also graduated from Simmons School of Management. Kathleen began her career with ABC in 1988 and has held various positions within the network, including positions in National TV sales, ABC Sports, and Broadcast Operations and Engineering. Kathleen joined Affiliate Relations in 1994 as an account representative. Subsequently she was promoted to associate director, Pacific/Mountain region, director, Southeast region, and director Pacific/Mountain region, where she launched the West Coast Satellite office for Affiliate Relations. Kathleen lives in Toluca Lake with her husband, Tim Von der Ahe, and her two children, Timmy and MaryJane Von der Ahe.

LOUISE J. WANNIER, a successful serial entrepreneur, founded and built three companies and is embarking on her fourth. My Shape.org is focused on making it easier to find fashion that fits and flatters your body. Enfish Software makes the "google" for your PC, offering personal search technology for solving the problem of information overload. Prior to establishing Enfish, Ms. Wannier was a cofounder, member of the Board of Directors, and chief operating officer of Gemstar Development Corporation, the makers of VCRPlus+, and then chief executive of Gemstar Europe. Gemstar grew to $65 million in revenues within three-and-a-half years with substantial profitability. VCRPlus+ is widely recognized as the most successful launch of a new consumer electronics product since the Sony Walkman. Gemstar is publicly quoted on NASDAQ, with a market capitalization of over $1 billion.

Previous to Gemstar, she founded Skillware, a multimedia, interactive learning systems venture for Chalmers Industriteknik in Sweden. She also spent six years in the management consulting services division of Ernst & Whinney (now Ernst & Young) in Los Angeles, where she was senior manager responsible for corporate planning and mergers and acquisitions services.

Ms. Wannier received a master of business administration degree with honors from the UCLA Graduate School of Management and a B.Sc. in astronomy with honors from the California Institute of Technology. She is also a Certified Public Accountant and was a member of TEC, an international organization of CEOs, for over 10 years. In 1993 she was recognized as one of the top 100 Marketers by *Advertising Age*. In December 2000 she received the Bridgegate20 Award, as one of the top 20 technologists in Southern California. Ms. Wannier is a director of Entretec, a nonprofit organization focused on supporting the growth of high-tech companies.

JACQUELINE E. WOODS has numerous years of experience and leadership as an educator, administrator, consultant, and senior executive. Currently, Woods spends most of her time in her governance capacities with the Institute for Higher Education Policy, Rentway, Inc. (corporate—NYSE), Pivot Point, Inc. (private family business), American University of Rome Board of Trustees, National Council for Women's Organizations, and *Ms.* magazine. She has an adjunct faculty appointment at the American University's School of Public Affairs and does board governance consulting. Recently, she served as the executive director of the American Association of University Women. She also actively participated in international affairs/women's rights for AAUW as part of the United Nations, UNESCO, and IFUW gatherings. She has long been active in supporting education and equity issues for nontraditional learners, with participation as a founding member and past-president of the Women Administrators in Higher Education; a speaker and consultant for the White House Office of Women; colleges and universities in the United States and throughout the world; and government agencies, community organizations, and executive groups nationwide.

Woods served as a presidential appointee in the U.S. Department of Education as the Director of the Community Colleges Liaison Office.

BOB WRIGHT became chairman and chief executive officer of NBC Universal in May 2004 in conjunction with the combining of NBC and Vivendi Universal Entertainment. He joined NBC as president and chief executive officer on September 1, 1986, and became chairman and chief executive officer on June 4, 2001. Mr. Wright has had one of the longest and most successful tenures of any media company chief executive. Under his leadership, NBC was transformed from a broadcast network into a global media powerhouse with leadership in television programming, station ownership, and television production. With the formation of NBC Universal, Mr. Wright takes the reins of one of the world's fastest-growing and most profitable media and entertainment companies. Mr. Wright serves as vice chairman of the Board and executive officer of the General Electric Company. Mr. Wright has received the Golden Mike Award from the Broadcasters' Foundation, the

Steven J. Ross Humanitarian of the Year award from the UJA-Federation of New York, and the Gold Medal Award from the International Radio and Television Society Foundation. Along with his wife, Suzanne, Mr. Wright serves as cofounder of Autism Speaks, a new initiative dedicated to raising public awareness and research funds to find the answers to autism.

WILLIAM A. WULF is currently the president of the National Academy of Engineering (NAE). Together with its sibling, the National Academy of Sciences, the NAE is both an honorific organization and an independent, authoritative advisor to the government on issues involving science and technology. Previously, Dr. Wulf was an assistant director of the National Science Foundation, founder and CEO of Tartan Laboratories, and a professor of computer science at the University of Virginia and Carnegie Mellon University. Dr. Wulf is a member of the National Academy of Engineering, a Fellow of the American Academy of Arts and Sciences, a corresponding member of the Academia Espanola De Ingeniera, a member of the Academy Bibliotheca Alexandrina (Library of Alexandria), a foreign member of the Engineering Academy of Japan, and a foreign member of the Russian Academy of Sciences. He is also a Fellow of five professional societies: the ACM, the IEEE, the AAAS, IEC, and AWIS. He is the author of over 100 papers and technical reports, has written three books, holds two U.S. patents, and has supervised over 25 Ph.D.'s in computer science.

HENRY YUEN, cofounder and previous CEO of Gemstar, along with Daniel Kwoh, invented the VCR Plus. To use this product, consumer electronic companies pay royalties for the privilege of incorporating Gemstar's program access code circuitry into its TV sets, VCRs, and set-top boxes. Publications like Murdoch's *TV Guide* pay for the privilege of publishing the one- to eight-digit VCR Plus codes in program listings, and then consumers use them to program their VCRs. Gemstar later merged with *TV Guide* to become Gemstar-TV Guide International, Inc. At the time of Yuen's departure in 2002, it was a leading global media and technology company involved in developing, licensing, marketing, and distributing products and services that simplify and enhance television guidance and consumer entertainment.

Henry Yuen was born in China but moved to Hong Kong when he was very young. Immigrating to the United States at the age of 17, Henry earned a B.S. degree in mathematics from the University of Wisconsin in Madison, then a Ph.D. from Caltech in 1973. He also earned a J.D. from Loyola Marymount University.

STUDYING POWER
MENTORING RELATIONSHIPS

PURPOSE OF THE STUDY

The overall purpose of this project was to investigate the mentoring relationships of high-profile individuals to learn about today's mentoring relationships and how they might differ from past traditional mentoring relationships. In reviewing the academic literature on mentoring, we realized that although many details of some of the more traditional views of mentoring exist, researchers have only begun to look at how the challenges in today's work world might call for different forms of mentoring relationships, or mentoring relationships that require different types of relationships skills. Moreover, the explosion of research in mentoring over the past 10 years teaches us much about what makes for successful mentoring relationships, but much of that information is used by human resource professionals in designing formal, corporate mentoring programs and is not as accessible to individuals who want to begin a mentoring relationship outside of a corporate program. Finally, in our own work in mentoring research and as mentoring program directors, we are continually asked by clients and students for a guidebook that details all the secrets of successful mentoring relationships. We often provide clients and students with articles written by us and by others, but we realized that undertaking a more methodological approach to understanding mentoring and summarizing this knowledge in a book that would reach a broader audience would be helpful to the careers of many.

Together these reasons brought us to focus on the following objectives in conducting the research for this book:

1. To describe in detail new forms of mentoring relationships that are critical for success in today's organizations and boundaryless career environment
2. To have an updated, seminal book on mentoring that tells the story of successful mentoring from diverse lenses and includes the perspectives and experiences of white men, white women, and people of color
3. To build a bridge between the knowledge gained from academic studies that tend to focus primarily on protégés, and practitioner experiences that emphasize how-to approaches for mentors, by drawing from both sides of the mentoring relationship
4. To teach lessons and strategies through inspirational stories and examples from our power mentoring pairs and clusters, thus making seemingly esoteric mentoring theory, knowledge, and new approaches appealing to a general managerial audience

THEORETICAL BACKGROUND

Mentoring as an academic field of inquiry resides within the literature on careers, leadership, and management development. Research on mentoring has explored many different facets of this valuable career development tool. One early book that bridged the academic and popular literature was by Michael Zey, *The Mentor Connection,* first published in 1984.[1] From his interviews, he derived the form and function of mentoring relationships and uncovered the many benefits. Kathy Kram's seminal piece in the *Academy of Management Journal* in 1983 and her book in 1985 published results of another important study that further outlined the developmental process that mentors and protégés experience.[2] The benefit of her qualitative approach gave aspiring professionals an appreciation of the importance of mentoring and the developmental stages and hurdles that one might expect to see when developing a relationship.

In the 1990s, many organizations adopted formal mentoring programs to increase the success of women and minorities. While some of these programs did much to advance careers, these formal mentoring programs did not fully replicate the spontaneous relationships that were so beneficial to protégés. Georgia Chao and her colleagues found, for example, that mentors in formal mentoring relationships received fewer benefits than did those in informal or spontaneous relationships.[3] Issues of mentor and protégé selection, training, and follow-up activities became very important in making sure formal relationships worked. Therefore, further research investigated what types of protégés might be more likely to have mentors, and whether issues of race and gender, or the similarity of race and gender for protégés and mentors, made a difference in relationship quality and the ensuing benefits.[4] Belle Rose Ragins, with her very comprehensive body of research, has made significant contributions to the field of mentoring by examining the impact of diversity and power; she inspired much of our thinking about issues of race, gender, and mentor functions in relation to mentoring.[5]

Scholars Lillian Eby, Stacey Blake-Beard, and Herminia Ibarra, as well as our own work published in 1999, highlight the proliferation of different types of mentoring relationships in organizations.[6] Other researchers investigating these different forms of mentoring relationships include Gayle Baugh and Terri Scandura, in 1999; Monica Higgins, 2000; David Thomas and Monica Higgins, 1996; Higgins and Kram, in an *Academy of Management Review* article from 2001, show the importance of shared networks of relationships in career success.[7] With the advent of increased communication technology in organizations, some mentoring relationships are taking new forms, such as those outlined by Ensher and colleagues in a recent article on e-mentoring.[8] Furthermore, we see new research on the link between managing and mentoring employees as many firms delineate coaching, mentoring, or both as a managerial responsibility.[9] Taken together, these ideas informed our inquiry and analysis of our interviews.

Although it has been comprehensive, mentoring research has three main shortcomings. First, HR practitioners or managers have not been privy to many of the academic research findings. For example, Joyce Russell and colleagues, in a special mentoring issue of the *Journal of Vocational Behavior,* counted more than 500 articles on mentoring, most of which came from academic journals.[10] To date, many of the empirical studies on mentoring have been gathered in books, but only a few new books bridge academic and practitioner material. Second, even though it is informative, much of the academic literature from the past 10 years relies on questionnaires and surveys to describe the nature and benefits of mentoring relationships. However, it is difficult for quantitative survey research to capture the richness of mentoring relationships. The third shortcoming of academic research is that it tends to focus almost exclusively on one side of the relationship at a time. The focus is on the protégés' perspective most often, the mentor's perspective is rarely gathered (with the exception of Allen, Poteet, and Burroughs in 1997), and never are both perspectives considered simultaneously.[11] Thus, the purpose of this current project was to address some of the gaps in the research knowledge by offering an integration of academic findings and real-life examples from data-rich, in-depth interview data from highly successful and well-known leaders, and give voice to both the mentors and the protégés, thus illuminating both perspectives.

In developing our interview protocol, we kept in mind a number of theoretical lenses that would come into play during data analysis. For example, using Kram's stage theory of attraction, cultivation, redefinition/separation, we wanted to explore in depth what predictors and processes were critical in each phase and how these led to the next.[12] We used a modified version of that model we published previously.[13] We were interested in ideas of how individuals came to their roles of mentor and protégés through the lens of role-making theory.[14] We were interested to what extent some of the mentoring relationships followed the precepts of social exchange theory, or what additional insight into the role of perceived similarity in values and attitudes in the mentoring exchange could be gained through knowledge of leader-member exchange theory of leadership.[15] Warren Bennis's work on leadership, particularly the emphasis he placed on crucible moments, also informed our thinking about defining moments for mentors and protégés.[16] We were also eager to consider how network constellations and alternative forms of mentoring suggested by Monica Higgins and Kathy Kram might play a role in today's mentoring, and how the mentor's perspective of the benefits of a relationship affected the types of mentoring that occurred.[17] And finally, we reviewed literature on important aspects of close relationship development as a method for understanding developing mentoring relationships.

STUDY PARTICIPANTS

Study participants were obtained by culling through lists such as *Fortune* magazine's top executives (including top women, top black executives, and so on) and specific industry publications (for example, *Hollywood Reporter*) to identify top leaders in our three target industries. Next, we did extensive background research on each of these individuals and their experiences as mentors and protégés. Next, we created a target list of those we felt were not only exemplary leaders but were also highly skilled at developing others via mentoring. As a final step, we employed a network of industry experts to provide feedback on participant worthiness to be included in the project. At this stage, we also began to have a series of approximately 40 contact meetings with key industry leaders who might provide us with a connection to those individuals we wished to interview. We also increased our sample by using the snowball technique.[18] With this technique, we asked each interviewee to recommend us to a colleague, usually at a different company, who met our criteria but had a different story to tell.

For our 50 interviewees, 17 were men (34 percent), 14 were people of color (29 percent), and the average age was around 48 years, ranging from approximately age 30 to 70. Individuals from three industries were primarily targeted for inclusion in the study. Many people would agree that the U.S. economic impact on the rest of the world, for better or worse, is strongly determined by our government, our television and movies, and our technological products. These industries impact how people govern, live their lives, work, and play, and they have an undeniable American imprimatur. We interviewed approximately equal numbers of individuals from these three broad industries. We felt that exploring how mentoring has been important to the prominent individuals in this study would be useful to workers in a variety of fields, as careers in nearly all industries are becoming increasingly more boundaryless. These three industries also all support virtual organizational structures or boundaryless careers. *Virtual organizational structures* are those in which individuals are linked together through technology by their product and service rather than by their organizational membership or geographical location. An example of this might be an independent political consultant who acts as a broker of services and relies on a cadre of colleagues with varying areas of expertise to respond to client needs. As authors such as Philip Mirvis, Tim Hall, and Michael Arthur have found, the *boundaryless career* is characterized by portable skills, knowledge, and abilities across multiple firms, personal identification with meaningful work, on-the-job action learning, the development of multiple peer-learning relationships, and individual responsibility for career management.[19] Career pundits predict that the wave of the future for many other industries and their workers is in boundaryless careers and organizational structures; therefore much can be learned from these three benchmark, boundaryless arenas. If new forms of mentoring can thrive in industries such as these, where there is enormous competition and amorphous career paths, then these new forms of mentoring should work well in other industries facing similar challenges.

Interview Method

Semi-structured interviews with the 50 participants were conducted over the course of a year and one-half. In-person interviews lasted approximately an hour, and the transcribed documents averaged about 25 pages in length, resulting in more than 1,250 single-spaced pages of text. Almost all of the interviews were conducted by both authors, so that in addition to having access to written transcripts, we were able to process the nonverbal aspects of the interview to aid in interpretation. All of the participants gave us permission to share their stories.

An initial set of questions was developed to ask generally about various aspects of interviewees' current mentoring relationships. Once initial themes about tests and challenges and specific mentor functions were mentioned in these preliminary interviews, we modified the interview protocol to further investigate these aspects. The final interview protocol included open-ended questions focusing on career history, mentoring relationship development, defining moments, and ideas about protégés and mentor characteristics; it is shown in Exhibit B.1. When the interview focused more on a protégé's relationships with his or her mentor, the protocol was changed slightly. Additional information about the participants was collected from their biographies, obtained by their staffs, and through information from newspapers, trade journals, and Internet resources.

ANALYZING THE INTERVIEWS

We used a qualitative data analysis technique suggested by Taylor and Bogdan.[20] In this technique, the authors argue that qualitative analysis should combine the purposes of identifying themes and finding new insights while also considering how these data fit within existing theories. So first, we used grounded theory to develop specific hypotheses regarding different forms of mentoring relationships, the role of tests and challenges, how defining moments strengthened relationships, and the role of trust.[21] The second approach we used to understand the interview data can most closely be defined as analytic induction. Within this approach, the purpose is to fit data to existing explanations of social phenomena. To assist us in the process of theory elaboration for mentoring relationships, we used NVivo, a qualitative software tool (QSR International). We used a combination of automated search function for words and phrases, and manual content analysis coding. Basically, the advantage of using the computerized program was for ease of handling the resulting content categories.

Our data analysis followed the following stages:

Stage 1: Once all the interviews were completed, the preliminary data analysis efforts involved reading the transcript of each interview at least two times in its entirety.

Stage 2: Transcripts were reviewed to generate underlying themes. An initial scan for themes used a grounded theory approach, where interesting themes emerged from the data. Many of these themes emerged not from a direct question but from an expanded answer to another question or to a seemingly unrelated question. For example, in our initial stages of analysis, several initial overall themes emerged such as:

- Support in terms of how you get it, who gives it, what you want it for
- Loyalty and trust
- Testing and key challenges
- How gender changed the conversation
- Being called or pushed out of comfort zone
- Mutual admiration and reciprocity

Stage 3: In the next stage of analysis, we went beyond answering "what is interesting, surprising, or similar" in looking for

EXHIBIT B.1   INTERVIEW QUESTIONS

Reflections on Becoming a Mentor

Please reflect on your first impressions of your protégés and how you met them. Is there any story that occurred early in your relationship that captures the essence of you two getting to know one another?

What would you say are the major similarities and differences between you and your protégés (for example, values, personal characteristics, negotiation style, management approach, how you solve problems, goals, and so on)?

What does it mean to be a mentor? That is, articulate your philosophy of mentoring. Are there any books, TV shows, or movies that relate to or inform your approach to mentoring? There is a fascinating new trend in management literature today on the integration of spirituality and management. To what degree does your spiritual practice reflect on your approach to mentoring?

Who was your role model for the type of mentor you are? What stories (that is, life lessons, proud moments, secrets of the trade, and so on) about your past mentors related to this? You may want to consider what you learned in areas like developing leadership agility, negotiation strategies, empowering employees, and life and work balance.

The Maturing Relationship

A lot of our past research on mentoring tells us that successful relationships are often an exchange in which both mentors and protégés give and get something, albeit something different. What do you think you give, and what do you get from your relationships with your protégés?

Trust between mentors and protégés is a common and compelling theme in our past interviews. Please reflect on trust between you and your protégés/mentors (you may wish to provide a story, relate observations, or simply reflect).

Research shows that oftentimes mentors play very distinct roles for their protégés, including those of sponsor, teacher, information provider, nurturer, advisor, and connector. Can you reflect on how you played the role of sponsor or teacher for your protégé(s)? What about information provider or nurturer? Finally, in what ways have you been an advisor and connector?

Summing It Up

Often we find that mentors and protégés, as they grow and develop, find that they need to redefine or transition in their relationship. How would you characterize where your relationship is now, and how will it transition? In other words, what's next? Was there a critical incident or event that caused this relationship redefinition?

If you were to write an ad for a protégé, what would it say and why (that is, what specific qualities or strategies should a good would-be protégé exemplify)?

There is a tremendous amount of research on issues of race and gender in mentoring. You have been a strong advocate and mentor to successful women and people of color. Do you think there are any advantages or disadvantages of having cross-gender or cross-race mentoring relationships? Or, more specifically, do men and women behave differently in mentoring relationships? If so, how?

General Reflections on Mentoring

Do you think the practice of mentoring varies across industries?

Whom do you think have been some mentoring superstars in your industry?

Is there anything that we have not asked you that you would care to tell us related to your career overall or your experiences with mentoring in particular?

patterns, and we used a more stringent approach. Here, we applied various theoretical lenses as described previously from the fields of mentoring, leadership, and social psychology to further analyze the data.

Stage 4: We used NVivo to sort data into thematic categories and then began an iterative process of refining the major themes. The models we used in guiding our research followed some of the existing models of mentoring relationship development we described in the theoretical background section, and specifically focused on:

- Defining moments
- The process of getting to know mentors
- What attracted them to their protégé or mentor
- Benefits both mentors and protégés receive or give in the relationships
- Role of tests and challenges

Once we had the data sorted into major theme documents, we were able to finalize our major categories of frequently occurring ideas, which then became the basis for the book chapters.

NOTES

Chapter One: Introduction to Power Mentoring

1. For a series of informative essays on this topic, see John De Graaf (ed.), *Take Back Your Time* (San Francisco: Berrett-Koehler, 2003); Anders Hayden, "International Work-Time Trends: The Emerging Gap in Work Hours," *Just Labour: A Canadian Journal of Work and Society* 2 (2003): 23–35.

2. Leslie H. Geary, "I Quit, Overworked Employees Are Fed Up: A Survey Finds 8 out of 10 Americans Want a New Job," *CNNMoney*, December 20, 2003. http://money.cnn.com/2003/11/11/pf/q_iquit/index.htm.

3. Jane Weaver, "Layoffs, Long Hours Taking Their Toll on Workers," *MSNBC*, September 1, 2003. http://www.msnbc.msn.com/id/3072410/.

4. Talk given by Bob Wright to Columbia Business School students on January 22, 2003, as part of the Silfen Leadership Series. Published March 12, 2003. http://www6.gsb.columbia.edu/cfmx/web/alumni/features/news/0303/wright.cfm.

5. James T. Bond, Cindy A. Thompson, Ellen Galinsky, and David Prottas, *Highlights of the 2002 National Study of the Changing Workforce* (New York: Families and Work Institute, 2003).

6. http://www.bls.gov/oco/oco2003.htm.

7. Report from the U.S. Chamber of Commerce, April 2004. http://www.uschamber.com/media/pdfs/outsourcing.pdf.

8. Steve Lohr, "Luddites Beware: It's a High-Tech World," *International Herald Tribune*, August 2, 2003. http://www.iht.com/articles/105014.html.

9. Global Reach, December 1, 2004. http://www.global-reach.biz/globstats/index.php3.

10. Lisa Hendrickson, "Email Outages Rise Significantly in 2003 According to Recent Survey: Email Essential Tool for High Income Earners and Mission-Critical for Business," December 16, 2003. http://www.messageone.com/news/nws_121603_1.

11. The U.S. Department of Labor's Bureau of Labor Statistics reported that the union membership rate has steadily declined from a high of 20.1 percent in 1983; January 15, 2004. http://www.bls.gov/news. release/union2.nr0.htm.

12. Wal-Mart is the biggest employer in Europe; see http://www.man power.co.uk/news/articles/article54_mainpage.asp. With 1.1 million employees, Wal-Mart is the largest private employer in the United States (and second overall to the federal government). (Lorrie Grant, "Retail Giant Wal-Mart Faces Challenges on Many Fronts," *USA Today*, November 10, 2003. http://www.usatoday.com/money/industries/retail/2003–11–10-walmart_x.htm).

13. Michael B. Arthur, Douglas T. Hall, and Barbara S. Lawrence (eds.), *Handbook of Career Theory* (New York: Cambridge University Press, 1989); in the preceding volume, see especially Michael B. Arthur, Douglas T. Hall, and Barbara S. Lawrence, "Generating New Directions in Career Theory: The Case for a Transdisciplinary Approach," 7–25.

14. Information available online from Bureau of Labor Statistics; see *Number of Jobs Held, Labor Market Activity, and Earnings Growth among Younger Baby Boomers: Results from More Than Two Decades of a Longitudinal Survey*, vol. USDL 04–1829, September 21, 2004. http//www.bls. gov/cps. See also a report on job change available from the Current Population Survey at http://www.bls.gov/cps/home.htm/cps, as well as Karen Hofferber and Kim Isaacs, *The Career Change Resume* (New York: McGraw-Hill, 2003).

15. Kahlil Gibran, *The Prophet* (New York: Random House, 1923).

16. This information is from a presentation given by Beverly Kaye to the Los Angeles Chapter of the American Society of Training and Development on October 21, 2004. A packet of readings is available on request at http://www.careersystemsintl.com.

17. Geary, "I Quit."

18. Beverly Kaye and Sharon Jordan-Evans, *The Retention and Engagement Drivers Report* (completed August 12, 2004); available on request from mailto:HQ@csibka.com or http://www.careersystemsintl.com.

19. Marcus Buckingham and Curt Coffman, *First, Break All the Rules: What the World's Greatest Managers Do Differently* (New York: Simon & Schuster, 1999).

20. Kathy E. Kram, *Mentoring at Work: Developmental Relationships in Organizational Life* (Glenview, IL: Scott, Foresman, 1985); Belle Rose Ragins, "Mentor Functions and Outcomes: A Comparison of Men and Women in Formal and Informal Mentoring Relationships," *Journal of Applied Psychology* 84 (1999): 529–550; Terri A. Scandura, "Mentorship and Career Mobility: An Empirical Investigation," *Behavior* 13

(1992): 169–174; Raymond A. Noe, "An Investigation of the Determinants of Successful Assigned Mentoring Relationships," *Personnel Psychology* 41 (1988): 457–479.

21. George F. Dreher and Ronald A. Ash, "A Comparative Study of Mentoring among Men and Women in Managerial, Professional, and Technical Positions," *Journal of Applied Psychology* 75 (1990): 539–546; George F. Dreher and Taylor H. Cox Jr., "Race, Gender, and Opportunity: A Study of Compensation Attainment and the Establishment of Mentoring Relationships," *Journal of Applied Psychology* 81 (1996): 297–308; Tammy D. Allen, Lillian T. Eby, Mark L. Poteet, Elizabeth Lentz, and Lizzette Lima, "Career Benefits Associated with Mentoring for Protégés: A Meta-Analysis," *Journal of Applied Psychology* 89 (2004): 127–136.

22. Allen and others, "Career Benefits Associated with Mentoring for Protégés."

23. See the following excellent mentoring reviews of the literature: Raymond A. Noe, David B. Greenberger, and Sheng Wang, "Mentoring: What We Know and Where We Might Go," *Research in Personnel and Human Resource Management* 21 (2002): 129–173; Connie R. Wanberg, Elizabeth T. Welsh, and Sarah A. Hezlett, "Mentoring Research: A Review and Dynamic Process Model," *Research in Personnel and Human Resources Management* 22 (2003): 39–124.

24. Julie Connelly, "Jack Moves On," *NYSE Magazine,* Winter 2002, 30.

25. Shelly Branch, "The 100 Best Companies to Work for in America," *Fortune,* January 11, 1999, 118–130.

26. Mentoring Organization's Mentor, 2003. Retrieved March 5, 2004, from http://www.mentoring.org/take_action/leg_alerts/legalert_12–12–03.

27. Belle R. Ragins, John L. Cotton, and Janice S. Miller, "Marginal Mentoring: The Effects of Type of Mentor, Quality of Relationship, and Program Design on Work and Career Attitudes," *Academy of Management Journal* 43 (2000): 1177–1194; Regina D. Langhout, Jean E. Rhodes, and Lori N. Osborne, "An Exploratory Study of Youth Mentoring in an Urban Context: Adolescents' Perceptions of Relationship Styles," *Journal of Youth & Adolescence* 33 (2004): 293–306.

28. Ellen A. Ensher and Susan Elaine Murphy, "Effects of Race, Gender, Perceived Similarity, and Contact on Mentor Relationships," *Journal of Vocational Behavior* 50 (1997): 460–481; Stacey D. Blake-Beard, "At the Crossroads of Race and Gender: Lessons from the Mentoring Experiences of Professional Black Women," in Audrey J. Murrell and Faye J. Crosby (eds.), *Mentoring Dilemmas: Developmental Relationships within Multicultural Organizations,* 83–104 (Mahwah, NJ: Lawrence Erlbaum Associates, 1999); Belle R. Ragins, "Power and Gender

Congruency Effects in Evaluations of Male and Female Managers," *Journal of Management* 15 (1989): 65–76.

29. Monica C. Higgins and Kathy E. Kram, "Reconceptualizing Mentoring at Work: A Developmental Network Perspective," *Academy of Management Review* 26, no. 2 (2001): 264–288; Richard L. Daft, *Organization Theory and Design* (Minneapolis/St. Paul: West Educational Publishing, 1995).

Chapter Two: The Many Faces of Power Mentoring

1. In Chapter One of this book we review some of the academic thinking on new networking forms of mentoring relationships described by Monica Higgins and Kathy Kram in their article "Reconceptualizing Mentoring at Work: A Developmental Network Perspective," *Academy of Management Review* 26, no. 2 (2001): 264–288. See also David A. Thomas, "Racial Dynamics in Cross-Race Developmental Relationships," *Administrative Science Quarterly* 38 (1993): 169–194; Elizabeth Wolfe, "Newcomers' Relationships: The Role of Social Network Ties during Socialization," *Academy of Management Journal* 45, no. 6 (2002): 1149–1162; and Monica C. Higgins and David A. Thomas, "Constellations and Careers: Toward Understanding the Effects of Multiple Developmental Relationships," *Journal of Organizational Behavior* 22 (2001): 223–247.

2. Kathy Kram, *Mentoring at Work: Developmental Relationships in Organizational Life* (Glenview, IL: Scott, Foresman, 1985); Michael Zey, *The Mentor Connection* (Homewood, IL: Dow Jones-Irwin, 1984).

3. Kram, *Mentoring at Work*. Others, including Raymond Noe and Terri Scandura, have developed scales to measure the extent to which these functions are incorporated into the relationship; see Raymond Noe, "An Investigation of the Determinants of Successful Assigned Mentoring Relationships," *Personnel Psychology* 41 (1988): 457–479; Terri Scandura and Ralph J. Katerberg, "Much Ado about Mentors and Little Ado about Measurement: Development of an Instrument." Paper presented at the annual meeting of the National Academy of Management, Anaheim, CA, August 1988.

4. Michael D. Eisner with Tony Schwartz, *Work in Progress: Risking Failure, Surviving Success* (Westport, CT: Hyperion, 1999); Ronald Grover, "An Eisner Exit Strategy? Don't Be Surprised If Disney's Board Announces Plan Soon to Start Searching for a Successor for Embattled CEO," *Business Week Online*, April 22, 2004. http://www.businessweek.com/bwdaily/dnflash/apr2004/nf20040422_6834_db035.htm; Sally Hofmeister, "Dealing for Disney: If Eisner Goes, Who Takes His Job?" *Los Angeles Times*, March 1, 2004; C. Bruce Orwall, "Disney

Says It Is Addressing Issue of Eisner Succession Plan," *Wall Street Journal,* February 11, 2004.

5. Jack Welch and John A. Byrne, *Jack: Straight from the Gut* (New York: Warner Books, 2001); Janet Lowe, *Welch: An American Icon* (New York: Wiley, 2001).

6. Kram, *Mentoring at Work.*

7. Tammy D. Allen, Marc L. Poteet, and Susan M. Burroughs, "The Mentor's Perspective: A Qualitative Inquiry and Future Research Agenda," *Journal of Vocational Behavior* 51, no. 1 (1997): 70–89. For the mentor's perspective, also see the review by Raymond A. Noe, David B. Greenberger, and Sheng Wang, "Mentoring: What We Know and Where We Might Go," in Gerald R. Ferris and Joseph J. Martocchio (eds.), *Research in Personnel and Human Resources Management,* 129–173 (Greenwich, CT: Elsevier Science/JAI Press, 2002).

8. Erik H. Erikson, *Identity and the Life Cycle* (New York: Norton [originally published 1959, New York International Universities Press], reissue 1994).

9. In 1997, Belle Rose Ragins summarized the findings of a number of research studies that focused on the importance and benefits of diversified mentoring relationships for minority employees; see her "Diversified Mentoring Relationships in Organizations: A Power Perspective," *Academy of Management Review* 21, no. 2 (1997): 482–521.

10. See, for example, Susan E. Jackson, "Team Composition in Organizational Settings: Issues in Managing an Increasingly Diverse Work Force," in Steve Worchel, Wendy Wood, and Jeffry A. Simpson (eds.), *Group Process and Productivity,* 138–173 (Thousand Oaks, CA: Sage, 1992).

11. For more about boundaryless careers in different industries and the different forms they can take, such as virtual organizations, see Michael B. Arthur and Denise M. Rousseau (eds.), *The Boundaryless Career: A New Employment Principle for a New Organizational Era* (New York: Oxford University Press, 1996).

12. See research by Terri A. Scandura and Chester Schriescheim that examines the behaviors of supervisors who also act as mentors: "Leader Member Exchange and Supervisor Career Mentoring: Mentoring as a Complementary Construct in Leadership Research," *Academy of Management Journal* 37, no. 6 (1994): 1588–1602. See also John J. Sosik and Veronica M. Godshalk, "Leadership Styles, Mentoring Functions Received, and Job Related Stress: A Conceptual Model and Preliminary Study," *Journal of Organizational Behavior* 21 (2000): 365–390; and Terri A. Scandura and Ethlyn A. Williams, "Mentoring and Transformational Leadership: The Role of Supervisory Career Mentoring," *Journal of Vocational Behavior* 65, no. 3 (2004): 448–468.

13. David Shaw, "Special Report/Crossing the Line: A *Los Angeles Times* Profit-Sharing Arrangement with Staples Center Fuels a Firestorm of Protest in the Newsroom—and a Debate about Journalistic Ethics; Preface: A Business Deal Done—A Controversy Born," *Los Angeles Times,* December 20, 1999.

14. Belle Rose Ragins and John Cotton, "Mentor Functions and Outcomes: A Comparison of Men and Women in Formal and Informal Mentoring Relationships," *Journal of Applied Psychology* 84, no. 4 (1999): 529–550.

15. See Jayne Gackenbach, *Psychology and the Internet* (San Diego, CA: Academic Press, 1998).

16. Ellen A. Ensher, Christian Heun, and Anita Blanchard, "Online Mentoring and Computer-Mediated Communication: New Directions in Research," *Journal of Vocational Behavior* 63 (2003): 264–288. See also Betti A. Hamilton and Terri A. Scandura, "Implications for Organizational Learning and Development in a Wired World," *Organizational Dynamics* 31, no. 4 (2003): 388–402.

Chapter Three: Mentoring as a Two-Way Street

1. See Marcus Buckingham and Curt Coffman, *First, Break All the Rules: What the World's Greatest Managers Do Differently* (New York: Simon & Schuster, 1999).

2. Evidence of more money: George F. Dreher and Josephine A. Chargois, "Gender, Mentoring Experiences, and Salary Attainment among Graduates of an Historically Black University," *Journal of Vocational Behavior* 53 (1998): 401–416; and for protégés with white mentors: George F. Dreher and Taylor H. Cox Jr., "Race, Gender, and Opportunity: A Study of Compensation Attainment and the Establishment of Mentoring Relationships," *Journal of Applied Psychology* 81 (1996): 297–308; and Georgia T. Chao, Pat M. Walz, and Phillip D. Gardner, "Formal and Informal Mentorships: A Comparison of Mentoring Functions and Contrast with Nonmentored Counterparts," *Personnel Psychology* 45 (1992): 619–636, which also contains evidence of enhanced career satisfaction. For evidence of positive career and job experiences, see, for example, Ellen A. Fagenson, "The Mentor Advantage: Perceived Career/Job Experiences of Protégés versus Non-Protégés," *Journal of Organizational Behavior* 10 (1989): 309–320; Terri A. Scandura, "Mentorship and Career Mobility: An Empirical Investigation," *Journal of Organizational Behavior* 13 (1992): 169–174; and William Whitely, Thomas W. Dougherty, and George F. Dreher, "Relationship of Career Mentoring and Socioeconomic Origin to Managers' and Professionals' Early Career Progress," *Academy of Man-*

agement Journal 34 (1991): 331–351. And better work-family balance was found for those with mentors in Troy R. Nielson, Dawn S. Carlson, and Melanie J. Lankau, "The Supportive Mentor as a Means of Reducing Work-Family Conflict," *Journal of Vocational Behavior* 59, no. 3 (2001): 364–381.

3. Tammy D. Allen, Marc L. Poteet, and Susan M. Burroughs, "The Mentor's Perspective: A Qualitative Inquiry and Future Research Agenda," *Journal of Vocational Behavior* 51, no. 1 (1997): 70–89.

4. "CNBC Ups Asofsky to Sr. VP," *Variety* online, July 17, 2001. http://print.google.com/print/doc?articleid=56aJqucvdb6.

5. Laurence Prusak and Don Cohen, "How to Invest in Social Capital," *Harvard Business Review,* June 2001, 86–93.

6. Susan Elaine Murphy and Ellen A. Ensher, *A Qualitative Analysis of Charismatic Leadership in Teams: The Case of Television Directors.* Paper presented at annual Academy of Management Meeting, New Orleans, LA, August 2004.

7. Andrew Walton, "Hilda Solis," in Caroline Kennedy (ed.), *Profiles in Courage for Our Time,* 269–291 (New York: Hyperion, 2002).

8. Michael Collopy, *Architects of Peace: Visions of Peace in Words and Images* (Novato, CA: New World Library, 2000).

9. Brigadier General Donald P. Pettit, Air Force Link, January 31, 2005. http://www.af.mil/bios/bio.asp?bioID=6747

10. See the following excellent mentoring reviews of the literature that highlight many of these benefits: Raymond A. Noe, David B. Greenberger, and Sheng Wang, "Mentoring: What We Know and Where We Might Go," *Research in Personnel and Human Resource Management* 21 (2002): 129–173; Connie R. Wanberg, Elizabeth T. Welsh, and Sarah A. Hezlett, "Mentoring Research: A Review and Dynamic Process Model," *Research in Personnel and Human Resources Management* 22 (2003): 39–124.

11. Louis V. Gerstner Jr., *Who Says Elephants Can't Dance? Inside IBM's Historic Turnaround* (New York: HarperCollins Business, 2002).

Chapter Four: The Mind of the Mentor

1. Mental models and prototypes are included in a research area in psychology called *social cognition,* which examines how individuals process information about people and social situations. For more on mental models, see Dedre Gentner and David R. Gentner, "Flowing Waters or Teaming Crowds: Mental Models of Electricity," in Albert Stevens and Dedre Gentner (eds.), *Mental Models* (Mahwah, NJ: Lawrence Erlbaum Associates, 1983); also see the following article on interpersonal relationship interactions that finds evidence that they

are dictated by relationship prototypes: Beverley Fehr, "Intimacy Expectations in Same-Sex Friendships: A Prototype Interaction-Pattern Model," *Journal of Personality and Social Psychology* 86, no. 2 (2004): 265–284.

2. Information gathered from Channel One Web site, http://www.channelone.com.

3. "Fran Allen: From 'Fair Lady' to Fellow: Mentor and First Female IBM Fellow Retires after Nearly 45 Years," January 31, 2005. http://domino.research.ibm.com/comm/pr.nsf/pages/news.20020806_fran_allen.html.

4. Catalyst, "2000 Catalyst Award Winners Focus on Corporate Culture Changes." Press release, January 6, 2000. http://www.catalystwomen.org/pressroom/press_releases/2000_catalyst_award_winners.htm.

5. Ellen A. Ensher, Elisa J. Grant-Vallone, and William D. Marelich, "Effects of Perceived Attitudinal and Demographic Similarity on Protégés' Support and Satisfaction Gained from Their Mentoring Relationships," *Journal of Applied Social Psychology* 32, no. 7 (2002): 1407–1430; Daniel B. Turban, Thomas W. Dougherty, and Felissa K. Lee, "Gender, Race, and Perceived Similarity Effects in Developmental Relationships: The Moderating Role of Relationship Duration," *Journal of Vocational Behavior* 61, no. 2 (2002): 240–262.

6. George F. Dreher and Taylor H. Cox Jr., "Race, Gender, and Opportunity: A Study of Compensation Attainment and the Establishment of Mentoring Relationships," *Journal of Applied Psychology* 81 (1996): 297–308. Dreher and Cox found that white male protégés were more likely to report relationships with white male mentors than were black or Hispanic protégés; they also found that men were more likely than women to form mentoring relationships with white men.

7. Ellen A. Ensher and Susan E. Murphy, "Effects of Race, Gender, Perceived Similarity, and Contact on Mentor Relationships," *Journal of Vocational Behavior* 50 (1997): 460–481.

8. Raymond A. Noe, "Women and Mentoring: A Review and Research Agenda," *Academy of Management Review* 13 (1988): 65–78; Belle Rose Ragins and Terri A. Scandura, "Gender Differences in Expected Outcomes of Mentoring Relationships," *Academy of Management Journal* 37 (1994): 957–971.

9. Tammy D. Allen, "Protégé Selection by Mentors: Contributing Individual and Organizational Factors," *Journal of Vocational Behavior* 65, no. 3 (2004): 469–483.

10. Michael Zey, *The Mentor Connection* (Homewood, IL: Dow Jones-Irwin, 1984).

11. Andrew Tobias, "How Much Is Fair?" *Parade,* March 2, 2003.

12. Daniel Goleman, *Emotional Intelligence* (New York: Bantam Books, 1995); Daniel Goleman, *Working with Emotional Intelligence* (New York: Bantam Books, 2002); Daniel Goleman, Richard Boyatzis, and Anne McKee, *Primal Leadership: Realizing the Power of Emotional Intelligence* (Boston: Harvard Business School Press, 2002).

13. With respect to tests and challenges, we did not initially include a question specifically asking about this aspect of the relationship. In an early sample of interviews, a number of mentors and protégés mentioned it, so we added it in all subsequent interviews. We describe this iterative interview process in more detail in Appendix B.

14. Joshua M. Sacco, Christine R. Scheu, Ann Marie Ryan, and Neal Schmitt, "An Investigation of Race and Sex Similarity Effects in Interviews: A Multilevel Approach to Relational Demography," *Journal of Applied Psychology* 88, no. 5 (2003): 852–865.

Chapter Five: The Protégé's Perspective

1. Earl Babbie, *The Practice of Social Research* (Belmont, CA: Wadsworth Publishing Company, 1986); and Steven J. Taylor and Robert Bogdan, *Introduction to Qualitative Research Methods: A Guidebook and Resource* (New York: Wiley, 1998).

2. With exception of the study by Tammy D. Allen, Mark L. Poteet, Joyce E. A. Russell, "Protégé Selection by Mentors: What Makes the Difference?" *Journal of Organizational Behavior* 21, no. 3 (2000): 271–282, only one previous study looked at protégé characteristics that attracted a mentor. See Judy D. Olian, Stephan J. Carroll, and Cristina M. Giannantonio, "Mentor Reactions to Protégés: An Experiment with Managers," *Journal of Vocational Behavior* 43 (1993): 266–278.

3. See, for example, Sandy J. Wayne and Robert C. Liden, "Effects of Impression Management on Performance Ratings: A Longitudinal Study," *Academy of Management Journal* 38, no. 1 (1995): 232–260; and William L. Gardner, "Lessons in Organizational Dramaturgy: The Art of Impression Management," *Organizational Dynamics* 21, no. 1 (1992): 33–46.

4. Anthony G. Greenwald, "The Totalitarian Ego: Fabrication and Revision of Personal History," *American Psychologist* 35, no. 7 (1980): 603–618.

5. Edwin A. Locke and Gary P. Latham, "Building a Practically Useful Theory of Goal Setting and Task Motivation: A 35-Year Odyssey," *American Psychologist* 57, no. 9 (2002): 705–717.

6. Veronica Godshalk and John J. Sosik, "Aiming for Career Success: The Role of Learning Goal Orientation in Mentoring Relationships," *Journal of Vocational Behavior* 63, no. 3 (2003): 417–437. And also see

Tammy D. Allen, "Protégé Selection by Mentors: Contributing Individual and Organizational Factors," *Journal of Vocational Behavior* 65, no. 3 (2004): 469–48, for other protégé characteristics that attract mentors.

7. Gary P. Latham and Colette A. Frayne, "Self-Management Training for Increasing Job Attendance: A Follow-up and a Replication," *Journal of Applied Psychology* 74, no. 3 (1989): 411–416; Colette Frayne and Gary P. Latham, "Application of Social Learning Theory to Employee Self-Management of Attendance," *Journal of Applied Psychology* 72, no. 3 (1987): 387–392; Charles C. Manz and Christopher P. Neck, "Inner Leadership: Creating Productive Thought Patterns," *Academy of Management Executive* 5 (1991): 87–95; Charles C. Manz and Henry P. Sims Jr., "Self-Management as a Substitute for Leadership: A Social Learning Theory Perspective," *Academy of Management Review* 5 (1980): 361–367; Charles Manz and Christopher P. Neck, *Mastering Self-Leadership: Empowering Yourself for Personal Excellence,* 3rd ed. (Upper Saddle River, NJ: Pearson, Prentice-Hall, 2004).

8. On the behavior of supervisors who also act as mentors, see Terri A. Scandura and Chester Schriescheim, "Leader-Member Exchange and Supervisor Career Mentoring: Mentoring as a Complementary Construct in Leadership Research," *Academy of Management Journal* 37, no. 6 (1994): 1588–1602, and Terri A. Scandura and Ethlyn A. Williams, "Mentoring and Transformational Leadership: The Role of Supervisory Career Mentoring," *Journal of Vocational Behavior* 65, no. 3 (2004): 448–468.

9. Matt M. Starcevich, "What Is Unique about Reverse Mentoring: Survey Results," November 28, 2004. http://www.coachingandmentoring.com/reversementoringresults.htm.

10. Kris Maher, "Reverse Mentoring Programs Can Bridge Generational Gaps," *Wall Street Journal,* November 11, 2003. http://www.online.wsj.com, retrieved January 31, 2005.

11. Maher, "Reverse Mentoring Programs."

12. Samuel Greengard, "Moving Forward with Reverse Mentoring—Sharing the Knowledge—Brief Article," March 2002. http://www.findarticles.com/p/articles/mi_m0FXS/is_3_81/ai_84148619.

13. Greengard, "Moving Forward with Reverse Mentoring."

14. Ellen A. Ensher, Christian Heun, and Anita Blanchard, "Online Mentoring and Computer-Mediated Communication: New Directions in Research," *Journal of Vocational Behavior* 63 (2003): 264–288. See also Betti A. Hamilton and Terri A. Scandura, "Implications for Organizational Learning and Development in a Wired World," *Organizational Dynamics* 31, no. 4 (2003): 388–402.

15. Ellen A. Ensher, Suzanne de Janasz, and Christian Heun, "E-mentoring: Virtual Relationships and Real Rewards," 2005. Manuscript under review.

16. Information about MentorNet can be found on their Web site at http://www.mentornet.net. See also Peg Boyle Single and Carol Muller, "When Email and Mentoring Unite: The Implementation of a Nationwide Electronic Mentoring Program." In L. Stromei (ed.), *Implementing Successful Coaching Mentoring Programs,* 107–122. Cambridge, MA: American Society for Training and Development.

17. Chance W. Lewis, "International Telementoring Program Report Evaluation Results from Teacher Surveys," 2002. http://www.tele mentor.org.pdf/Research-2002–1.pdf.

18. Susan E. Murphy and Ellen A. Ensher, "The Role of Mentoring Support and Self-Management Strategies on Reported Career Outcomes," *Journal of Career Development* 27, no. 4 (2001): 229–246.

Chapter Six: Unlocking the Secrets of Great Power Mentoring Relationships

1. "100 Most Influential People of the 20th Century," *Time Magazine,* June 8, 1998. http://www.time.com/time/time100/artists/profile/winfrey.html.

2. "Oprah Winfrey Tops Bush, Gore as Preferred Travel Companion, Survey Says," *CNN.com,* October 26, 2000. http://archives.cnn.com/2000/TRAVEL/NEWS/10/26/fodors.survey/.

3. Nancy L. Collins and Brooke C. Feeney, "An Attachment Theory Perspective on Closeness and Intimacy," in Debra Mashek and Arthur Aron (eds.), *Handbook of Closeness and Intimacy,* 163–187 (Mahwah, NJ: Lawrence Erlbaum & Associates, 2004).

4. John M. Gottman and Nan Silver, *The Seven Principles for Making Marriage Work* (New York: Three Rivers Press, 1999). Gottman's research has been used successfully not only in keeping marriages together, but also keeping them happy and healthy.

5. Daniel B. Turban, Thomas W. Dougherty, and Felissa K. Lee, "Gender, Race, and Perceived Similarity Effects in Developmental Relationships: The Moderating Role of Relationship Duration," *Journal of Vocational Behavior* 61, no. 2 (2002): 240–262.

6. Ellen Berscheid and H. Reis, "Attraction and Relationship Development," in Daniel T. Gilbert, Susan T. Fiske, and Gardner Lindzey (eds.), *Handbook of Social Psychology,* Vol. 2, 4th ed., 193–281 (New York: McGraw-Hill, 1999).

7. John Grey, *Men Are from Mars, Women Are from Venus: A Practical*

Guide for Improving Communication and Getting What You Want in Your Relationships (New York: HarperCollins, 1992).

8. John Bowlby, *Attachment and Loss,* Vol. 1: *Attachment* (New York: Basic Books, 1969).

9. For a discussion of these ideas of relationship interdependence, see review by Caryl E. Rusbult, Madoka Kumashiro, Michael K. Coolson, and Jeffrey L. Kirchner, "Interdependence, Closeness, and Relationships," in Debra Mashek and Arthur Aron (eds.), *Handbook of Closeness and Intimacy,* 137–161 (Mahwah, NJ: Lawrence Erlbaum & Associates, 2004).

10. Warren G. Bennis and Robert J. Thomas, *Geeks and Geezers* (Boston: Harvard Business School Press, 2002).

11. Jim Lukaszewski, "Inside the Mind of the CEO," *Strategy* 14, June 18, 2001. www.e911.com/monos/articles/14.pdf.

12. Classic study by Robert Rosenthal and Lenore Jacobson, *Pygmalion in the Classroom: Teacher Expectation and Pupils' Intellectual Development* (New York: Holt, Rinehart & Winston, Inc., 1968).

13. Diane Brady, "Rethinking the Rat Race," *Business Week Online,* August 26, 2002. http://www.businessweek.com/magazine/content/02_34/b3796646.htm.

14. Stephanie Armour, "More Americans Put Families ahead of Work," *USA Today,* December 5, 2002; Wayne Cascio and Cliff E. Young, "Work-Family Balance: Does the Market Reward Firms That Respect It?" in Diane Halpern and Susan Elaine Murphy (eds.), *Work-Family Balance to Work-Family Interaction: Changing the Metaphor* (Mahwah, NJ: Lawrence Erlbaum & Associates, 2005).

15. Bureau of Labor Statistics, "Special Tabulations Based on Analyses of March Current Population Surveys," 1980, 1988, 1990, 1994–2001, unpublished work (Washington, DC: Bureau of Labor Statistics, 2004).

16. Troy R. Nielson, Dawn S. Carlson, and Melanie J. Lankau, "The Supportive Mentor as a Means of Reducing Work-Family Conflict," *Journal of Vocational Behavior* 59, no. 3 (2001): 364–381.

17. Bill Hogan, "Alone on the Hill," MotherJones.com, September 20, 2001. http://www.motherjones.com/news/feature/2001/09/lee.html.

18. Gottman and Silver, *Seven Principles for Making Marriage Work.*

19. Daniel Goleman, *Emotional Intelligence* (New York: Bantam Books, 1995); Daniel Goleman, *Working with Emotional Intelligence* (New York: Bantam Books, 2002); Daniel Goleman, Richard Boyatzis, and Anne McKee, *Primal Leadership: Realizing the Power of Emotional Intelligence* (Boston: Harvard Business School Press, 2002).

20. Winifred Gallagher, *How Heredity and Experience Make You Who You Are* (New York: Random House, 1996).

21. Gottman and Silver, *Seven Principles for Making Marriage Work*.

22. Mayta A. Caldwell and Letitia A. Peplau, "Sex Differences in Same-Sex Friendship," *Sex Roles* 8, no. 7 (1982): 721–732.

23. Bennis and Thomas, *Geeks and Geezers*.

24. See, for example, Susan Elaine Murphy, Sharon Goto, and Ellen A. Ensher, "Advising Young Women of Color," in Sara Davis, Mary Crawford, and Jadwiga Sebrechts (eds.), *Coming into Her Own: Educational Success in Girls and Women,* 244–259 (San Francisco: Jossey-Bass, 1999).

25. Lillian T. Eby, Stacy E. McManus, Shana A. Simon, Joyce E. A. Russell, "The Protege's Perspective Regarding Negative Mentoring Experiences: The Development of a Taxonomy," *Journal of Vocational Behavior* 57, no. 1 (2000): 1–21.

26. Daniel Levinson with Charlotte N. Darrow, Edward B. Klein, Maria H. Levinson, and Braxton McKee, *The Seasons of a Man's Life* (New York: Knopf, 1978).

27. See Kathy Kram, *Mentoring at Work: Developmental Relationships in Organizational Life* (Glenview, IL: Scott, Foresman, 1985) on ending mentoring relationships that do not transition into friendship.

28. Belle Rose Ragins and Terri A. Scandura, "The Way We Were: Gender and Termination of Mentoring Relationships," *Journal of Applied Psychology* 82 (1997): 945–953; cited in Terri A. Scandura, "Dysfunctional Mentoring Relationships and Outcomes," *Journal of Management* 24 (1998): 449–467.

29. Lillian Eby and Stacy McManus, "The Protégé's Role in Negative Mentoring Experiences," *Journal of Vocational Behavior* 65 (2004): 255–275; Lillian T. Eby, Marcus Butts, Angie Lockwood, and Shana A. Simon, "Protégés' Negative Mentoring Experiences: Construct Development and Nomological Validation," *Personnel Psychology* 57 (2004): 411–447.

30. Terri Scandura, "Dysfunctional Mentoring Relationships and Outcomes," *Journal of Management* 24 (1998): 449–467.

Chapter Seven: Power Mentoring and You

1. Richard Bolles, *What Color Is Your Parachute? 2004* (Berkeley, CA: Ten Speed Press, 2003); Julia Jenson, *I Don't Know What I Want, But I Know It's Not This: A Step-by-Step Guide to Finding Gratifying Work* (New York: Penguin Books, 2003).

2. Cynthia McCaulay, Russ Moxley, and Ellen Van Velsor, "Our View of Leadership Development," in Cynthia McCauley, Russ Moxley, and

Ellen Van Velsor (eds.), *The Handbook of Leadership Development,* 1–25 (San Francisco: Jossey-Bass, 2000).

3. Many Web sites offer the Myers-Briggs Type Indicator (MBTI). Check out the original site at http://www.myersbriggs.org/. Kolb Learning Style Inventory (LSI) is available at http://www.hayresourcesdirect. haygroup.com.

4. For example, for the benefits of a happy disposition, see Martin P. Seligman, *Authentic Happiness* (New York: Free Press, 2002).

5. Martin P. Seligman, *Learned Optimism: How to Change Your Mind and Your Life* (New York: Free Press, 1990 and 1998).

6. See, for example, Tammy D. Allen and Lillian T. Eby, "Factors Related to Mentor Reports of Mentoring Functions Provided: Gender and Relational Characteristics," *Sex Roles* 50, nos. 1–2 (2004): 129–139.

7. This phrase was borrowed from the movie titled *Field of Dreams,* starring Kevin Costner. Released 1989 by Universal, directed by Phil Alden Robinson, produced Lawrence Gordon and Charles Gordon.

8. Ronald E. Riggio, *Manual for the Social Skills Inventory: Research Edition* (Palo Alto, CA: Consulting Psychologists Press, 1989); Ronald E. Riggio and Dana R. Carney, *Social Skills Inventory Manual,* 2nd ed. (Redwood City, CA: MindGarden, 2003).

9. Check out the soon-to-be-available online version of Social Skills Inventory at www.mindgarden.com.

10. For a review of research on the Social Skills Inventory, see Ronald E. Riggio and Heidi R. Riggio, "Self-Report Measures of Emotional and Nonverbal Expressiveness," in Valerie Manusov (ed.), *The Sourcebook of Nonverbal Measures: Going beyond Words,* 105–111 (Mahwah, NJ: Lawrence Erlbaum Associates, 2005).

11. One assessment is available at http://www.hayresourcesdirect. haygroup.com/Competency/Assessments_Surveys/Emotional_Com petency_Inventory_University/Overview.asp.

12. See, for example, Raymond A. Noe, "An Investigation of the Determinants of Successful Assigned Mentoring Relationships," *Personnel Psychology* 41 (1988): 457–479; and Belle Rose Ragins and John L. Cotton, "Mentor Functions and Outcomes: A Comparison of Men and Women in Formal and Informal Mentoring Relationships," *Journal of Applied Psychology* 84 (1999): 529–550.

13. Terri Scandura and Ralph J. Katerberg, "Much Ado about Mentors and Little Ado about Measurement: Development of an Instrument." Paper presented at the annual meeting of the National Academy of Management, Anaheim, CA, August 1988.

14. Aneil K. Mishra, "The Centrality of Trust," in Roderick Kramer and Tom Tyler (eds.), *Trust in Organizations,* 261–287 (Thousand Oaks, CA: Sage, 1996).

15. Lillian Eby and Stacey McManus, "The Protégé's Role in Negative Mentoring Experiences," *Journal of Vocational Behavior* 65 (2004): 255–275; Lillian T. Eby, Marcus Butts, Angie Lockwood, and Shana A. Simon, "Protégés' Negative Mentoring Experiences: Construct Development and Nomological Validation," *Personnel Psychology* 57 (2004): 411–447.

16. Terri A. Scandura, "Dysfunctional Mentoring Relationships and Outcomes," *Journal of Management* 24 (1998): 449–467.

Chapter Eight: Conclusion

1. Kathy E. Kram, *Mentoring at Work: Developmental Relationships in Organizational Life* (Glenview, IL: Scott, Foresman, 1985); Georgia T. Chao, Pat M. Walz, and Phillip D. Gardner, "Formal and Informal Mentorships: A Comparison on Mentoring Functions and Contrast with Non-mentored Counterparts," *Personnel Psychology* 45 (1992): 619–636; Terri A. Scandura, "Mentorship and Career Mobility: An Empirical Investigation," *Behavior* 13 (1992): 169–174; Raymond A. Noe, "An Investigation of the Determinants of Successful Assigned Mentoring Relationships," *Psychology* 41 (1988): 457–479; Tammy D. Allen, Lillian T. Eby, Mark L. Poteet, Elizabeth Lentz, and Lizzette Lima, "Career Benefits Associated with Mentoring for Protégés: A Meta-Analysis," *Journal of Applied Psychology* 89 (2004): 127–136.

2. George F. Dreher and Ronald A. Ash, "A Comparative Study of Mentoring among Men and Women in Managerial, Professional, and Technical Positions," *Journal of Applied Psychology* 75 (1990): 539–546; George F. Dreher and Taylor H. Cox Jr., "Race, Gender, and Opportunity: A Study of Compensation Attainment and the Establishment of Mentoring Relationships," *Journal of Applied Psychology* 81 (1996): 297–308; Belle Rose Ragins and John Cotton, "Mentor Functions and Outcomes: A Comparison of Men and Women in Formal and Informal Mentoring Relationships," *Journal of Applied Psychology* 84 (1999): 529–550.

3. Kram, *Mentoring at Work*; Raymond A. Noe, David B. Greenberger, and Sheng Wang, "Mentoring: What We Know and Where We Might Go," *Research in Personnel and Human Resource Management* 21 (2002): 129–173; Ellen A. Fagenson, "The Mentor Advantage: Perceived Career/Job Experiences of Protégés versus Non-Protégés," *Journal of Organizational Behavior* 10 (1989): 309–320.

4. Monica C. Higgins and Kathy E. Kram, "Reconceptualizing Mentoring at Work: A Developmental Network Perspective," *Academy of Management Review* 26, no. 2 (2001): 264–288; Richard L. Daft, *Organization Theory and Design* (Minneapolis/St. Paul: West Educational Publishing, 1995); Monica C. Higgins and David A. Thomas,

"Constellations and Careers: Toward Understanding the Effects of Multiple Developmental Relationships," *Journal of Organizational Behavior* 22 (2001): 223–247.

5. Kathy E. Kram and Lynn A. Isabella, "Mentoring Alternatives: The Role of Peer Relationships in Career Development," *Academy of Management Journal* 28 (1985): 110–132; and Ellen A. Ensher, Craig Thomas, and Susan E. Murphy, "Comparison of Traditional, Step-Ahead, and Peer Mentoring on Protégés' Support, Satisfaction and Perceptions of Career Success: A Social Exchange Perspective," *Journal of Business and Psychology* 15 (2001): 415–438.

6. Franklin S. Lunding, George E. Clements, and Donald S. Perkins, quoted in Eliza G. C. Collins and Patricia Scot, "Everyone Who Makes It Has a Mentor," *Harvard Business Review,* July-August 1978, 89–101; mentioned in Gerard R. Roche, "Much Ado about Mentors," *Harvard Business Review,* January-February 1979, 1–10.

7. Linda Hill and Nancy Kamprath, "Beyond the Myth of the Perfect Mentor: Building a Network of Developmental Relationships," Harvard Business School Case, Case No. 9–491–096, 1991. https://harvardbusinessonline.hbsp.harvard.edu/b01/en/common/item_detail.jhtml?id=491096.

8. Tammy D. Allen, Marc L. Poteet, and Susan M. Burroughs, "The Mentor's Perspective: A Qualitative Inquiry and Future Research Agenda," *Journal of Vocational Behavior* 51, no. 1 (1997): 70–89.

9. See Belle Rose Ragins, John Cotton, and Janice Miller, "Marginal Mentoring: The Effects of Type of Mentor, Quality of Relationship, and Program Design on Work and Career Attitudes," *Academy of Management Journal* 43 (2000): 1177–1194. According to these authors, "marginal mentoring" describes relationships where mentoring is not destructive but is also not really beneficial. They also cite other researchers who developed the same ideas earlier. For example, Kathy E. Kram, *Mentoring at Work: Developmental Relationships in Organizational Life* (Glenview, IL: Scott, Foresman, 1985), claimed that mentoring relationships should be viewed as dynamic and changing. And see Daniel Levinson with Charlotte N. Darrow, Edward B. Klein, Maria H. Levinson, and Braxton McKee, *The Seasons of a Man's Life* (New York: Knopf, 1978).

10. Tammy D. Allen, Marc L. Poteet, and Susan M. Burroughs, "The Mentor's Perspective: A Qualitative Inquiry and Future Research Agenda," *Journal of Vocational Behavior* 51, no. 1 (1997): 70–89.

11. Lillian Eby and Stacy McManus, "The Protégé's Role in Negative Mentoring Experiences," *Journal of Vocational Behavior* 65 (2004): 255–275; Lillian T. Eby, Marcus Butts, Angie Lockwood, and Shana A. Simon, "Protégés' Negative Mentoring Experiences: Construct

Development and Nomological Validation," *Personnel Psychology* 57 (2004): 411-447; Terri Scandura, "Dysfunctional Mentoring Relationships and Outcomes," *Journal of Management* 24 (1998): 449–467.

12. Joann S. Lublin, "Protégé Finds Mentor Gave Her a Big Boost, But Shadow Lingers," *Wall Street Journal,* September 7, 2004.

13. Shelly Branch, "The 100 Best Companies to Work for in America," *Fortune,* January 11, 1999, 118–130.

14. Branch, "100 Best Companies; cited in Tammy D. Allen, Lillian T. Eby, Mark L. Poteet, Elizabeth Lentz, and Lizzette Lima, "Career Benefits Associated with Mentoring for Protégés: A Meta-Analysis," *Journal of Applied Psychology* 89 (2004): 127–136.

15. National Women's Business Council, "Women's Business Mentoring Programs Demonstrate Unique Characteristics." News release, July 24, 2003. http://www.nwbc.gov/documents/finalmentoringte lease71003.pdf.

16. Information on mentoring as part of career development at IBM is available at http://www-8.ibm.com/employment/th/life/mentor ing.html.

17. David Giber, Louis Carter, and Marshall Goldsmith, (eds.), *Best Practices in Leadership Development Handbook* (San Francisco: Jossey-Bass/Pfeiffer, 2000); see especially 439–447.

18. Beverly Kaye, "Coaching and Mentoring: New Twists, Old Theme—An Introduction," in Louis Carter, David Giber, and Marshall Goldsmith (eds.), *Best Practices in Organizational Development and Change,* 438–441 (San Francisco: Jossey-Bass/Pfeiffer, 2001); and see also in same volume chap. 16, "Dow Corning," 442–487.

19. KABC-TV Los Angeles Annual EEO Public File Report August 1, 2004. http://abclocal.go.com/kabc/aboutus/073004_EEOfile.html.

20. Jim Welp, "How to Set Up a Formal Mentoring Program," May 8, 2002. http://techrepublic.com.com/5100-6317_11-1051313.html? tag=search#.

21. MentorNet Web site address: http://www.mentornet.net.

22. Ellen Goodman and Patricia O'Brien, *I Know Just What You Mean: The Power of Friendship in Women's Lives* (New York: Simon & Schuster, 2000).

Appendix B: Studying Power Mentoring Relationships

1. Michael Zey, *The Mentor Connection* (Homewood, IL: Dow Jones-Irwin, 1984).

2. Kathy E. Kram, "Phases of the Mentor Relationship," *Academy of Management Journal* 26, no. 4 (1983): 608–625; Kathy E. Kram, *Mentoring at Work: Developmental Relationships in Organizational Life* (Glenview, IL: Scott, Foresman, 1985).

3. Georgia T. Chao, Pat M. Walz, and Phillip D. Gardner, "Formal and

Informal Mentorships: A Comparison on Mentoring Functions and Contrast with Nonmentored Counterparts," *Personnel Psychology* 45 (1992): 619–636.

4. See, for example, Ellen A. Ensher and Susan E. Murphy, "Effects of Race, Gender, Perceived Similarity, and Contact on Mentor Relationships," *Journal of Vocational Behavior* 50 (1997): 460–481. Other research on this topic is contained in Chapter Six of this volume.

5. Belle R. Ragins, "Power and Gender Congruency Effects in Evaluations of Male and Female Managers," *Journal of Management* 15 (1989): 65–76.

6. Lillian Eby, "Alternative Forms of Mentoring in Changing Organizational Environments: A Conceptual Extension of the Mentoring Literature," *Journal of Vocational Behavior* 51, no. 1 (1997): 125–144; Stacey D. Blake-Beard, "At the Crossroads of Race and Gender: Lessons from the Mentoring Experiences of Professional Black Women," in Audrey J. Murrell and Faye J. Crosby (eds.), *Mentoring Dilemmas: Developmental Relationships within Multicultural Organizations,* 83–104 (Mahwah, NJ: Lawrence Erlbaum Associates, 1999); Herminia Ibarra, "Race, Opportunity, and Diversity of Social Circles in Managerial Networks," *Academy of Management Journal* 38, no. 3 (1995): 673–703.

7. S. Gayle Baugh and Terri A. Scandura, "The Effects of Multiple Mentors on Protégé Attitudes Toward the Work Setting," *Journal of Social Behavior & Personality* 14, no. 4 (1999): 503–521; Monica C. Higgins, "The More the Merrier? Multiple Developmental Relationships and Work Satisfaction," *Journal of Management Development* 19, no. 4 (2000): 277–296; David A. Thomas and Monica C. Higgins, "Mentoring and the Boundaryless Career: Lessons from the Minority Experience," in Michael B. Arthur and Denise M. Rousseau (eds.), *Boundaryless Careers: A New Employment Principle for a New Organizational Era* (New York: Oxford University Press, 1996); Monica C. Higgins and David A. Thomas, "Constellations and Careers: Toward Understanding the Effects of Multiple Developmental Relationships," *Journal of Organizational Behavior* 22, no. 3 (2001): 223–247; Monica C. Higgins and Kathy E. Kram, "Reconceptualizing Mentoring at Work: A Developmental Network Perspective," *Academy of Management Review* 26, no. 2 (2001): 264–288.

8. Ellen A. Ensher, Christian Heun, and Anita Blanchard, "Online Mentoring and Computer-Mediated Communication: New Directions in Research," *Journal of Vocational Behavior* 63 (2003): 264–288. See also Betti A. Hamilton and Terri A. Scandura, "Implications for Organizational Learning and Development in a Wired World," *Organizational Dynamics* 31, no. 4 (2003): 388–402.

9. On the behavior of supervisors who also act as mentors, see Terri A. Scandura and Chester Schriescheim, "Leader-Member Exchange and Supervisor Career Mentoring: Mentoring as a Complementary Construct in Leadership Research," *Academy of Management Journal* 37, no. 6 (1994): 1588–1602, and Terri A. Scandura and Ethlyn A. Williams, "Mentoring and Transformational Leadership: The Role of Supervisory Career Mentoring," *Journal of Vocational Behavior* 65, no. 3 (2004): 448–468.

10. Joyce E. A. Russell and Danielle M. Adams, "The Changing Nature of Mentoring in Organizations: An Introduction to the Special Issue on Mentoring in Organizations," *Journal of Vocational Behavior* 51, no. 1 (1997): 1–14.

11. Tammy D. Allen, Marc L. Poteet, and Susan M. Burroughs, "The Mentor's Perspective: A Qualitative Inquiry and Future Research Agenda," *Journal of Vocational Behavior* 51, no. 1 (1997): 70–89.

12. Kathy E. Kram, "Phases of the Mentor Relationship," *Academy of Management Journal* 26, no. 4 (1983): 608–625.

13. Susan Elaine Murphy and Ellen A. Ensher, "The Effects of Culture on Mentoring Relationships: A Developmental Model," in Stuart Oskamp and Cheryln Granrose, *Cross-Cultural Work Groups*, 212–233 (Thousand Oaks, CA: Sage, 1997).

14. George B. Graen, "Role Making Processes within Complex Organizations," in Marvin D. Dunnette (ed.), *Handbook of Industrial and Organizational Psychology*, 1201–1245 (Chicago: Rand-McNally, 1976); George B. Graen and Terri Scandura, "Toward a Psychology of Dyadic Organizing," in Barry Staw and Lawrence L. Cummings (eds.), *Research in Organizational Behavior*, Vol. 9, 175–208 (Greenwich, CT: JAI Press, 1987).

15. George C. Homans, *Social Behavior: Its Elementary Form* (New York: Harcourt, Brace, and World, 1974); George Graen and William Schiemann, "Leader-Member Agreement: A Vertical Dyad Linkage Approach," *Journal of Applied Psychology* 63 (1978): 206–212.

16. Warren G. Bennis and Robert J. Thomas, *Geeks and Geezers* (Boston: Harvard Business School Press, 2002).

17. Monica C. Higgins and Kathy E. Kram, "Reconceptualizing Mentoring at Work: A Developmental Network Perspective," *Academy of Management Review* 26 (2001): 264–288.

18. Earl Babbie, *The Practice of Social Research* (Belmont, CA: Wadsworth Publishing Company, 1986).

19. Philip Mirvis and Douglas T. Hall, "Psychological Success and the Boundaryless Career," *Journal of Organizational Behavior* 15, no. 4 (1994): 365–380; Michael Arthur and Denise M. Rousseau, "The

Boundaryless Career as a New Employment Principle," in Michael B. Arthur and Denise M. Rousseau (eds.), *The Boundaryless Career,* 3–20 (New York: Oxford University Press, 1996).

20. Steven J. Taylor and Robert Bogdan, *Introduction to Qualitative Research Methods: A Guidebook and Resource* (New York: Wiley, 1998).

21. Barney G. Glaser and Anselm L. Strauss, *The Discovery of Grounded Theory: Strategies for Qualitative Research* (Chicago: Aldine, 1967); Anselm Strauss and Juliet Corbin, "Grounded Theory Methodology: An Overview," in Norman K. Denzin and Yvonna. S. Lincoln (eds.), *Strategies of Qualitative Inquiry,* 158–183 (Thousand Oaks, CA: Sage, 1998).

ACKNOWLEDGMENTS

What a tremendous relief and enormous pleasure it is to thank our own network of family, friends, mentors, supporters, advisors, and angels who helped us along the way to completing this book. This book represents the culmination of a three-year process. During the three years we worked on our book, our work-family balance challenges ramped up as Susan got married and Ellen had a baby. We would not have been able to manage all that we did without the support of all of those we mention here.

In this book we share stories about mentoring. Often these are stories about what makes their relationships so successful or what they learned from each other. So, it is appropriate to first and foremost thank our 50 participants, without whom this book would not have been possible. We were inspired by their examples and passion for their work.

Behind the mentoring stories are the stories of how we connected to each individual. While those stories are too numerous to recount here, the overall theme is that so many people graciously gave us their time, thoughts, connections, and help to make this book happen. Help always seemed to appear in the nick of time, just as we reached a dead end.

Before we recognize the many individuals who helped us, we need to gratefully acknowledge the American Association of University Women, who provided us with a grant (American Fellowship) to fund this work. Moreover, they also provided us with ample opportunities for speaking engagements that gave us the chance to test our early ideas. The members of AAUW in Southern California lent endless encouragement and enthusiasm for this project.

The other institutions that we want to gratefully acknowledge are Claremont McKenna College—particularly the Kravis Leadership Institute—and Loyola Marymount University (LMU).

CLAREMONT MCKENNA COLLEGE
(A SPECIAL THANK YOU FROM SUSAN)

I have had the great fortune to work with a wonderful group of colleagues at the Kravis Leadership Institute at Claremont McKenna College. These include Ron Riggio, Institute Director, who over the years has let me bounce ideas off of him from across the hall and shared my enthusiasm for this project. Sandy Counts, our Institute secretary, spent countless hours pulling together travel reports and other administrative aspects of the project, with no complaints. I appreciate the help given by Kravis students, including Katherine Hall, Eric Arnold, and Anne Pearl, who read drafts of the manuscript and offered insightful suggestions from their early career perspective. Jennifer Hartwell, our postdoctoral research fellow, also reviewed chapters and offered important insights. I also thank my good friend and former student Stefanie Halverson, who helped out in the later stages of the project, making sure that we adequately acknowledged the important mentoring research that others have completed. Many individuals also helped brainstorm connections to our interviewees; these include members of the Kravis Institute Board of Governors; the dean of faculty, William Ascher; and Pamela Gann, president of Claremont McKenna College. In addition, I thank the Kravis Leadership Institute and Claremont McKenna College for the generous financial support of the project.

I must also thank my collaborator Ellen Ensher for the special opportunity to work together throughout all phases of this immensely worthwhile project. Not only did we gain fascinating insight into the way today's mentoring relationships work, we also had the opportunity to hear great and inspiring stories from our mentors and protégés. I could not ask for a better research partner in this endeavor. Complementary skills make our research efforts productive, but friendship makes all our collaborations a true joy.

And very important, I thank my dear husband for his unwavering patience while I traveled and made him endure my late night reading and writing.

LOYOLA MARYMOUNT UNIVERSITY
(A SPECIAL THANK YOU FROM ELLEN)

I thank my academic community at LMU and in particular key individuals who were so gracious about providing assistance. Colleagues like Jerry Adler, Ed Gray, my department chair, Joe Jabbra, our former academic vice president, Mark Leach, Annie Liu, Cathleen McGrath, and Sister Peg all provided me with invaluable resources, connections, advice, and encouragement.

The research and administrative work that were behind the creation of this book would not have been possible without the dedication of our two faculty secretaries, Cissy Easter and Kathe Segall. Cissy, thank you for your help with this book and for keeping me going every single day with all of my teaching, service, and writing responsibilities. I so appreciate your calm manner and ability to keep up with all my requests. I also want to thank Kathe Segall for her relentless enthusiasm, excellent editing, and endless patience with the third-floor interloper! What an amazing team of undergraduate and graduate students that I have been lucky enough to have worked with on this book. These terrific students and alumni include Steve Bowen, Jane Dikdan, Julia Fehrenbach, Jory Jimenez, Cecilia Ruvalcabon, Christy Swanson, and Pauline Tetangco. A special thank you to Tyler Lamb, who mastered the intricacies of the QSR software and whose dedication went far above and beyond the call of duty.

There are three LMU colleagues who were absolutely pivotal to the success of this project. The first is Fernando Guerra, director of the Center for the Study of Los Angeles, who is my former professor and now colleague. Fernando believed in this project and provided us with some of our very best contacts and advice. Second is Father Robert Lawton, LMU president, who entrusted me with his valuable connections and whose gracious manner and eloquent words never cease to inspire me. And finally, I want to recognize John Wholihan, my dean in the College of Business, who shared my vision and excitement from the very beginning and has provided me with constant support and encouragement all along the way.

Along with my LMU community, I am fortunate to have a network of professional contacts and friends who were absolutely instrumental to this book. These include my past and present peer, step-ahead, traditional, and inspirational mentors.

Jeanne Hartley and Charlie Vance deserve special recognition. They were my first mentors, who taught me by example what mentoring is really all about. I have spent most of my 20-year professional career working with one or both of them in some capacity or another. They are my treasured friends and a constant in my chaotic life. I can always count on Jeanne and Charlie to be there for me, and they both were very helpful in the development of this project.

Before my life in academia, I was a corporate trainer and consultant. I am fortunate to have a circle of my consulting buddies, also known as the "designing women/spa ladies," who read early drafts and provided us with much needed reality checks during the production of this book. In addition to Jeanne, they include Joy Hawkins, Larry Kutcher (an honorary spa lady), Lupe Morales, Sue Padernacht, Yesmean Rihbany, and Karen Russo.

It is with great joy that I recognize family and friends who were absolutely steadfast in their support.

A big thank you to my husband, Sean, who alleviated my mommy guilt by being an exemplary daddy during way too many crunch times and for being a relentless promoter of this book even while doing press for your own projects. Thank you for shamelessly using your connections and for being there at 2:00 a.m. during those times of pure panic. And thank you to my son, Mark, who was born in August 2003, for your endless cheer, good humor, and patience. Your mommy has been working on this book your whole life, and I promise to stop soon.

Thank you to Sister Barbara Browne, my high school English teacher, who taught me to write no matter what. A special thank you also to Father Ken Deasy, who gave me the courage to pursue this project in its very early stages.

Thank you to Elena Lugo, who has helped Sean and me take care of Mark since he was just a few weeks old. Her loving presence and excellent advice has made it possible for me to write and teach without worrying, as I know my baby is in excellent hands. She has made me a better mom. She is truly my mommy mentor.

A special thank you also goes to my three nieces (Megan, Tarren, and Amanda), who were my very first protégés. A special thanks to Megan and the baby-sitter club (Ashleigh, Kate, and Holly).

Thank you to Mom and Dad, who instilled in me a love of learning, a passion for books, a commitment to balance, and the belief that I can do anything.

And finally, a big thank you to my coauthor, Susan. She began as my step-ahead mentor in 1993, and as the best mentoring relationships often do, our relationship evolved into so much more. For more than 12 years, she has been my most excellent writing partner, research collaborator, dear friend, and sister of my heart. I am so glad we took this ride together, and I am looking forward to many more years of creative projects.

A FINAL THANK YOU FROM BOTH OF US

We also acknowledge others in our circle of dear friends and trusted colleagues who gave of their time, advice, and contacts. Their help was absolutely indispensable, and we are more grateful than they will ever know for their help. They are Lilian Abrams, Gerald Alcantar, Jan Bowler, Chris Christenson, Suzanne de Janasz, Michelle De Rosa, Ellen Fagenson-Eland, Elisa Grant-Vallone, Rachel Isgar, Patrick Kerwin, Troy Nielson, Peg Boyle Single, and Joye Swan.

It is our pleasure also to acknowledge two leaders in the field of mentoring, Carol Muller and Belle Rose Ragins, who were absolutely unflagging in their support of this project and who provided invaluable connections, advice, and stimulated our thinking. Belle Rose Ragins was an early inspirational role model mentor, as her talk at Claremont McKenna in the 1990s piqued our interest in mentoring and started us on our way.

We also acknowledge Warren Bennis, who is truly our inspirational mentor and whose work has continued to enlighten us.

And finally, a big thank you to Rob Brandt, our editor at Jossey-Bass, whose persistence, enthusiasm, and dedication to this project has been remarkable.

We are certain that in our haste to put this book-baby to bed we may have inadvertently left out individuals who were helpful to us, so please forgive any omissions and know that our gratitude is deep and sincere.

THE AUTHORS

ELLEN A. ENSHER, PH.D., is an associate professor of management at Loyola Marymount University in Los Angeles, California. Dr. Ensher earned her master's degree in public administration at the University of Southern California in 1990 and completed her doctorate in organizational psychology at Claremont Graduate University in 1997.

Dr. Ensher currently teaches human resource management and related courses, including employee and labor relations, organizational development, and training and development. She has been consistently evaluated by her students as being in the top 5 percent of business professors at LMU.

Dr. Ensher's key areas of research include careers, diversity, and mentoring. Along with frequent collaborator Susan Murphy, Ensher has written about mentoring and issues of race, gender, and culture, types of mentoring relationships, career outcomes and benefits, leadership, and more recently, e-mentoring. In 2001, Ellen was honored to be named Ascendant Scholar in recognition of her early career achievement and in 2002 received the award for Best Paper from the Western Academy of Management. In 2002, Dr. Ensher was awarded the competitive American Fellowship Award from the American Association of University Women. She received a 2004 faculty research grant to fund an investigation of Mentor-Net's online peer mentoring forums. Dr. Ensher has received numerous LMU faculty grants and currently serves on the advisory board for MentorNet, a nationally recognized e-mentoring program.

Dr. Ensher has published 25 articles and book chapters and made more than 70 professional presentations. She has published in journals including *Academy of Management Executive, Human Resource Development Quarterly, Journal of Career Development, Journal of Vocational Behavior,* and *Organizational Dynamics.*

Ellen has consulted for a number of organizations both domestically and abroad, including Arco, the *Los Angeles Times,* Petronas (Malaysia), and the University of Southern California. Ellen lives in Los Angeles with her husband, Sean McNamara, and their son, Mark McNamara.

SUSAN ELAINE MURPHY, PH.D., is an associate professor of psychology at Claremont McKenna College and the associate director of the Henry R. Kravis Leadership Institute in Claremont, California. Dr. Murphy earned her Ph.D. and M.S. from the University of Washington in organizational psychology, where she also earned an MBA in the School of Business. Dr. Murphy currently teaches in organizational psychology and organizational development and is also an adjunct professor at Claremont Graduate University, where she teaches courses in industrial psychology and teams and leaders.

She has published more than 25 articles and book chapters on leadership, leadership development, and mentoring. Her current works include two edited books, *The Future of Leadership Development* (with Ron Riggio) and *Work-Family Balance to Work-Family Interaction: Changing the Metaphor* (with Diane Halpern). Susan is actively involved in the development, delivery, and evaluation of youth mentoring programs in the Los Angeles area, both through her service-learning college course on mentoring, and her evaluation of youth-based mentoring programs, including *TeamWorks.* These efforts provide mentoring to hundreds of students. Her other area of research looks at leadership effectiveness and the application of education to leaders at the high school, undergraduate, and adult levels. She has recently published two studies on the importance of charismatic leadership in increasing group motivation. Susan was recently honored to be chosen, because of her background in and dedication to mentoring, to be a Posse Foundation mentor to incoming Claremont McKenna College students. She previously worked for Battelle as a research scientist, consulting in the areas of leadership and management education, as well as organizational change, for clients in the United States and Japan. She continues designing and delivering leadership development programs as well as other organizational development activities for organizations such as Toyota Motor Sales, RGL Gallagher, Bain & Co., the Los

Angeles City Fire Department, and the City of Claremont. She resides in Los Angeles with her husband Copil Yáñez.

In addition to their work on power mentoring, Professors Ensher and Murphy have several other ongoing research studies and writing projects. They are currently working on a project that uncovers the management secrets of film and television directors. In interviews with 25 directors, they uncover the nature of leadership from the director's chair. This work was presented at the 2004 Academy of Management meeting in New Orleans. In 2003, Professors Murphy and Ensher presented at the National Summit for Youth Mentoring Research. They also accepted an invitation to contribute to a leading scholar's handbook of mentoring, *The Handbook of Mentoring* (to be published in 2007).

INDEX

mentoring initiative announced by, 167; reverse mentoring conceptualized by, 68; Wright as protégé of, 6
Wells, Frank, 34
West, Alice, 43
Willingness to learn, mentors attracted by, 120
Willis, Mark, 48
Wilson, Pete, 6, 149
Winfrey, Oprah, 170–171, 172–173, 175
Wise, Robert, 62
Women: comfort of, with female mentors, 117; female bonding between, 147–149. *See also* Gender
Women's Technology Cluster, 50, 263
Woods, Jacqueline E., 12, 203, 299
Work: changing context for, 13–14; characteristics of great places to, 15–16; identity and life satisfaction's relationship to, 1–2; time U.S. workers spend at, 1
Work-family balance, 13, 69, 192, 193
Workforce, changing, 13

Wright, Bob, 12; attractions of protégés to, 119–120; biography of, 71–72, 299–300; initial connection of protégé with, 182–183; as master mentor, 5–6; on observing people in nonwork contexts, 197; as power mentor, 34; reciprocity in power mentoring relationships of, 72–76; testing of mentor by, 129–130; trust in mentoring relationship of, 143, 144–145, 150–151; in Welch mentoring lineage, 153
Wright, Fred, 27
Wulf, William, 12, 158, 300

Y

Yuen, Henry, 12; biography of, 117, 300–301; peer-mentoring relationship of, 166; reason peer mentor attractive to, 119, 124

Z

Zey, Michael, 29, 121–123, 304